Gurus for Hire, Enlightenment for Sale

An insider's guide into the relationship between spiritual teachers, students and centres

Tsem Tulku Rinpoche

Edited by Jamie Khoo

Kechara Media & Publications
2009

Copyright © 2009 Tsem Tulku Rinpoche

All rights reserved. No part of this book may be used or reproduced in any manner whatsoever without written permission from Kechara Media & Publications except in the case of brief quotations embodied in critical articles and reviews.

Kechara Media & Publications
5-1, Jalan PJU 1/3G
SunwayMas Commercial Centre
47301 Petaling Jaya
Selangor, Malaysia

Tel: [+603] 7805 5691 Fax: [+603] 7805 5690
Email: kmp@kechara.com
Website: kechara.com/kmp

The moral right of the author has been asserted.

ISBN 978-983-43399-8-2

First published by Kechara Media & Publications in 2007

Cover design by Justin Ripley / 1am Concept

INTERNATIONAL ACCLAIM FOR *GURUS FOR HIRE, ENLIGHTENMENT FOR SALE*

Tsem Tulku Rinpoche presents spiritual practice to the contemporary reader in a way that is accessible, uplifting and practical. He shows us how very possible it is to incorporate spiritual practice into our daily lives, without having to compromise our modern 21st-century responsibilities and commitments.

Martin Barrow
Company director
London, United Kingdom

When a friend gives you a book and you reach for it with excitement, it means something, so be aware; when that very book you began to read with enthusiasm evokes a panoply of feelings and appurtenance takes place, take heed; when you are moved to tears, search for the meaning; I did!

Although evident, there is less to support us in our practice "anywhere in the world that does not have mass Buddhist consciousness". But that does not mean we cannot pursue it. We should dedicate 50% for our present life and 50% for our future lives, as HH the Dalai Lama was quoted. I wiped my tears and came round. I made again an effort and I know if I slack, I will try again and again and again. *Gurus for Hire Enlightenment for Sale* is a very inspiring book. May it be of benefit to all beings.

France Berveiller Choa
Disciple of Lama Norbu, Repa Sang-Ngag Gompo
New York, USA

In the wake of the crumbling banking system, outlandish bonuses and severance packages and, more generally speaking, blatant greed, modesty comes as a refreshing word. This unique quality permeates Tsem Tulku Rinpoche's guide for the open-minded "newbie" in search of something the material world obviously can't give him.

François de Witt
Author
Paris, France

Tsem Tulku Rinpoche's teachings come from a place of good, and all you have to do is listen with your heart to know that he speaks Truth. Gurus are not there to teach us, but rather, to help us remember and awaken the Truth that is within all of us.

Dr Stuart Koe
CEO and founder, fridae.com
Singapore

Tsem Tulku Rinpoche, much like the enlightened teachers of ancient times, untangles the maze of confusion for those seeking spirituality in today's times. Touching on a wide range of issues that confuses the seeker, he clears the mist and reveals the path leading to higher consciousness. Tsem Rinpoche, the Guru of today, manages to re-state the ancient wisdom of spiritual pursuit in the contemporary context with a clarity that is accessible to all.

Vikram Lall
Partner & Principal Architect, Lall & Associates
Delhi, India

How refreshing and inspiring it is to see a book that celebrates the fundamentals not just of Buddhist practice, but of all faiths, beliefs and philosophies for living. Through his supreme gift of understanding and eloquence, Tsem Tulku Rinpoche presents eternal values in contemporary terms, showing us what it means to truly develop qualities of awareness, commitment, dedication and self-effacement, bringing inner happiness, peace, strength and Enlightenment. His teachings are real and relevant. He is a modern and eternal Guru.

Kai-Yin Lo
Designer & Art/Cultural Advocate and Consultant
Hong Kong, People's Republic of China

It is very refreshing to see such a clearly written book on what it means to be spiritual today. Malaysia, a multi-racial country, respects all religions as one of the fundamental pillars of national unity, stability and progress. The words of compassion, love and regard for all religious beliefs as taught by His Eminence Tsem Tulku Rinpoche ring with truth, and are precisely the values that make a caring nation.

H.E. Dato' Seri Dr. Ng Yen Yen
Minister of Women, Family and Community Development
Kuala Lumpur, Malaysia

In this modern age of instant gratification, we still need to have spiritual well-being. This, however, does not come instantly; we should allow ourselves quality time to investigate and find what suits each one of us. It is a pleasure to find that we now have a modern-day teacher to talk to us in a way that we can understand!

Nora Sun
President, Nora Sun Associates Ltd
Shanghai, People's Republic of China

This book is dedicated to all the great Gurus and teachers who have left the cultural comforts of their own society and braved the tremendous task of bringing Dharma to the "Outside World". It is also dedicated to all the practitioners, students and committed people of the "Outside World" who work so hard to bring the ancient teachings of Buddha to their lands.

May both have freedom from inner and outer hardship and gain the necessities and paths for their work to come to fruition. May the teachings of the enlightened Buddha pervade the ten directions.

Tsem Tulku of Gaden Shartse Monastery

His Eminence Tsem Tulku Rinpoche: A Short Biography

Beloved for his unconventional, contemporary approach to Dharma, H.E. Tsem Tulku Rinpoche brings more than 2,500 years of Buddhist wisdom and teachings to the modern spiritual seeker by connecting ancient worlds with new people, cultures, attitudes and lifestyles.

A Mongolian-Tibetan heritage, a childhood in Taiwan and in the United States of America, intensive monastic studies in India and now the spiritual guide of Kechara in Malaysia – these are but some of the many factors that contribute to Tsem Rinpoche's unique ability to bridge the East and the West, Disco and Dharma, Tantra and the 21st-Century.

Tsem Rinpoche has been strongly inclined towards Dharma since his early childhood, and has studied under many great Buddhist masters of the Tibetan tradition. Rinpoche eventually went on to receive his monastic education at Gaden Shartse Monastery, currently located in south India.

Following the advice of his beloved Guru, H.H. Kyabje Zong Rinpoche, Tsem Rinpoche took his vows as a monk from H.H. the Dalai Lama and joined Gaden Shartse Monastery in India when he was in his early twenties. His two preceding incarnations, Gendun Nyedrak and Khentrul Rinpoche Thubten Lamsang, had also studied at Gaden Shartse Monastery when it was then in Tibet. There, they obtained Geshe Lharam degrees before completing their studies at Gyuto tantric college.

Gendun Nyedrak went on to become the lead chanter and, later, abbot of Gaden Monastery, while Khentrul Rinpoche brought the Dharma to the laypeople of the Phari district of Tibet. The tremendous and virtuous work of his previous lifetimes can perhaps be seen again in Tsem Rinpoche's present-day activities, where he continues this practice of teaching vast numbers of non-monastic communities in places where the Dharma has yet to bloom.

During his nine years in Gaden, Tsem Rinpoche was involved in extensive charitable works including building schools for refugee children in India, building dormitories, upgrading living conditions for the monastic community, and providing long-term assistance to the poor lay community of Mundgod.

Now, based in Malaysia and Nepal, Rinpoche continues this immense work to benefit many. Through creative and engaging approaches, Rinpoche continuously shares new methods of bringing happiness and relief to people from all walks of life. Rinpoche also maintains close contact with Gaden Monastery, and through his constant practice of generosity and deeply altruistic motivation, continues to frequently sponsor Gaden's work and activities.

Be inspired by H.E. Tsem Tulku Rinpoche's work and life at www.tsemtulku.com.

"WE WANT TO BE EFFICIENT AND BENEFICIAL, AND WE WANT TO MAKE OUR DHARMA CENTRES RUN WELL. THIS APPLIES TO EVERY CENTRE IN THE WORLD. THE ONLY WAY WE CAN DO THIS IS TO UNDERSTAND THE PHENOMENON OF DHARMA CENTRES, THE FUNCTIONS OF DHARMA CENTRES, THE PEOPLE WHO ARE THERE AND WHAT WE ARE SUPPOSED TO DO."

– TSEM TULKU RINPOCHE

CONTENTS

Tsem Tulku Rinpoche: A Short Biography

Foreword: Tsem Tulku Rinpoche

Editor's Introduction

A Note on Editing

MOTIVATION
- 024 Motivation
- 025 Guru Yoga

GURU
- 034 H.H. Kyabje Zong Rinpoche
- 042 The Guru
- 045 The Root Guru
- 047 Why We Need a Guru
- 049 Taking a Guru
- 054 The Crazy Wisdom of the Guru
- 056 Guru Devotion: What Submission Really Means
- 060 Outer Protocol: The Fifty Stanzas on Guru Devotion
- 066 The Inner Qualities of a Dharma Student – Practising Guru Devotion with the Nine Attitudes
- 080 *Samaya*
- 085 Spiritual Conviction, Spiritual Commitment
- 089 Doubting the Guru
- 094 Switching Gurus
- 098 Questions and Answers

CENTRE
- 106 Milarepa
- 107 The Phenomenon of Dharma centres › Dharma Centres • The Dharma Centre Building • Retreat Centres
- 114 The Difference between a Centre Related to a Mother Monastery and One That is Not
- 116 The Challenges
- 121 The "Roles" of the Guru
- 128 Serving the Dharma centre
- 130 Committees
- 135 **Volunteers** › Contributing to the Centre as a Volunteer • Inspiring and Helping New Volunteers

138	Working for the Dharma centre
141	**Students** › New Students • The Buddy System • Unhappy Students • Students Who Take Advantage of the Centre • High-Profile or Well-known Students or Visitors
149	Effective Communication
151	Encouraging People to Join the Centre
153	**Protocol** › What is Protocol? • Making Offerings • Requesting for Teachings • Public Teachings • Educating others on Protocol
160	**Promoting the Guru** ›The Image • Promotion
165	Centres with High-Ranking, Well-Known Gurus
169	**Centre Bashing** ›The Phenomenon of Centre Bashing • The Damage • How to Handle it
176	**Guru Bashing** › The Phenomenon of Guru Bashing • How to Handle it
182	The Other Tactic: Encouraging Others In Their Practice
184	Other Students, Your Centre
186	**Sectarianism** › What it Means to be Sectarian • The New Sectarianism • How to Handle it
193	**Ordination Vows** › Why There are Vows (or not) • Disrobement – What it Means • Giving and Taking Back Robes
200	Supernatural Phenomena
203	**Succession** › The Samaya that Hooks the Guru Back • The Preparation, the Commitment • The Pujas • When the Guru Returns
210	Questions and Answers
	SELF
222	**Refuge: Freedom** › The Refuge Vows • The Refuge Commitments • The Benefits of Taking Refuge
232	Questions and Answers
	Glossary
	Bibliography
	Acknowledgements
	Index

EDITOR'S INTRODUCTION

The Guru has become a commodity and "Enlightenment" something that comes nicely packaged like an instant cake mix, in DIY manuals to be found in all New Age bookshelves and quick-fix websites. A spiritual path has become easy and far too accessible for us to really understand what it means (or entails) to bring out that Buddha nature and actualise it into something more meaningful than the glamorous concept now so easily adopted by cosmopolitan bars and CD covers for acid jazz.

When we finally decide to awaken that Buddha slumbering inside us and traverse the path, we realise how much personal effort, work and even pain is involved in the process. It is a rude and terrible shock. Often, we get angry, we hurt, we suffer more than we did when we were romping about in the outside world and soon, we bat our eyelids at the lure of quitting.

And, as if our own egos and temptress fickleness weren't enough to contend with, we find ourselves caught up in a difficult (but very human) web of gossip, rumour-mongering and politics in the only place we go to for peace – the Dharma centre. Contemporary catfights and the paranoid neurosis of 21st-Century angst find themselves pitted against ancient wisdom and thousand-year-old traditions of monks, nuns and mystics. The combination is potent either way – it forces us towards Enlightenment or it makes us clamber back deeper into our old, awful selves. So just how does a girl like me, you or the aspiring yogi next door ever get anywhere?

H.E. Tsem Tulku Rinpoche, embodying all that is amber and ancient of 2,500-year old teachings, links it all together, into a path that is uncomplicated and full of that special clarity we seek within and without. It's not so hard, after all. While talking about refuge and taking on a spiritual path, one of his students said to him, "If I don't do it now, I'll never do it. I've just got to jump in the deep end". He answered, "And then you find it's not so deep after all."

We rediscover, through these teachings, that the pool isn't as dark and murky as we think. We go back to that proverbial saying, that whatever we're looking for is right under our noses (a fitting metaphor, since we are taught to look exactly at the tip of our noses during meditation). Eventually, we realise that the Guru-disciple relationship – so incredibly difficult for the independent, contemporary self to comprehend – is actually all about, well, ourselves. We understand that the Dharma centre becomes a physical manifestation of the teachings, embodied through the students and, eventually, ourselves. Practice, submission, the initial suffering, inner peace and world peace is all, Rinpoche emphasises, about the self and (paradoxically) freeing ourselves from it. So we are given the option: you can choose to make your spiritual path easy, or you can choose to make it difficult.

This book was born out of a three-day teaching given by His Eminence Tsem Tulku Rinpoche in Tsem Ladrang[1] (in Kuala Lumpur, Malaysia) to a group of students who were directly involved in committees within the centre or who worked in affiliated departments (the Dharma stores, arts department and publishing house). The talks were initiated by Rinpoche, who wanted to highlight and give a thorough explanation of the Guru-disciple (teacher-student) relationship for modern practitioners, and the intricate workings, politics and sensitivities within a Dharma centre. In this second revised edition, we have also added further material from other Dharma teachings given by Rinpoche about the Guru-disciple relationship and commitment to Dharma work and practice.

As Dharma centres continue to mushroom, Rinpoche's own Dharma centre in Kuala Lumpur, Malaysia – Kechara – finds itself at a pivotal point of expansion and growth. The idea for this book came out of the need to address issues that members in our own centre will come to face (if they had not already), and that invariably affect the operations and activities of other Dharma centres around the world.

Having had a fervent passion for Dharma since his earliest childhood, Rinpoche has studied, worked and taught in Dharma centres in America, Nepal, Gaden Shartse Monastery in India, and various centres throughout Malaysia and Singapore. Much of what he speaks about in this book is garnered from his experiences from his volunteering,

---

1 A Guru's ladrang is his personal residence and administrative office. In all Tibetan Buddhist organisations, the ladrang forms the headquarters of the centre and all its activities.

work, study and teaching in all these centres, making it incredibly relevant for centres anywhere, for members at all levels.

At the end of the third day, one of Rinpoche's senior students, and then-president of the centre's committee, raised a further question about refuge, which brought out an additional, completing part of the whole Enlightenment puzzle – the practice and the path of each individual, embodied in the formalised ceremony of taking refuge. Unexpectedly, the talks that Rinpoche had given on the Guru and the centre, found its most fitting, inspiring conclusion in the self, the illusive "I" that we all constantly struggle with in any spiritual endeavour and relationship with our Dharma teachers and peers.

Ultimately, as he tells us, it is entirely and only about gaining freedom. The last few lines of the book conclude, "Once you take the vows, you are not entailed to do anything except to be the best person you can be," which is what it is all about – from the Guru through to the centre, landing back, eventually, on ourselves.

Jamie Khoo
Editor

A NOTE ON EDITING

The content of this book was extracted from a series of talks given by His Eminence Tsem Tulku Rinpoche over three days in December 2006. The complete talks (except for a few minutes of tantric ritual that Rinpoche did not allow to be filmed) are also available on DVD, which includes many wonderful, heart-warming moments.

The talks were transcribed and edited into the separate sections and chapters of this book. As such, though it is encouraged that you read this book together with watching the DVDs of the talks, please bear in mind that the sequencing of the book does not correspond exactly to that of the talks.

In this second revised edition, additional material from Rinpoche's other Dharma teachings has also been added to complement and enhance what was taught in this three-day teaching.

FOREWORD

As far as I know, no book of this nature has ever been written but what I have to say is necessary and very applicable for all of us today.

There are certain things I would like to talk about, beginning with the relationship with the Guru. This leads to many other issues, such as how to see someone as your teacher, the qualities of a Dharma student, people who promote their Gurus at the expense of other Gurus, people who go against their Gurus, Guru-bashing, centre-bashing, sectarianism and how to deal with all these issues with day-to-day, practical methods.

Some of these topics are quite sensitive but they need to be talked about so that they can be cleared. These are things we all think about but dare not ask or discuss for fear of offending others. These are hurdles that all Dharma centres need to overcome.

Because we live with other human beings and we are always with each other, politics invariably arise due to the different dispositions that people have. Rather than always suppressing these problems or keeping quiet about them, it would be better to speak openly and create understanding, so that Dharma centres everywhere can grow.

We are not in places where the mass consciousness has been Buddhist in thought for a long time. Since the mass consciousness is not Buddhist in thought, it is hard for us arrive at a Buddhist way of thinking, although we are in Buddhism. Therefore, it would be better if we talk about these issues and create this kind of consciousness – at least among ourselves – so that Dharma work and practices to benefit others will be more effective in the future.

We want to be efficient and beneficial, and we want to make our Dharma centres run well. This applies to every centre in the world. The only way we can do this is to understand the phenomenon of Dharma centres, the functions of Dharma centres, the people who are there and what we are supposed to do.

This book has been inspired by my many, many years of being involved with Dharma centres and seeing many things that I have kept quiet about, out of respect. However, I have now found a way to talk about these issues without incurring negative karma, breaking *samaya* or damaging anyone. My intention to speak about this is not to talk about sensitive issues and political issues. It will sound like that but I am not speaking with a political motive; I am actually using politics to clear politics.

I do not mean for these things to be sensitive. I do not mean for what I say to be a put-down, to hurt people, to criticise or to say which culture is good or not. I am simply explaining the phenomenon of Dharma centres, their difficulties and what they go through. I hope it can provide practical information for all of us on a personal level, and for our centre and its growth.

Tsem Tulku Rinpoche

Motivation

REMAIN IN ONE-POINTED AWARENESS – TEMPTATIONS WILL SCATTER WITH THE WIND.

REMAIN ALONE – A HOLY FRIEND WILL FIND YOU.

REMAIN STILL WHILE HURRYING – SOON YOU WILL ARRIVE.

REMAIN AS THE LOWEST – EXALTED YOU WILL BECOME.

REMAIN FREE OF THIS LIFE'S GOALS – THE SUPREME YOU WILL ATTAIN.

– JETSUN MILAREPA

MOTIVATION

> We should learn
> Dharma for the
> sake of practice.

In Dharma talks or when we are receiving the Dharma, we should not be like the three pots. One pot faces upwards with holes, so that whatever goes in just comes out. We should not be like the second pot which faces upwards but is dirty and contaminated – whatever teachings go in are unusable because they become contaminated. And, do not be like the third pot, which faces downwards – it is like close-mindedness, so that whatever teachings come to us dribble away to the side.

When listening to the Dharma teachings, we should have a good motivation, stay alert, be awake and focus. We are listening to our teachers repeat what Lord Buddha taught 2,500 years ago. Our teachers are not motivated by money, fame or reputation, and definitely not to receive anything from the students. Our teachers are motivated purely by transferring knowledge from a vase to a pot, from one container to another container.

If we make the time to come to teachings but fall asleep once we are there, what is the point of all the effort that we made before the teachings? We did not make all that effort to come to the teachings to have a good nap! Alertness is very important.

We should listen to the teachings as personal advice, not as entertainment or as something fun; not as something that is just for intellectual, absorption of information. If we listen for intellectual satisfaction, then it remains as that and intellectual satisfaction does not match spiritual progress. Intellect, and practice and transformation are related, but not the same. We should listen with concentration and focus without distraction. We should learn it for the sake of practice, absorb it and also have a lot of compassion. We should listen and go over the teachings again and again, so we may share them with others.

The centre does not grow by the Guru teaching every single person who walks in. The students have a greater responsibility to share the Guru's teachings with others – this is achieved by listening, contemplating, practising and then sharing with others.

GURU YOGA

> Start your day
> with the Buddha.

It is very auspicious to start teachings or special events by reciting Lama Tsongkhapa's *Guru Yoga*. I learnt this from the great *Mahasidda*, Geshe Tsultim Gyeltsen[2] in America, who has passed away.

Sometimes Geshe-la and I would go for big inter-faith Buddhist gatherings in Los Angeles, with Buddhists from all countries, sects and backgrounds. Once, Geshe-la went to one of these gatherings with three or four of us from the centre. Before the meeting started, each tradition or country did a very beautiful, special chant – some were quite ritualised, some recited their prayers with bells and staccato rhythms. Then it came to the Tibetan tradition. Geshe-la represented the whole Tibetan tradition and I thought it was now our time to show off since Tibetans are known for their long rituals!

I wondered what Geshe-la was going to do – maybe some Yamantaka prayers, maybe he would chant and impress them with his memory, his *mudras*, his recitation, his great chanting.

I waited. Geshe-la folded his hands in front of everybody and recited Lama Tsongkhapa's Guru Yoga without any melodious chanting. When he got to *Migtsema* he chanted it very slowly. He finished with the dissolution. It only took him about ten minutes.

When we left the gathering, I asked, "Geshe-la, those people did all that fancy chanting and stuff. Why did you do just Tsongkhapa's *Guru Yoga*?" He looked at me and said, "Just?"

He explained that all the 84,000 teachings of Lord Buddha are planted in the *Guru Yoga* of Lama Tsongkhapa. If you are a master, you will be able to explain all of Buddha's teachings completely from each line of Lama Tsongkhapa's praise.

---

2 Geshe Tsultim Gyeltsen was the resident Guru of Thubten Dhargye Ling and Tsem Tulku Rinpoche's second Guru.

He said that to recite that – simply, from the heart and purely – would plant seeds of Enlightenment in everybody's mind, and bless everybody in the congregation. What practice is more superior to that? I shut up real fast! Here was a grand Dharma master who was already in his seventies, with a PhD in Buddhist studies, (a Geshe Lharam of Gaden Shartse) who knew the rituals of Sutra and Tantra inside out, who had everything memorised, who could stand in front of the Dalai Lama and make long life offerings or recite long verses from memory. Even grand masters of our monastery prostrate to him when they see him. And he told me that the most complete practice is that of Lama Tsongkhapa.

Before starting Dharma teachings, he would do Lama Tsongkhapa's *Guru Yoga*, a *mandala* offering, the short form of the Heart Sutra and a few minutes of meditation on motivation.

When I heard that, it made a huge impact on my life, so I have followed this tradition of reciting Lama Tsongkhapa's *Guru Yoga* before anything, for anything. I would advise everybody to memorise Lama Tsongkhapa's *Guru Yoga*, in English or Tibetan, and recite it.

The minute you get up in the morning – before you start making calls, scream for tea or think about work – recite Lama Tsongkhapa's *Guru Yoga*. Start your day with the Buddha.

After you have completed the prayers, think that your mind is clear and bright, your body is clear and your temporary obstacles are removed. You feel very happy, you feel very light. You should think like that very strongly, and affirm this again and again. All arises from the mind. Then you can continue with your work for the rest of the day.

> "After you have completed the prayers, think that your mind is clear and bright, your body is clear and your temporary obstacles are removed."

When we do Lama Tsongkhapa's *Guru Yoga* with awareness, concentration, confidence, faith and the visualisation I have described below, we open a doorway that connects us with a real enlightened Being who abides in and comes from compassion, skilful means and omniscient wisdom. It is a real, existent Buddha.

Secondly, by invoking such a Being with those qualities, we open up the same potential within ourselves. When we invoke that Being, we are invoking that same Being within ourselves to come out by their blessings. We all have the seed of Buddhahood that needs to be cultivated. Seed means potential. It does not mean it is there, latent or dormant. It means the potential is there.

When we invoke Lama Tsongkhapa, it is a two-fold prayer. Firstly, we invoke the blessings of the outer Lama Tsongkhapa, who is a real enlightened Being. Secondly, the prayers are an environmental factor for us to open up the Lama Tsongkhapa within us. When we create that environment – with retreats and meditation, dedications, offerings, practice of the six paramitas and association with Lama Tsongkhapa – we will open up the Lama Tsongkhapa within us, stage by stage.

We will see ourselves open up, becoming less miserly, more generous; we will see our skills and speech grow; we will see our ability to forgive and accept, increase. All these qualities embodied by the six paramitas will increase and grow, in dependence on our practice of Lama Tsongkhapa's *Guru Yoga*.

Guru Yoga means the yoga that finds one's Guru. We call it the *Guru Yoga* of Lama Tsongkhapa because when we submit to an outer Guru such as Lama Tsongkhapa, we find our inner Guru.

*

LAMA TSONGKHAPA'S
Guru Yoga

GA-DEN HLA-JI NGON-JYI THUG-KAY-NEY
RAP-KAR SHO-SAR PUNG-DEE CHU-DZIN TSER
CHO-KYI GYEL-PO KUN-CHEN LOZANG DRAG
SEY-DANG CHE-PA NE-DIR SHEG SU SOL

My Lord Guru comes from Tushita Heaven, emanating forth from Lord Maitreya's heart, and he is assembled before me with his two spiritual sons, Khedrup Rinpoche and Gyaltsap Rinpoche. Please come to this place at this time.

DUN-JYI NAM-KAR SING-TI PEE-DEE TENG
JE-TSUN LA-MA JYEH-PI DZUM-KAR CHYEN
DAG-LO DE-PE SO-NAM SHING-CHOG TU
TAN-PA JYEH-SHIR KAL-DJAR JUG-SU SOL

My beautiful Guru smiles with great delight, he sits before me on a lion throne with a lotus and a moon seat. I request you to remain for a hundred eons in order to spread the teachings and be a supreme merit field for my mind's faith.

SHEY-JYEH CHONG-KUN JAL-WEY LO-DO THUG
KAL-ZANG NA-WEY JYIN-JUR LIK-SHEY SUNG
DRAG-PI PEL-JYI HLAM-MER DZEY-PI KU
THONG-THO DRAN-PI DON-DHAN LA-CHAG TSAL

Your mind has the intellect to comprehend all to the full extent to be known. You are omniscient. Your speech with its excellent explanation becomes the ear ornament of those with good fortune. Your body is radiant and handsome, with glory and renown. I prostrate to you, Lama Tsongkhapa, who to behold, to hear or to recall, is worthwhile.

YIH-WONG TCHO-YON NA-TSOG ME-TOG DANG
DRI-JEM DUG-PO NANG-SAL DRID-CHAB SOG
NGO-SHAM YIH-TUL TCHO-TIN GYA-TSO DI
SO-NAM SHING-CHOG CHE-LA CHO-PA BUL

Pleasing water offerings, various flowers, fragrant incense, light and scented water, an ocean of actual and visualised cloud of offerings – I present to you, Oh great merit field, Lama Tsongkhapa.

DAG-GI TO-MEY DU-NEH SAG-PA YI
LU-NGAG YIH-KYI DIG-PA CHI-JYI DANG
CHEY-PA DOM-PA SUM-JI MI-TUN SHO
NYING-NEH JO-PA TAH-PO SO-SOR SHAG

Whatever negativities I have committed with my body, my speech and my mind that I have accumulated for many lifetimes, and any transgressions of my vows, I confess to you, Lama Tsongkhapa, a fully enlightened Being. Please forgive me and may I purify my negative actions.

NIK-MI DU-DIR MANG-THO DRUP-LA TSON
CHO-JYED PANG-PI DAL-JOR DON-YO SHYE
NGON-PO CHEY-KYI LAP-CHEN DZE-PA LA
DAG-CHAG SAM-PA TAG-PEH YI RANG NGO

From my heart, great Lama Tsongkhapa, by reading your biographies and listening to your deeds, I rejoice in your waves and oceans of great merits and the great actions that you committed in your life. You strove to learn and practise in this degenerate age and made life meaningful by abandoning the eight worldly Dharmas.

JE-TSUN LA-MA DAM-PA CHEY-NAM KYI
CHO-KU KA-LA CHEN-TI TIN-TIK NEY
JI-TAR TSAM-PI DUL-SHIH DZIN-MA LA
ZAB-JI CHO-KYI CHAR-PA WHAP TU SOL

Great Lama, without you, Dharma is not possible, attainments are not possible. From the void of the *Dharmakaya* sky-like wisdom, please rain down a vast Dharma and train me according to my needs.

NAM-DAG WO-SAL YING-LEY JING-PA YI
ZUNG-JUG KU-LA CHAR-NUM MI-NGA YANG
THA-MAL HNANG-NGOR ZUG-KU RAG-PA NYI
SEE-THEE BAR-DU MI-NUM TAN PAR SHUG

My root Guru, all the great Gurus and teachers in the world, I request you again, through Lama Tsongkhapa, to please stay and remain until *samsara* ends.

DAG-SOG JIN-NYEH SAG-PA GE-WA DEE
TAN-DANG DRO-WA KUN-LA GANG-PHAN DANG
CHE-PA JE-TSUN LO-ZANG DRAG-PA YI
TAN-PI NYING-PO RING-DU SAL-SHEH SHOG

I dedicate whatever virtues I have collected for the benefit of the teachings to grow, for all sentient beings to receive it, and in particular for the essential teachings of the Venerable Lobsang Drakpa, Lama Tsongkhapa, to shine forever.

MANDALA OFFERING

SA-ZHI PO-KYI JUG-SHING ME-TOG-TRAM
RI-RAB LING-ZHI NYI-DAY GYAN-PA-DI
SANG-GYE ZHING-DU MIG-TAY UL-WAR-GYI
DRO-KUN NAM-DAG ZHING-LA CHO-PAR-SHOG

By directing to the field of the Buddhas this *mandala*, a base resplendent with flowers, saffron, water, incense, adorned with Mount Meru, the four continents, the sun and the moon, may all sentient beings be led to the holy fields of Buddha.

IDAM GURU RATNA MANDALAKAM NIRAYATAYAMI

MIGTSEMA

MIG-MEY TZE-WAY TER-CHEN CHENREZIG
DRI-MEY KHYEN-PI WANG-PO JAMPAL YANG
DU-PUNG MA-LU JOM-DZEY SANG-WEY DAG
GANG-CHENG KE-PEY TSUG GYEN TSONGKHAPA
LO-SANG TRAG-PEY SHAB-LA SOL-WA DEB
(recite seven times, 21 times, 108 times or more)

DISSOLUTION

PAL-DAN TSA-WEY LA-MA RINPOCHE
DAG-SOG CHI-WOR PE-ME DAN-JUG LA
KA-DRIN CHEN-PO GO-NEY JE-ZUNG TE
KU-SUNG THUG-KYI NGO-DROP TSAL-DUL SOL

Lama Tsongkhapa's two sons dissolve into Lama Tsongkhapa. They become one. Lama Tsongkhapa's throne, his lotus and moon disc – all made of light – all dissolve inside Lama Tsongkhapa. Then, Lama Tsongkhapa, for the benefit of ourselves and our perception, shrinks to the size of a thumb, and turns around to face the direction we face. He lands on top of our head, very gently, with a smile.

PAL-DAN TSA-WEY LA-MA RINPOCHE
DAG-SOG NYING-KHAR PE-ME DAN-JUG LA
KA-DRIN CHEN-PO GO-NEY JE-ZUNG TE
CHO-DANG THUN-MONG NGO-DRUP TSAL-DU SOL

By reciting the second line of invitation, Lama Tsongkhapa, as a fully enlightened Being, very happily and very gently dissolves through our central channel. He enters the lotus at our hearts and the lotus closes, symbolising he has become one with our mind. The lotus is our mind, full of light, bright and clear. Do not focus on the heart area – just think that it is there. From the top of the lotus, where the petals have closed, a stream of cloud goes through our central channel, leaves the crown of our heads, and directly connects back to Lord Maitreya's heart. This gives us a connection, always, with Lord Maitreya.

PAL-DAN TSA-WEY LA-MA RINPOCHE
DAG-SOG NYING-KHAR PE-ME DAN-JUG LA
KA-DRIN CHEN-PO GO-NEY JE-ZUNG TE
JANG-CHUB NYING-PO BAR-DU TAN-PAR SHUG

Lama Tsongkhapa and us become one. He stays with us until the end of time. In this life and future lives, we will meet Lama Tsongkhapa again and again and again, the teachers of this tradition, and the teachers of Lama Tsongkhapa, to receive Dharma teachings.

Guru

YEARS AND YEARS OF
CHANTING AND MEDITATION
CANNOT COMPARE
WITH ONE INSTANT OF
REMEMBERING THE GURU.

– TANTRIC TEACHING

H.H. KYABJE ZONG RINPOCHE

> I felt I was collecting merits with a person without faults, that everything that I did would accelerate my Dharma practice and my Dharma attainments.

When I was 17, I was elected by the centre in Los Angeles[3] to be the assistant to His Holiness Kyabje Zong Rinpoche, my root Guru.[4] A few powerful sponsors in the centre were totally against it. They told Geshe-la,[5] "No way! He's such a bad representation of Zong Rinpoche. He's just a kid! Look at the way he looks! His hair! The way he dresses! That is going to represent one of the greatest living Dharma teachers of Tibet? Certainly we can do better!" I looked like a freak, I admit it, but when I heard it, I was very hurt. I almost cried but it made me push myself much more.

I served Rinpoche in the centre – I cooked for Rinpoche, his entourage, my Geshe-la and their guests. I made seven trays of food every single day for six months. Each tray would have food for Rinpoche, two of Rinpoche's German students, the translator, the translator's uncle and two monks who were Rinpoche's assistants. I remember laying out seven trays every day in the kitchen. I had to prepare everything for them because they were Rinpoche's entourage and I needed to take care of them. I did not know how to cook, so I had to ask anyone who had time to show me how to cook. I could not talk to Zong Rinpoche directly in the beginning so I asked translators to find out what food he liked and what his schedule was like.

---

3 Thubten Dhargye Ling, Los Angeles

4 Rinpoche refers here to a time when the previous incarnation of H.H. Zong Rinpoche had come to stay at Thubten Dhargye Ling for six months to give teachings and initiations. This was the first time that Tsem Rinpoche met Zong Rinpoche but he very quickly developed immense faith and devotion which he holds until today. The current incarnation of H.H. Zong Rinpoche is now in his twenties and resides in Gaden Shartse Monastery, South India.

5 Geshe-la: Geshe Tsultim Gyeltsen, who was also a disciple of H.H. Zong Rinpoche.

I would serve Rinpoche first. I would get up early in the morning and bring breakfast to Rinpoche. I would offer him the breakfast and make three prostrations immediately. I made prostrations because I did not know how long I could be with him, and I did not want to prostrate to a statue; I wanted to prostrate to the living Buddha.

Then I would go to my teacher, Geshe-la, offer him breakfast and make sure everything was alright. After that, I would offer breakfast to the translator, his uncle, Rinpoche's two assistants and the two German ladies. By the time I finished offering breakfast to the last person, I would go back up and wait by Rinpoche while he was eating.

If there was something left, I would ask his permission to eat his leftovers. I wanted his saliva, I wanted something he had bitten every day. I would even eat crumbs because I believed very much in my Guru.

I would wash his cups and his plates first, clean them and put them in the highest shelf in the kitchen, without damaging anything. Sometimes I would wash his silverware twice, wipe it very carefully so that none of it was dirty or sticky. I would put everything away in a special place so no one could touch his items. I even put up a sign in case anybody made a mistake. This was an opportunity to serve my Guru.

Then, I would do the same with Geshe-la's and everyone else's breakfast. If there were any leftovers, I would give them to the dogs outside and feed the cat at the centre. If I had time, I would clean the kitchen and put everything away.

I would take a shower quickly, get dressed and go to work until about 2 or 3 o'clock. I would come home by about 3 o'clock and start cooking dinner. I also had to run to the store to do the shopping, wash, prepare and cook everything. I knew only a few dishes and it was a challenge to cook for seven people each day! Sometimes, if I burned the food, I would have to do it all over very quickly. I hated cooking but Geshe-la wanted me to do it.

I would cook dinner and make seven trays of food again with drinks. Rinpoche liked Tibetan tea and there was a certain way he liked it so I would make it that way, with just the right amount of butter.

Then I would serve Zong Rinpoche – I would go upstairs, offer dinner to him and make three prostrations. Sometimes, when I was not in such a big rush, I would have the luck to sit near him and massage his feet.

I would do my best to massage his feet every day. And I would kiss his feet because I read in an Indian tantric manual that to show the deepest respect to someone very high is to touch the lowest part of their body.

Rinpoche made it a game after a while. He would show me his foot, and when I tried to grab it, he would quickly pull it back and laugh! When I grabbed it, I would put it on my head and I would kiss it. Tibetans do not kiss. I did it because I had grown up with American culture. It was my way to show my reverence to him because I could not speak his language.

No one taught me all this. I wanted Dharma. I ran away from home three times to learn Dharma, to serve a Guru. I tried hitchhiking from New Jersey to New York, and from New York to California, to learn the Dharma. I was successful the third time.[6] So when I came across such a great master, I was not going to lose my chance.

After serving Rinpoche dinner, there would be Dharma teachings which started between 6pm and 7.30pm every evening and finished between midnight and 2am. There were teachings every day for six months in Thubten Dhargye Ling centre in Los Angeles, and the place was always packed.

After cleaning the kitchen, I would run upstairs and make sure everything in Rinpoche's room was alright. If Rinpoche had an audience or people coming to meet him, I would vacuum his room and make sure everything was clean and in order. Then I would go downstairs, ask them to please wait a few minutes and confer with Rinpoche's assistant to see if it was okay.

When they said it was okay, I would assist the person into Rinpoche's room. I made sure I did not wait for Rinpoche to come out to call them in. When they went inside Rinpoche's room and had an audience, I would stay nearby quietly, as alert as possible, in case Rinpoche needed anything. I would make sure I never let Rinpoche be without anyone close at hand.

---

[6] Rinpoche spent his childhood with a foster family in New Jersey, where he often received tremendous physical and emotional abuse from his foster parents. They forbade him from pursuing the Dharma but his passion for the teachings led him eventually to run away from home. He hitchhiked penniless and alone all the way across the United States to Los Angeles, where he found Thubten Dhargye Ling centre.

After Rinpoche's interviews or divinations, I would assist him downstairs, carry incense, carry his hat, help him to sit on the throne and fix his robes. When he was sitting on the throne, I would not leave his side. Even before he sat down, I would make sure everything was straightened.

Then I would sit for Dharma teachings. I had notebooks and more notebooks filled with notes; the notes that I wrote down then are still very useful to me now. In between teachings, if Rinpoche needed anything, I would attend to him; I made sure his thermos was always filled with whatever he needed. If the teachings were exceptionally long, I would assist Rinpoche upstairs after they were finished. If I had to help, explain or talk about some questions with the Dharma students, I would do so. If Geshe-la needed something, I would attend to him. If not, I would go upstairs and give Rinpoche a massage.

Usually if I could, I would give Rinpoche a massage nightly. Once in a blue moon, Rinpoche had a headache so I would have the honour to touch his head. I would wash my hands, purify them with incense and make three prostrations before I massaged his head. Whether I was clean or not would not affect Rinpoche but to be conscientious about what I was doing and who I was serving would affect me and my awareness. Why? Because I wanted attainments.

I would massage Rinpoche's head very gently. I would make sure my nails were cut so I would not puncture his skin. I would be very careful and very aware because I was touching my Guru's head – my Guru, the one who confers on me Dharma! That was the reason I left my home and school: to learn the Dharma.

After Dharma teachings, everyone would go home. I lived at the Dharma centre, so I would stay up to clean the kitchen, wash the floor, mop and clean the cabinets. I did it to make the place clean for when people came to see Zong Rinpoche and Geshe-la, so my Gurus would not be misrepresented. I did it to make the place clean for Zong Rinpoche's feet to step on, if he walked downstairs and past the kitchen. I wanted to be sure of that.

Every once in awhile, Geshe-la would come downstairs, on his way somewhere. He would look at what I was doing but he would not say anything to me. He would just pat me on the back, which meant he was very pleased. I did not get any gifts, flowery praises or any of that stuff. That was the reward I got. It was more than enough.

I did not care about the people who were not happy about me in the beginning and thought I would "misrepresent" Rinpoche. I proved them all wrong and silenced them. After that, no one had a complaint. No one even talked about the burned chicken I offered Rinpoche or the uncooked potatoes that Rinpoche patiently ate!

I will never forget those days. I never look back on those days as work. I have never regretted, felt tired or felt I did not want to do it. Never. Not even once in my life for the last 20 years. Oh my god, it was so much work! But I do not remember being in pain, or being sick. I felt I was collecting merits with a person without faults, that everything that I did would accelerate my Dharma practice and my Dharma attainments. In that one year, I did not go out to any clubs or meet any of my non-Dharma friends, and the year passed so quickly.

I cannot explain to you how wonderful those days were of cooking, cleaning and serving my teacher, and receiving Dharma every single night. Sometimes, I cannot believe I was there.

I was in mortal fear that Rinpoche would leave. I could not even think of the day he was leaving. When Zong Rinpoche passed away, I did not recover for months, almost for years. Even though going to India was exciting, it was empty. I felt empty going to Dharamsala and to Gaden in India.[7] And when I went to his house, I felt empty because I expected him to come out, to walk around or to be there. But he was not. I kept my promise because I said I would enter his house, I would go to India and I would join Gaden.

There was a time, after Zong Rinpoche passed away, that I thought I was not going to do that anymore. I was going to pursue acting and entertainment. But one day, I sat down and I asked myself, "Do I believe he's Heruka or not?" It was a very difficult question because it was a very easy way to escape and to say, "Well, my Guru died, I can't go to India and join him anymore."

The answer came out that, yes, he is not physically in front of me but Buddha Heruka is all-pervasive. If I made a promise to him, I must keep it, whether he was directly watching me or not. I told myself that I was going to do it, so I packed up everything and went to India.

---

7 Tsem Rinpoche made a promise to Zong Rinpoche that he would become ordained as a monk and join Gaden Shartse Monastery to pursue his Dharma studies. Rinpoche eventually joined Gaden in 1987.

Zong Rinpoche taught me the Dharma, his lineage was pure, he conferred on me the highest initiations, and he gave me my Dharma Protector practices and all the paths of Dharma from the *Lamrim Chenmo* to the highest practices. He scolded me, he shouted at me, he gave me so much love that everything I am doing today is totally a result of his kindness. He is the only person I miss every single day, and I do not have much attachment to people.

The retreats that I was able to do and the little bit of improvement I have experienced all stem from him. I will never, ever give up my vows, and the commitments and promises I made to my root Guru, even at the cost of my life.

One big reason that I teach Dharma today is because of Zong Rinpoche and the promise I made to him. If I break my promise to Rinpoche, then there

> **"One big reason that I teach Dharma today is because of Rinpoche and the promise I made to him."**

are no more Buddhas for me. The Buddhas do not exist anymore. If I cannot commit to the person who has taught me the Dharma and shown me so much kindness, who *can* I commit to? A wife? A friend? A business partner? What is the long term benefit of that?

I am committed to my Guru, I have an "attachment" for him because I have not met anyone like that. I am committed to my Guru because he has given me the highest empowerments and I know their benefits. I know how important they are and how rare they are, and to get it from such a master is incredible!

I wish so *much* that I could learn more from him, be near him and serve him. I would not mind being his servant for the rest of my life – to travel with him and to be his servant, quietly, to sit on the floor near him, so he can teach the Dharma. There is no difference if he teaches or if I teach, as long as the Dharma is taught.

When I read the manuals of Guru devotion and how we should conduct ourselves with the Guru, I resolved that I would follow it all the way. I have not made any infractions of my Guru devotion, not that I know of. I have never spoken against my Gurus; I have never argued or fought with my Gurus. I would not dare.

In the presence of my Rinpoche, I never slouched, because that is what the *Fifty Verses on Guru Devotion*[8] advises and I know why now. It is to create awareness. It would be good manners not to slouch in front of anybody, wouldn't it? My Guru was teaching me good manners so that when I went out into the world, I could be more effective in whatever I want to do with others. I never slouched in front of my teacher, I never farted, I never burped. If I coughed, I covered myself. I did not scratch myself, twist my body around, massage myself, or crack my knuckles because that is what the *Fifty Verses* instructs.

It is about awareness and manners. If we cannot do that in front of our Dharma teacher, who can we do that in front of? That is the whole purpose of having a Dharma teacher – to bring that awareness to the forefront. I would be very aware of that. I will keep my commitments to someone who is giving me the most powerful initiation – whether he is around or not around. I have promised him and I said "yes". When we say "yes" and when we promise something, we have to do it. Our integrity, our reputation, our self-growth and our spiritual growth lies behind that. Our lineage, our face, our parents, and everything good that we represent lie behind that. When we say "yes", we have to do it.

I have met many masters and they were all very kind and I have received so much from them but the one who left the greatest impact, an indelible mark on me for the rest of my life was Zong Rinpoche. This is what has made me go on for many years and this is why I encourage people towards Guru devotion.

I am not interested in being people's Guru. I am interested in people having Guru devotion. Whatever Gurus they have, I am not interested in taking them away or separating them because how would I feel? How did I feel when I separated from my Guru? I would not want that feeling for anyone.

It still shocks me when people make promises to me, as their Dharma teacher, and they break their promises, because I am not able to do that. I am not able to be rude to my Gurus, young, old, or reincarnated.

How can we be rude, lie to, talk about or scorn someone who has taught us the Dharma from their heart? It is a knowledge that we can use to better our lives. If we can scorn our Guru, say negative things, make

[8] A text written by the Indian pandit Ashvaghosha that gives us guidelines for how we should conduct ourselves in front of our Gurus.

him upset, fight, whisper things behind his back, retaliate or break our promises to him, then everybody else is just below that. Then we can do it to everybody and anybody.

I encourage Guru devotion practice, I encourage devotion to one's teacher, I encourage people to keep their *samaya* and keep their commitments clean. If we do not, then where does our spiritual practice go? What can having no commitment equate to?

I am wishy-washy about everything else but not with the Dharma, Guru devotion, commitments and promises I made to my Guru. I cannot be wishy-washy on that. I want attainments, I want to make my mind ascend another level and I want to get the results of my practice, so I am going to follow the hard and fast rules that will bring the result.

All the Gurus from Tibet, all the Gurus from India, all those great *Mahasiddhas* cannot be wrong. Guru devotion cannot be wrong because every master I have met talks about it and the very attained ones take that as the pith of their practice. They cannot be wrong.

THE GURU

> No one has ever become Enlightened without a teacher.

Guru comes from the combination of two Sanskrit words: *Guna*, meaning "good qualities," and *Ruchi*, meaning "a collection". So, *Guna* and *Ruci* is "a collection of good qualities". Temporarily, for now, we need a Guru on the outside but the outer Guru leads us to the inner Guru. Without the outer Guru there is no guideline for our practice; it is impossible.

In worldly life, we need teachers, we need help. Everything we have in life has been acquired from a teacher or someone who has taught us – a parent, at school, a relative, etc. Whenever we want to achieve anything in ordinary, worldly situations, we must have someone to guide us and lead the way. We respect that person, and we speak nicely and politely to them. If we fight back, show no respect, do not listen and do the opposite of what the teacher tells us to do, then we will not be able to learn or perceive as quickly.

This is just for our ordinary lives, which is only for about 60 to 80 years. For our spiritual lives, when we want Enlightenment – where the roads and direction are much more complicated, difficult, longer and even dangerous at times – how can we achieve this without a teacher? There is no way we can achieve this without a teacher.

Not everything can be learnt from books. I was just reading a commentary about spiritual teachers which said very clearly that if we only read books to study, we can only reach a very low point. Many questions cannot be answered. We need a teacher with experience to explain these things to us.

If books were enough, then the Buddha would have emanated as books and he would never have spoken a single word of teaching. If teachers were not necessary, Buddha would have never manifested as a universal teacher.

No one has ever become enlightened without a teacher. It is impossible without a teacher – not in this world, in this age, at this juncture. There may be other world systems where Buddhas have manifested, turned the Wheel of Dharma and given other sets of teachings where those beings could run on their own for a while. According to what I have studied, it is not like that in this place.

In this fortunate eon, 1,000 Buddhas will appear. The fourth Buddha was Shakyamuni, who manifested 2,500 years ago. Even after Shakyamuni, many superior Buddhas and *Bodhisattvas* have appeared to teach and benefit, such as Manjushri and Chenrezig. Many great saints and masters like Jesus Christ and Mohammad have manifested all over the world.

We have not had – and probably will not have – the opportunity to attend their teachings at this time. At our stage, at this point in our lives, we will probably never see the Buddha. (This does not mean that the Buddha does not exist. We just do not have the karmic affinity to see an enlightened Being.)

So how can we receive the Dharma if we cannot get the Buddha to teach? In our present pitiful state, where we cannot see the Buddhas, nor receive their teachings and hear from them, who will be compassionate enough to teach us and give us guidance and help? Who will put up with our delusions, our anger, our complaints and childish problems? Who would do that all day, into the night, free of charge, with no expectations?

Here is an analogy: during a famine when you are very poor, someone might come along and give you a little bit of money, which you use to start a business. When you become very wealthy from that business, many rich patrons come to your shop and many people do business with you. Who is kinder to you? The rich patrons that come later or that single person who helped you in the beginning?

That person is like our Guru, while the Buddhas are like the patrons that come later. We can only see the Buddhas by practice; the practice can come only via our teacher. Without our teacher's

"We can only see the Buddhas by practice; the practice can come only via our teacher."

blessings, practice, instructions and his giving us the Dharma, how will we ever reach a state where we can actually see the Buddhas, perceive and listen to them directly? In order for wood to catch fire from the sun, we need a magnifying glass. That sun is like the Buddha, the magnifying glass is like your Guru, and the timber or the wood is like yourself. If you just stick the wood under the sun, it will never catch fire. It works in this way.

The Guru never teaches in a way that he expects things back from us. Our Gurus give out of compassion, with the motivation that we may be free. Our Guru teaches us on the basis of compassion and on the basis of reality. He has spent his whole life studying, he has given up his pleasures and worldly pursuits, and anxiety for money, position and status, so he can study the Dharma, practise it and convey it to us to change our lives.

When we put our Gurus on the throne, it is to show our respect for the Dharma. Monks and teachers are put on a throne in all Buddhist countries to show respect for the holy Dharma, our second refuge. It is not to uplift that person. How beautiful or ornate the throne is reflects the devotion you have toward the Dharma, the Dharma talks and the Dharma that is being conveyed from these thrones.

THE ROOT GURU

> From the root Guru, all roots of attainments arise.

Our root Guru is the person who made an indelible and powerful impact in our minds, to turn away from worldly actions and to engage in Dharma actions. The root Guru is someone who associates very closely with us, takes care of us, talks to us and helps us. Our root Guru is the Guru who inspires us the most, who has given us a lot of Dharma and who has changed our life.

A root Guru may not necessarily be the person we take refuge with. There is often that wrong view. Someone is not our root Guru just because of his status, because he is famous, he has a great publicist who advertises him very well, his books are all over the place and he is in the media. He is not a qualified Guru just because of these things. He may be qualified. He may not be. He may not even be the Guru for us, even if he is qualified. Whether he is the right Guru for us or not will depend on what we need, our personality and the type of Guru that will suit us. That is an individual decision, something we have to examine in our heart. No one can tell us this.

It is important to check this because there is a huge Dharma supermarket out there – all types of Gurus in all types of shapes, colours, types of hats and robes, and backgrounds are available. You want a Guru with a big, long lineage? You got one! You want a tall Guru with a medium lineage? You got one! There are all types out there.

Do you want a Guru who is famous so you can run around, be in the limelight and have pictures taken with him? Or do you want a Guru who is not very well-known? Who cares? There is no difference. As long as this Guru touches our heart, opens our mind and makes an indelible impact on our mind to turn us towards doing virtuous work, he is our real root Guru.

We should not pick a Guru on the basis of appearance, status, wealth, whether he has a centre or a temple or a long lineage, whether he is a reincarnation of a high teacher or not. We should not choose our teacher based on any of those things. We should base our decision on whether the teacher has compassion and teaches us Dharma and whether the teacher changes our mind and helps us towards Dharma practice with his teachings. It depends on his relationship with us and how he affects our mind.

That is why they are called "root" Gurus – they change the root of our thinking, they change our whole basis of life, the whole basis of where we come from. They change everything.

And from the roots, the whole tree grows; from the root Guru, all roots of attainments arise.

WHY WE NEED A GURU

A Guru is someone who challenges us, pushes us, tells us ugly and nasty things and tells us things about ourselves that are both true and untrue. When we are challenged, we will see where our mind is.

Let me tell you a secret. The real reason we have a Guru is for him to scold us, to tell us off, to point out our weaknesses, to tell us ugly things, to tell us things we don't like to hear, to push us to do things we do not want to do, to make us achieve something we did not think we could and to give us something inside that he can perhaps see through experience, divination, dreams and revelations, which we did not know we could do. A real Guru is not someone who praises us, gives us gifts and tells us nice things. It is the person who scolds us, tells us off and tells us what is wrong.

We should not fight back or make excuses. We should achieve whatever our teacher tells us to do – no matter how impossible and difficult it may seem. That is what a Guru is for.

Think about our teachers at school. They made us do everything we did not want to do and they gave us all those difficult, ugly assignments! Think about our parents. They made us do everything we did not want to – eat vegetables, take vitamins, go to sleep early, wash up, brush our teeth, not watch bad television shows, not to be rude to our neighbours or not to fight. Everything that we have now comes from being made to do what we did not want to do.

A Guru is not someone who is supposed to be kind, nice, gentle, easy and all smiling to us. That is not a Guru, that is a big Shangri-la man who comes once every three years, gives initiations, pats us on the head, throws some flowers and tells us how wonderful we are. Of course if we see these Gurus once every few years for just a few days, we will think he is holy and wonderful, and we will cry when someone just mentions his name.

A real Guru is not someone who is nice to us. He might do that in the beginning to train us and prepare us. But a real Guru is someone who challenges us, pushes us, tells us ugly and nasty things, and tells us things about ourselves that are both true and untrue. When we are challenged, we will see where our mind is. A Guru will press all our buttons to help us see our minds; and to help him see our minds so he can help us. We want a Guru to bring us to Enlightenment and we achieve Enlightenment by destroying the qualities in our mind that block us from Enlightenment. We destroy those negative qualities by recognising them; and we are led to recognise them when our Guru brings them forth to us.

"How we react, what kind of face we show to the Guru and behind the Guru shows us our level of practice."

When we reach a higher level of practice, when our minds are more stable, our Guru may even accuse us of things that are not true. How we react, what kind of face we show to the Guru and behind the Guru shows us our level of practice. Ultimately, through this training, we will get to a point where nothing disturbs us.

When nothing disturbs us, we have acquired a wish-fulfilling jewel just like what Avalokiteshvara holds in his hands. This wish-fulfilling jewel is a mind that creates no negative karma, a mind that fulfils all our wishes. That mind arises when nothing disturbs it anymore.

TAKING A GURU

It is not the Guru's action but the motivation behind the acts that counts.

CHECKING THE GURU

Students sometimes have doubts as to whether their Guru is harmful or beneficial. This is why it is very important for us to check our Guru before we take him as our Guru. We are advised that we can take up to 12 years to check the Guru, while the Guru checks us for 12 years.

As it says in the *Fifty Verses on Guru Devotion*:

In order for the words of honour of neither the Guru nor the disciple to degenerate, there must be a mutual examination beforehand to determine if each can brave a teacher-disciple relationship.

A disciple with sense should not accept as his Guru someone who lacks compassion or who is angersome, vicious or arrogant, possessive, undisciplined or boasts of his knowledge.

Verses 6 & 7[9]

It tells us very clearly to check beforehand, not after we have taken refuge. It is our choice. The verses tell us that if we come across someone with those negative qualities, we should stop right here. We do not need to go for refuge and we do not need to take this person on.

Do not check afterwards. Do you check your car after you buy it? Do you check your husband after you marry him? Do you check your house carefully after you buy it? Then why would you check the Guru after you have taken refuge?

Most Gurus will not confer initiations, higher practices or higher vows until we are connected to them. Real Gurus will tease us, play with us, jest with us, push us around, scream at us, shout at us, put us down,

---

[9] This version of the *Fifty Verses on Guru Devotion* is extracted from *buddhism.kalachakra.org*. All subsequent citations are also from this website.

give us gifts, make us happy, help us and shout at us, back and forth, so we can see each other's characteristics and qualities. If we have the good fortune to be near a teacher on a personal basis, then we can examine his character and his daily actions all the time. Realise that whether the daily activities of the Guru are mundane or Dharmic, it is not the activity but the motivation behind it that counts.

Verse 8 of the *Fifty Verses* on Guru Devotion explains:

A Guru should be stable in his actions, cultivated in his speech, wise, patient and honest. He should neither conceal his shortcomings nor pretend to possess qualities he lacks. He should be an expert in the meanings of the Tantra and in its ritual procedures of medicine and turning back obstacles. Also, he should have loving compassion and complete knowledge of the scriptures.

A Guru's consistency or "stability in his actions" refers to his perseverance for Dharma – spreading the Dharma, giving us the Dharma and transforming us for Dharma. That is what it means to be "stable in his actions." If he changes his clothes, hair-style and food, it does not mean he is unstable because those things do not matter. It is his intention towards the Dharma that matters.

We can check the long-term results of his actions and his motivation. We can check out our Gurus by their students, by what they do for the monastery and their Dharma organisation. We can see how much they give up for others – how much sleep, love, care, finances and reputation they can give up for others. We can see if the result matches the person's motivation.

I cannot go around examining some high Gurus to check if they are pure or not, so I look at his actions, his people, what he does, how he acts. If he is totally obnoxious and loud, I look at the effect that his actions have on the students. Even if some students run away, we can ask if they have regrets, if they still love the Guru, how they feel. Only then will we know the Guru's motivation.

We can check if the Guru surrounds himself with material items for himself, such as jewels, beautiful houses, beautiful women and lots of money; or if he tries to surround himself with Dharma, such as Dharma objects, Dharma people, Dharma motivation, Dharma work, Dharma projects. If he is always talking about Dharma projects and work, and speaks of a Dharma motivation; if he is always moving us through and with Dharma, then he must be without an ulterior agenda.

In this degenerate time, it is hard to find a Guru we can view perfectly. Therefore, the criteria for us today should be whether this person, whom we take as a Guru, concerns himself more with this life or future lives. If this person concerns himself more with future lives, then his actions will be in accord. If this person is more concerned with this life, his actions will be in accord and it should not be a qualification that we should go for. If this person is more concerned about his future lives, he will not be after wealth, appearances and good places. He will be studying the Dharma, practising morality, teaching, praying. If he is more concerned about future lives and he can convey the Dharma; if he can inspire us and we benefit from his Dharma, then we can take him as a Guru.

A true Guru will hide his qualities and will not tell you what his attainments are. He will tell you that he is stupid, full of anger, lazy, not advanced in his practice and not qualified.

A false Guru will tell us he floats in the sky, he sees Kuan Yin and he can talk to Amitabha. This is a sign of a false Guru because a real Guru has modesty and has humility. These would be some of the qualities he has cultivated in his practice. If he does not have that, how can he be preaching qualities like humility?

Of course, we should not be fooled by his humble talk. We should not think that he really is stupid, full of anger, is lazy, that he does not have attainments and does not know what he is doing. We should not think it is that simple just because he said so, because a true Guru will never, ever reveal his attainments.

For example, we know that His Holiness the Dalai Lama is Avalokiteshvara but he would never say that. He says, "I'm just a simple Buddhist monk. My name is Tenzin Gyatso." A true Guru will never, ever reveal his qualities to us. It is only by our practice, meditation and attainment that we can slowly see the qualities of our Guru.

After we receive the vows from our Guru, we should hold them, we should be conscientious about them – we should read teachings like *The Fifty Verses on Guru Devotion, Relating to a Spiritual Teacher*[10] or *Dangerous Friend*[11] on how we should interact with, talk to and treat our Guru.

Taking refuge with a Guru is not a game and once we take refuge, we cannot turn against our Guru, or say nasty and ugly things about him. It is presumed that we have used our wisdom to check them out. If we say things about him, it is then assumed that everyone must see our Guru as evil and rotten. If everybody else does not see that and we see that, it is our own wrong perception. We will look stupid and ridiculous; we will look like we were in haste, in a momentary fad and did not check.

If we hastily take a person as a Guru and we act out of line, the responsibility falls on us, not on the Guru. *The Fifty Verses on Guru Devotion* warns,

> Having become the disciple of such a protecting Guru, should you despise him from your heart, you will reap continual suffering as if you have disparaged all the Buddhas.
>
> Verse 10

We will collect the karma of not meeting a Guru, or not meeting or following the proper teachings in the future.

Also, we should not just cultivate a Guru relationship with someone who has a high, big name and a big entourage. We should not develop a relationship with a Guru because he is charismatic or attractive, or because he is a scholar and teaches the Dharma eloquently, or because he is wealthy, has a lot of disciples and people praise him. Our Guru devotion and the person we receive Dharma from have nothing to do with the person's status, form, appearance, name or position.

We should develop an affinity with a teacher because we can understand the teachings from this person, we can relate to this person and he can guide us to Enlightenment, whether he is a layperson or a monk, whether he has a high name or a low name, whether he is attractive or not, or scholarly or not.

---

10 Alexander Berzin, *Relating to a Spiritual Teacher: Building a Healthy Relationship* (New York: Snow Lion Publications, 2000)

11 Rig'dzin Dorje, *Dangerous Friend: The Teacher-student Relationship in Vajrayana Buddhism* (Shambala Publications, 2001)

It is better to take as our Guru a simple monk who does not have a lot of knowledge but who inspires us and helps us to practise, than to take a high scholar who does not practise anything he says and who will probably end up in hell anyway!

TAKING A GURU

There is no formal ceremony for taking a Guru, or for the Gurus to accept us as their students. The Dalai Lama for example, cannot say, "I accept you, I accept you, I accept you as my student" to every person who goes up to him. Each Kalachakra initiation has 40,000 people! However, if anyone in the audience thinks, "I take this person as my Guru from now on," then the bond is sealed. It is nothing verbal or spoken. It can be a spoken or unspoken bond; that is up to us.

However, if we wish to take a second teacher, we must have the permission of the first. Without the permission of our first teacher, we cannot get teachings from the second. If we do, no attainments will arise. It is for us to show respect.

If for any reason our teacher should say no to us going to another Guru, we should not think that our Guru is being mean to us and that he just wants to keep us for himself. If we think like that, we may as well forget the whole thing!

There are many books that benefit us and talk about the relationship with the Guru. Instead of relying on hearsay from here and there, we should read these guides and be sure. We have to ask ourselves if we treasure this relationship and if it is important to us. We read up, check and surf the net for everything else that is important. We should do the same for this.

THE CRAZY WISDOM OF THE GURU

> The Guru will do things that are completely the opposite of what you expect.

The Guru will do things that are completely the opposite of what you expect. He uses what we might call unconventional, crazy wisdom.

It is crazy in the way we think that another culture's habits are crazy. Craziness is culturally conceived and whether something is crazy or not is a reference point which we are born with. For example, in this country, you might think that eating dogs is crazy and disgusting. In other countries, they think you are crazy for *not* eating dogs.

It is not whether something is right or wrong. When we operate at a certain level and someone is judging us from a lower or different level, they will think it is crazy. For example, when we were kids, we could not understand some of the things that our parents told us – we thought they were crazy for sending us to school or telling us to do certain things. Now that we have grown up and we are more at their level of thinking, we understand what they were doing for us and why. It is the same with our Gurus. We are not yet at a level where we are able to directly examine why he is doing what he is doing.

High Gurus can manifest incredible crazy wisdom. You might ask why he does this, why he would act like that to embarrass himself. We wonder, "Why doesn't the Guru act the way I feel a Guru should act?" It is precisely because we are so attached to the way a person should act, that the Guru does not act that way – it is to break our attachments.

We must realise that the Guru puts himself at risk to lose our respect, our confidence and our faith. But he has no ego and he has no agenda to get something from us, like money, praise, or admiration. The Guru is out to save us. He is willing to risk having us "hate" him if he can benefit us by doing something that looks controversial or crazy. The

> **"He is willing to risk having us 'hate' him if he can benefit us by doing something that looks controversial or crazy."**

Guru may use very wrathful means in certain situations. For example, if he knows that you are doing something very negative, which will bring many negative effects to others, and he knows that you will not do any spiritual practice to purify it, he may use very wrathful methods to make the karma manifest now, so you do not have to suffer it later.

He might send us on assignments that we do not understand. It does not have to be complicated. Sometimes our Gurus might use very simple ways, using simple things like food, to train his students. For example, he might send several people out at the same time, at 4am in the middle of the night, to find a certain type of food.

We may start to have doubt, or wonder if the Guru is crazy. If he was actually crazy, he would be like that all the time, with every person. Usually, he is selective with whom he is "crazy". If he is selective, it means that he is training that particular person. If the Guru was like that with everybody, then he is not training anyone – he really is crazy! (A really crazy person will act crazily with whomever he comes across, whether it is the president, a beautiful lady or a bum off the street.)

You might ask, if we are not at the level to understand why our Guru does what he does, then how do we check him? It is, again, by checking the result of his actions and the motivation of his actions. We look at whether he is more concerned about this life, or whether he has great concern for our future lives; we can see whether he is always excited about material things, cars, houses, women or if he is excited about something higher like Dharma work, Dharma practice, Dharma things and benefiting people.

GURU DEVOTION: WHAT SUBMISSION REALLY MEANS

> Devotion leads to your inner Guru, your natural state of mind.

Guru devotion is not cooking, cleaning, washing and giving money to the Gurus. Guru devotion is not just about crying, feeling sad or getting emotional when you talk about your Guru. Those are small, small parts of it, an extension of Guru devotion.

When you think about your Guru, you think about a person who is extraordinary. Therefore, you cry because you have never met such a person who has had such an impact on you. You cry because you are connected to him as a disciple, and therefore you should push yourself towards your commitments.

Real Guru devotion is about developing and keeping your spiritual qualities. You do not let go of your commitments, you develop the qualities that you see your Guru embodies, that make you cry. Guru devotion is about keeping your promises and doing your *sadhanas* at all cost. Guru devotion is about not harming another person, being very kind to others and becoming better and better. Real Guru devotion is about destroying the self-cherishing mind. All that is Guru devotion because that devotion leads to your inner Guru, your natural state of mind – kindness, commitment and clarity.

People think that when they submit themselves to the Guru, they become a slave. No way! If you were an indentured servant in the olden days, you may have been made into a slave. But this is not the olden days! And you have to ask yourself who you are "indenturing" yourself to. A wealthy land owner? Some noble who owns 500 acres and makes you work in the fields every day? Or are you "indenturing" yourself to a spiritual person who is training you like a spiritual athlete, to put you in the ultimate competition so you do not lose out at the time of death?

We thought that going to school every day was a prison but we gained freedom from that – we gained education so we can do what we want now. Submitting to a qualified Guru or a Guru who cares about us, who is sincere and who has love, is like everything else in life – by submitting and listening to someone who can give us knowledge and show us the methods to benefit and develop ourselves, we will advance in anything we want to do.

If we need to be told the same thing again and again, it reflects our selfishness. If the Guru gives us instructions to do something and we say no, then we have not submitted. If we show anger to our teachers, we fight back, we ignore our teachers; if we always turn around the instructions they give us, forget, and have to be reminded, won't that be the same with everything else that we do in our lives?

If these people choose to be purely selfish, and they come up against a Guru who challenges that selfishness, they either submit or they run. Some students are smart and they do a little at a time. It starts off as little but they push themselves to do it all the way eventually. There is no student who comes in and is immediately perfect in all his actions but his aspiration, and working towards it, makes a very big difference.

We must remember that the whole purpose of the practice is to destroy arrogance. When we submit to the Guru, it is not to lose our freedom; it is to gain full freedom. Through the practice of Dharma and Enlightenment, we gain full freedom. It is not just about getting money, long life or protection from obstacles. We gain full freedom – we gain control of where we go, what we do, our rebirth and how we benefit. We gain full benefit.

If, in our next rebirth, we want to have money, we will be born into money. We will be born where we want to be born. We gain full control. This is why we submit to the Guru. It is just like submitting to school, to training, to our teachers, to our parents, to our counsellors, to our psychiatrists and doctors.

We all submit, we are already always submitting! We submit to our doctors to invade our bodies. We only have one body – if he messes up, we're finished! We submit to our beautician. One wrong jab and some of the muscles in our face will never move again! We submit to our teachers, we submit to our wives and husbands, we submit to our children. Some of us even submit to our dogs and cats; our lives are controlled by them! We cannot go anywhere nor do anything because we are completely controlled by our pets. We put ourselves into those situations, whether we do it deliberately or not. We are always submitting to others. It is nothing new to submit. Only now, it is to a person who helps us on the ultimate, highest level.

> "Devotion to and submission to our Guru is the beginning of us becoming independent – of our ego, of *samsara* and of our afflictive emotions."

Devotion to and submission to our Guru is the beginning of us becoming independent – of our ego, of *samsara* and of our afflictive emotions. It may look like we have imprisoned ourselves, but if he is a real Guru, the minute we submit to him, believe, trust, let go and do as he says, it is the first step towards total freedom. The Guru will push us, give us assignments and design work for us that will help us achieve the six *paramitas*, *Bodhicitta* and compassion, which are the necessary prerequisites of higher practices that give us total freedom.

When you sacrifice, submit and do things for the Guru that you ordinarily would not do, you collect merit. Psychologically, you open up because this person will challenge you to become better. If we look at people who are close to the Guru, we will see that no matter how bad they are, they become better or they get some benefit – physical, monetary or emotional – most of the time. We will also see people who are forthright, improving and becoming better and better, year after year when they are around the Guru.

The minute you submit to your Guru, you immediately win your first day of independence. The day you meet a real Guru is the day he starts to separate you from him, to make you independent of him.

Real Gurus do not become clingy with us. They make us more and more independent. Their goal is to make us a Buddha, not to have companions around him. You may think you were working with your Guru last year, doing this and that with him, and question why you are not this year. You think, "Poor me, poor me. I did so much for you but you don't let me do anything anymore this year. It's so unfair. It's so bad." This shows that the student does not know the purpose of a Guru-disciple relationship.

Do you think the Guru has to be clingy with you? Do you think that the Guru does not like you or that he has rejected you when he switches your job or responsibilities around? Perhaps the initial methods were not working, so he does something else to help you. Perhaps you have already done and mastered a task so he may give you something else to help you develop your mind. Sometimes a Guru will let you be clingy, sometimes the Guru will make you not be clingy – it is your level that the Guru is looking at.

People do not understand Guru devotion. They think it is slavery. They think it is indoctrination or a loss of freedom but it is absolutely the opposite. When I hooked up with my teachers, I gained freedom. Look what I am doing now. Guru devotion was and is my main practice. When I had obstacles and problems, because I had so much faith in my Guru, my Dharma Protector in Gaden[12] told me in an audience with him, "Don't recite any mantras, recite your Guru's mantra and you will be fine." So I did; I recited my Guru's mantra 100,000 times and my sickness healed. I did not need to do any *pujas*.

If you think this is slavery or induction, or the forcing of another culture, you are absolutely wrong. I will not be diplomatic about it. I will be diplomatic with everything else and give concessions because I know we are all trying, but not in the case of Guru devotion. There are no concessions. That is the pith of the path. Without an instructor, without a teacher, without someone to guide you, and without your cooperation with this person, what benefit can you derive?

If you are studying under a music teacher but you are always late, you forget your music scores, you do not do your homework, you do not practise, you break your guitar, you do not restring it, you forget your appointment, you are rude to your teacher, you pick your nose in front of him, you do not listen to instructions, how is he going to teach you how to play the guitar? And that is just for playing a guitar! Imagine how much more alert we must be if we want to learn how to attain Enlightenment.

Even with normal teachers who teach us writing and arithmetic, we have to be respectful because arithmetic and writing will benefit us. But we want benefit that will help us in many lifetimes. If we have an instructor for that – our Guru – and cannot be respectful or submissive, or even trust or try, then how will we gain that benefit?

---

12 Dharma Protectors, enlightened beings who work specifically to clear obstacles in our spiritual path and work, can manifest through a specially trained person known as an oracle and speak directly to us.

OUTER PROTOCOL – *THE FIFTY VERSES ON GURU DEVOTION*

It is to remind us of the correct conduct towards a being who teaches us Enlightenment or represents the state of Enlightenment that we wish to achieve.

Verse 48 of the *Fifty Verses on Guru Devotion* by Ashvagosha states:

After a disciple has taken refuge in the Triple Gem and developed a pure Enlightened motive, he should be given this text to take to his heart how to abandon his own arrogant self-will and follow in his Guru's footsteps along the Graded Path to Enlightenment.

In this day and age, when we give this text to people in countries without Buddhist mass consciousness, they will reject it (even after they have taken Refuge), run away, or find it fanatical. They may not accept it because they do not know the real causes for refuge and how to act after taking refuge.

However, the reason we follow this text is stated very clearly: it is to let go of our arrogance. Although the verses seem to be restrictive and tell us that we cannot do a lot of things, the basic purpose of the whole text is to let go of arrogance.

The whole point of being polite in front of a Guru – such as to stand up for the Guru or to serve and help the Guru – is to hone and refine our outer actions to be polite with everybody. How we sit or act, and how alert we are is very important. A person's outer action reflects his inner mind. If we can control ourselves internally, then controlling our external behaviour becomes very easy.

When we attend Dharma talks, according to the *Fifty Verses on Guru Devotion*, we are not supposed to twist our bodies, crack our knuckles, stretch or point our feet to the Guru, play with our nails, look around, fall asleep and move about to get comfortable. It shows our flippancy. If we are not even at a level where we can control our outer bodies, how can we control our inner bodies or our mind? If we cannot even control our feet, fingers or spine, how are we going to meditate? If we cannot even control this body and we go around telling people we are spiritually advanced, we will look ridiculous!

When His Holiness Kyabje Zong Rinpoche gave teachings in Los Angeles, I watched my old Geshe[13] (who was Zong Rinpoche's student) sitting right in front of the room, fully aware, with his eyes half open, not looking left and right, never moving. He sat through eight to 10 hours of teachings like this, everyday. If Kyabje Zong Rinpoche said something funny, he would cover his mouth and laugh, just like a geisha. Now I know why people say he has good manners and why he is so advanced in his tantric practice – it is because he can control everything.

I have seen my great masters and how they act with their Guru. They are like a newly-wed bride (as it says we should be in the *Fifty Verses*). When they speak, they talk pleasantly and in such a way that their voice is clear; if their teacher shows any difficulty in hearing, then they speak louder. They are humble, they always smile, they are always pleasant and they make sure they pronounce their words well; they never make their Gurus suffer by having to ask them to repeat what they said.

If during a Dharma talk, we cannot be alert or polite, we cannot concentrate and focus – even if the Guru makes lots of jokes to keep us awake, the air conditioner is on and everything is provided – then what kind of spiritual pioneer or spiritual devotee are we?

Having said that, in a country that does not have this type of mass consciousness, respect comes in different ways. For example, students may make the effort to change their schedule or move their personal attachments around in order to attend the teachings – that is respect. Here, if you do not sit on the floor with your feet in a yogic position, it does not mean you do not have respect, it means your body is not able to or not used to it.

It is not about whether prostrating to our Gurus is Guru devotion. Whether or not we prostrate is not Guru devotion. Those things are cultural. Some people in other countries just bow – that is equivalent to a full Tibetan prostration. Guru devotion is not a fanatical practice which makes us do things that we physically cannot do. It is about the

13 Geshe Tsultim Gyeltsen

attitude of the mind. It is okay if you have not been sitting through hours of teachings with your back bent and hands folded for the last 40 years. If, instead, you sit on a chair comfortably, you are alert and do not fall asleep, that is very good. But to crack our knuckles, twist our bodies around, pick our noses, talk to our neighbours or fall asleep is rude across all cultures. Those are basic human manners that we need to be aware of.

Verse 45 says:

> If because of sickness, you are physically unable to bow to your Guru and must do what normally would be prohibited, even without his explicit permission, there will be no unfortunate consequences if you have a virtuous mind.

There is no bad karma if we do something wrong when we are sick, not able to do something, do not know the protocol or if it is not in our culture. These verses are not fanatical. The most important thing is that our mind remains virtuous.

What the *Fifty Verses on Guru Devotion* does is to use our physical, outer body to train our awareness. When it trains our awareness, it also trains us to be well-mannered. If we are mannered, alert and awake, we can dress and talk well, we will be able to bring other people to the Dharma.

People watch our devotion and interaction with the Guru. How we interact with and react to the Guru can be regarded as *tenzin*, "holder of the Dharma", or *tenshi*, "destroyer of the Dharma". Our bad actions and rudeness can destroy the Dharma among people around us because they will see that although we have been around the Guru for years, we are still behaving badly. They will immediately think that the Guru is ineffective.

If we want to talk about our Guru to anybody in the centre, it begins with our physical manners. That is the first sign of whether we really have conviction in our spiritual practice. You might ask what that has to do with inner meditation: everything and nothing. It is everything because if we are controlled within, then to control our behaviour on the outside is very easy.

We are taught not to argue with our Gurus and not to argue with others near his presence. We do not disturb our Guru's mind with our delusions. This is because he is there is to control our delusions, so if we are practising delusion next to him, what is the point of being near him? When he is with us or around us, we should control ourselves to the best of our ability and not argue, fight or engage in negative actions around him.

We do all this in our Guru's presence to train our mind to be aware, to be alert. It is training for us – we learn to do it once, twice, thrice, we become accustomed to it and we can then apply it to any situation. Dharma practitioners of the highest order are very polite, very mannered and groomed. Their body, their speech and their mind are used to hook people to the Dharma. Everything about their countenance evokes wondrous admiration in others, so that they ask, "What are you about? What is your history?" They talk to them, and they come to the Dharma. All that is for development; and all that is for compassion.

These are things that senior students should be able to teach others. Senior students should be able to take care of the new ones and the ones who always slip. Senior students should not just blindly ignore bad behaviour by other students, not do anything, say that they tried and leave it. Senior students should take the responsibility for this and not leave it for the Guru to correct other students; if we do that, we bring the Guru down to the level of a disciplinarian or a parent.

As it says in Verse 44,

Be diligent in all your actions, alert and mindful never to forget your word of honour. If fellow disciples transgress what is proper in their behaviour, correct each other in a friendly manner.

When I lived with Kensur Jampa Yeshe Rinpoche,[14] I took control of handling all the students' discipline. I would never bring it to Rinpoche because that would have been a distraction to take my Guru away from his real purpose of teaching. When other students and other disciples do not do what they are supposed to do, it is our responsibility as the Guru's disciple to let them know. If senior students keep quiet about other students who are always errant and full of mistakes, they allow this behaviour to continue or they let someone else talk about it, it is

---

14 One of Rinpoche's Gurus, the abbot emeritus of Gaden Shartse Monastery, who still resides in Gaden Monastery in south India.

a clear reflection of the senior students' lack of Guru devotion, care, compassion and commitment. It becomes another way of expressing that we do not care or that we do not want to look bad or lose face – that is ego.

Then, as it says in Verse 49, after training in the *Fifty Verses* and mastering them, we become a proper vessel of the Dharma. When we become a proper vessel of the Dharma, the Guru may give us empowerments, initiations and the tantric path.

> By studying the prerequisite trainings of Guru-devotion and the Graded Path, common to both the Sutra and Tantra, you will become a suitable vessel to hold the pure Dharma. You may then be given such teachings as Tantra. [...]

A real Guru would never give us empowerments or the tantric teachings without us first mastering the *Fifty Verses on Guru Devotion*.

These fifty verses train us in our spiritual practice, which is the best and ultimate offering to our Gurus. There are three types of offerings we can make to our Gurus: offering of material gifts or items, offering of service and offering of our spiritual practice. The offering of spiritual practice and transformation is the best out of the three and the one that our Gurus actually expect and want from us.

If we have taken refuge in our Guru, we should decrease hateful, bad states of mind, delusions and we should offer that up to our Guru. If we have recited the *Heart Sutra* one million times, or if we have gotten rid of or lessened our anger, we should offer that up to our Guru. The Guru wants our practice. If we just offer material things, we will still get merits and positive potential, and we will still make a connection with the Buddha. However, making material offerings is not actually the purpose of Guru devotion.

Reciting and meditating on the *Fifty Verses on Guru Devotion* is not a torturous act. It is not to brainwash or torture us, or to make us follow a Guru mindlessly. It is to remind us of the correct conduct towards a being who teaches us Enlightenment, and who is enlightened or represents the state of Enlightenment that we wish to achieve. The proper conduct towards the Guru is not fanatical. It is based on logic, and on our physical and mental capabilities.

> **"If we can practise all the qualities that are mentioned in the *Fifty Verses* with our Guru, we will be able to practise all this with all sentient beings."**

The Guru is the greatest training ground for us to destroy our delusions, illusions, hatred, anger and all the ten non-virtuous acts that we have engaged in since we were born, from our previous lives until now. Our Guru is the greatest training ground for us to become enlightened Beings. If we can practise all the qualities that are mentioned in the *Fifty Verses* with our Guru, we will be able to practise all this with all sentient beings. And finally, when we are able to practise this with *all sentient beings* without any feeling, hurt, attachment or detachment, then we will have realised Emptiness and gained compassion.

Our Guru is our battleground. The best thing about this is that he does not expect anything from us, except our Dharma practice. Anything we do in relation to him – offering food, material items or service, or assisting him – is not for him, it is for *us*.

THE INNER QUALITIES OF A DHARMA STUDENT – PRACTISING GURU DEVOTION WITH THE NINE ATTITUDES

> "The root of all that is auspicious and good,
> In this life and all of my future lifetimes,
> Is to enthusiastically devote myself, correctly, in thought and deed,
> To my Spiritual Guide who reveals the path."[15]

We are always talking about the qualities of a Guru – what the Guru should be, how the Guru can be criticised, helped or not helped. The Guru is always in the spotlight and there are always a lot of criticism and comments about the Guru.

We must also consider the qualities of the student. A real student is not necessarily a student of a Rinpoche, a Geshe or a Guru. A student is someone who happens to be learning Dharma from that person. A real student is a student of his own mind, of the Dharma.

A real student should follow the *Fifty Verses on Guru Devotion* which are fifty verses that explain outer protocol. This outer protocol is to train the inner mind in awareness and in service of the Dharma, spiritual practice and our Guru, to make it easier for the Guru to give us the Dharma teachings.

For those who cannot serve the Guru well, who are not aware and who are always making mistakes, it is very important for them to read, study and memorise the *Fifty Verses on Guru Devotion*. It is not to be a slave to a Guru. Every part of that text is for us to develop awareness. In fact, most of it is common sense.

---

[15] This version of *Practising Guru Devotion with the Nine Attitudes* was translated by David Molk for Kechara Media & Publications.

Then, if we condense those fifty verses, we have the *Nine Attitudes* of devotion to the Guru that, as students, we should have in receiving Dharma from our teacher and for our spiritual practice to advance.

Practising Guru devotion with the nine attitudes

Practising Guru Devotion with the Nine Attitudes begins:

Seeing that the root of all that is auspicious and good,
In this life and all of my future lifetimes,
Is to enthusiastically devote myself, correctly, in thought and deed,
To my Spiritual Guide who reveals the path:
Never giving him up even for the sake of my life,
I shall delight him with the supreme offering
Of practising in accordance with his instructions!

1) With an attitude like a good son: Who does not enter into activities independently but checks his father's demeanour first and then, sensitive to that, acts in accordance with his father's instructions.

If we accept a person as a teacher, we are submitting to our own mind and the Dharma practices to improve our mind, to bring us further and faster in our spiritual evolution.

Having a teacher who can give us living experience, talk, answer questions and who has the empowerments, lineage, blessings and oral transmissions to pass on to us is something very rare and very precious. In order to receive these teachings, our relationship with our Guru should not be that of a boss to someone subservient, or that of an employer to an employee, or that of an older brother scolding a younger brother. It should not be that of a husband or a wife, in the way that they sometimes fight and sometimes have harmony.

It should be like that of an obedient son acting exactly in accordance with the Guru's wishes. If we meet an abusive, scary, ill-motivated Guru, we could, of course, be taken advantage of. This is definitely so, and it has happened in the past to people. But if we have examined our Dharma teacher over time to avoid this problem, we should have no problem being as obedient as we can, like a son. What does it mean for us to have obedience to our Guru like a son? It means that if our Guru is a real Guru, he will not give us work that we cannot do. He will not exploit us. He will not use us. He will not harm us in any way, shape or form. If we meet a good Guru, and we are obedient like a son, he will only give us exercises, activities or practices that will make us excel. We have to cooperate with our teacher to excel.

2) With an attitude like a vajra: Indestructibly, such that no *mara*, harmful companion, or anything at all could ever separate you from the Guru.

Who are these harmful companions?

There are inner and outer *maras*. A *Mara* is an obstacle or a demon, but the demon is not always on the outside. In general, *maras* represent spirits or ghosts, or people on the outside that may come and say negative things to us about the Dharma or the Guru and push us off the path. Or they could be inner *maras* – a lot of anger, impatience, ineptness, laziness, irresponsibility. Those are very, very big *maras*. Those inner *maras* – laziness, selfishness, anger – stop us from carrying out the Guru's spiritual instructions to us. They are very dangerous. After we have checked out our Guru and accepted him as our Guru, we should see them as *maras* and avert them whenever they come to our minds.

If they are outer *maras*, we should push them away and the most effective way for this is meditating on *Bodhicitta*, great compassion. If they are inner *maras*, we let the anger, jealousy or lack of faith come and go, come and go. *Let it go*. We should not get attached or be attracted to it; we cannot get rid of anger overnight and if we let it take over us, it can take us away from our spiritual practice.

Then, there are "the harmful companions". Harmful companions are not people who come with daggers, clubs and hammers; they are not beings with fangs, red faces, long hair and long fingernails, dishevelled and bloody! A harmful companion is anyone who takes our time and energy away from thoughts of Enlightenment.

The people who overtly and directly criticise their Guru are harmful companions. If we hang out with them, we face the danger of losing our confidence and faith, and not progressing in our positive spiritual practice. Harmful companions are people who make us turn against or away from, or lose confidence in our Guru. They could do it on purpose or accidentally. They could also inadvertently make us lose confidence through their own practice or example.

Inadvertently (which is not accidental) means that they break their commitments and their vows, avoid, dislike or do not praise the Guru.

We have positive and negative dispositions in our mind. These dispositions will open according to the environmental causes or environmental triggers around us. If we are around Dharma students or people with the same intentions and same goals, and they encourage us, it triggers the positive dispositions to open. If we are around people who have broken their *samaya*, (even if they are not against our Guru but against *their* own Guru), they have broken-*samaya* energy which is very dirty. When they come around us, they will affect us – their energy will bring us down. Their coming around us, talking negatively about their Guru or our Guru, or not encouraging us towards our Guru in any way, triggers negative dispositions in our mind to open.

A new student needs a kicker-upper to encourage them and their practice. They need someone to talk about the Guru's good qualities, past good actions and what has been done. When we meet someone who does not encourage our relationship with our Guru, who has had a "fall out" with their Guru or broken their own commitments, then even if they do not say one word about the Guru – positive or negative – simply being around those people brings us down immediately. Their objective is already different from ours.

Over time, they will wear us down and make us lose confidence. They will make us see flaws in the Guru. We might think that they cannot make us see flaws that we have not already seen but they can lie and they can manipulate.

When *maras* or harmful companions try to split us from the Guru, they sometimes talk very nicely, they sometimes sound negative or they sometimes make us feel sorry for them. When those people associate with weak-minded people, or people with low merits, they will split them from the Guru. They will begin to see the Guru less often, avoid the Guru or think negative things about the Guru.

What benefit can a person obtain when, influenced by a harmful companion, he starts thinking negative things about his Guru? The harmful companion destroys his own chances for Dharma, and he destroys other people's chances for Dharma.

If they have broken off with our Guru but we met them through our Guru (or through our Guru's centre or friends), why do they still hang around us? Is their life so empty without Dharma friends? If they have no other friends outside of Dharma, what does that tell us about them?

There are also the friends who like our Guru, our practice and they follow our tradition but they do not practise, they break their commitments, they are lazy, they do not do their *sadhanas* or serve their Gurus. They do not hate the Gurus; they like the Gurus. Or they might flip back and forth. They might say, "My Guru is my Guru" one day, and then say, "He's my friend" another day. They are confused about what they are doing in their own lives, lazy, flippant and very irresponsible. Those are harmful companions too.

To say they are harmful does not mean that they are implicitly harmful; it could also be a distracting kind of harm. They are not harmful by nature; they are harmful by action because when we hang around them, they distract our time away from spiritual practice. They may ask us out to a movie every night, not because they want to hurt us or take us away from our practice but because their own minds are untamed, uncontrolled and unable to allow any type of Dharma to go in.

These people are not harmful by character, but are extremely irresponsible and set a very bad example for new students because the new students will not know what to do: to be devotional? To follow or not to follow?

Staying away from harmful companions

Most of us have more negative dispositions than positive, otherwise we would not be in *samsara*. When the negative dispositions from our previous lives open, we cannot do Dharma practice. In the tantric vows, we are not even allowed to talk to those who scourge, scorn and dislike our Guru. We are not allowed to share food with them, share our instruments or our *vajras* and bells, or talk about tantric secrets or tantric practice with them anymore. We cannot perform certain prayers or rituals with them anymore because their energy can pollute us, bring us down and trigger the opening of negative energy, negative karma.

You might be thinking that Buddha is not very compassionate. Of course he is compassionate! If, at this level, we allow someone to disturb our practice, how will we become a Buddha to help them? By avoiding them, we are being very compassionate. We send a message to them that we are not happy with what they are doing and unless they reform, we cannot support them and their actions. On a spiritual level, if someone disturbs our practice and pushes us off, how will we become an attained being or a Buddha to benefit them?

At our level, these people's disturbance and broken *samaya* can push us off the path, influence us and make us think negatively. There might even be other disciples of the teacher that these people always say negative things to and push away from the Guru. When these people push disciples away from the teacher, who suffers? The teacher or these people who push others away? Of course it is these people who suffer.

Staying around, associating, communicating with or being close to people who have broken their *samaya*, against their teachers or our teacher is very dangerous if we do not know how to handle them. We have to be advanced to handle them. After all, if our teacher cannot tame them and control them, how can we?

If we allow them to continue their negative talk or actions, we are not being very compassionate. If we think we can handle them and turn them around, we would have been able to turn them around by now. If we allow them to continue their little games, they will go on for years and years and years. They do not have merits to dig themselves out, and we would actually be helping them to create even heavier negative karma for themselves.

They present a danger to us and to themselves and this is why this text specifically tells us to avoid harmful companions who might try to split us from our teachers.

3) With an attitude like the earth: That carries all burdens without ever becoming tired.

The Guru may give us a very small assignment or work designed to help us, push us to become better and better (not better in our view, but better in terms of Dharma, for our future lives). The Guru might make us do something that is very difficult but is that what we are concerned about?

We have checked out the Guru and sworn our refuge with the Guru. Then after the big refuge ceremony and the big offerings, the feelings, the pictures, the lights, candles, incense and effort, when the Guru asks us to please cut our hair about two inches shorter, we reply that we cannot and give 25 reasons *why not*.

What happened to the whole ceremony, the vows, the allegiance? What happened to Guru devotion? Do we follow Guru devotion only when it is convenient for us? Does the practice of Guru devotion only apply during a certain time of the month, when we do not have friends, when things are going well for us or when we are not angry?

The whole point of the Guru giving us work – no matter how difficult it is – and us actually doing it, is to break through our ego. When the Guru helps us break through our ego, then when he gives us a higher level practice, such as practices for controlling our death, we will be able to achieve everything that is included within that practice.

But if we cannot even control our devotion to our Guru, how are we going to control something much higher? If we find it so difficult controlling our speech, our body, and the minor assignments that the Guru asks us to do, how will we be able to do those practices that require us to be free of the ego, to have *Bodhicitta* and to practise the six *paramitas*?

A real Guru, who is compassionate and cares, will be very careful to give us assignments and work. The Guru thinks very carefully – he considers our aptitude, who we are, what we can and cannot do. He then gives us all types of work, duties and jobs to develop the six *paramitas*, such that we can purify our karma and break our ego, our level of perception and our wrong perception of reality. This is for us to reach the next level. Then when he confers higher practices on us, we will get results.

The Guru might also give us jobs or assignments to help us avoid something negative that might happen later on. If we do not believe it and we go against it, we will suffer the result. The Guru will not be happy and he will keep trying to find other ways to lessen what will happen to us later. If we do what he says the first time, the bad effects may be lessened by 100%. However, even if the Guru cannot help us avoid the bad incident fully, he would still try to lessen the result for us by ten percent.

Our Guru might tell us to work in the centre once a month. We say we cannot do that but at the same time, we ask for initiations, retreats, 10 million mantras, and we can actually do these retreats and mantras. There is no difference! Why are we able to do 10 million mantras but unable to work once a month in the centre?

If we do not cooperate, why do we need a Guru or a teacher? A Guru or a teacher is someone who is supposed to be compassionate and kind and is out to serve and help us. When we always reject everything the

Guru tells us, we have excuses, we are late for everything we are assigned and we never finish anything we are given, that reflects on us and our practice.

Yes, the Guru is a human being who will be disappointed, feel sad and angry and shout at us or tell us off, but the ultimate person who is disappointed is ourselves. The Guru will have even more and greater wisdom than our own mothers and fathers to set us on the right path. The whole point of having a Guru is that the Guru is supposed to have more wisdom to see past our weaknesses, see into our gifts, understand our karma and what is happening to us so he can give us specific practices – both meditative and active – to help us overcome our personal problems, difficulties and sufferings.

"It is precisely because we think we cannot do it that we are given that assignment!" However, when assignments are given and out of habit, we immediately say, "No, I can't do it. I don't think I can do it," it is very bad. It is precisely because we think we cannot do it that we are given that assignment! The Guru can see something more.

For example, the Guru might tell us to be generous, to give and not to be miserly. The Guru might tell us to buy silver bowls and to offer them to the Buddha but we have 101 excuses why we cannot. It is not because we cannot afford the silver bowls but because we are extremely miserly and have had many lifetimes of habituation. The Guru can see the result of that and he does his best to break it because no one else can. If other people could have, they would have already done so.

It is like seeing a therapist. First, we check out the reputation of the therapist. We listen and we see some of the results of her clients. When we see that this therapist is wonderful and we hear that she has results, we walk in, pay the fees and we submit, open, surrender and tell her everything, week after week. After a few processes, depending on our problem, we start to find healing. If we resist all the way and do not let go or submit to the therapist, why would we even go for therapy and how would we get the result of therapy? It is the same thing with the Guru.

If we resist, fight, we do not do the assignments the Guru gives us and we covertly cover, or we try to make up things, use sweet words and go round and round, we may have been able to trick our Guru but we cannot trick ourselves and we fail our service, our devotion and ultimately, our own spiritual practice.

Submitting to the Guru is gaining independence, gaining freedom from our ego, *samsara* and ourselves. That is what a real and qualified Guru helps us to do. When we find such a Guru, we should devote ourselves with folded hands to him. Whatever work he gives us and whatever sufferings there may be, we should endure the work he gives us. We have to be accepting.

4) When carrying out activities on behalf of the Guru, perform them with an attitude like an iron mountain, unmoving, no matter what suffering occurs.

If our Guru gives us work, we do it and it creates suffering – it makes us sleepy, tired, sick, it drains our pockets, we get financially or emotionally set back – we should accept it without bragging to people that we have done it. Showing off is not Guru devotion and we set a bad example.

When we have to endure any type of suffering that the Guru has given us, we should endure it happily. We do it whether our Guru is watching us or not because by doing it, it does not become difficult or suffering anymore. We have overcome.

By enduring our Guru's work and assignments, we will also purify our karma tremendously. The Guru's intent behind giving us the assignment is to overcome something, so we can use the skills or qualities gained as a tool to become a Buddha. If we do it, we collect merit because our motivation and intent for doing it is to achieve Buddhahood.

The Guru might tell us to run up and down the hill every day, to make sure we stay slim and healthy so something does not happen to us. (The Guru might know that we will have a heart attack later.) We may say it is okay because we are going to die anyway but we might burden the people around us or, if we die prematurely, we might take a lower rebirth. The Guru may tell us to exercise and lose weight because his intention is for us to have a healthy body, for us to discipline ourselves, so we can do Dharma practice. If we do make the effort to lose weight, losing weight itself becomes a collection of merit because of the higher intention that goes into achieving it.

If our Guru tells us to force and discipline ourselves to stay awake, he may be trying to help us avoid something else that may arise due to our sleepiness – a car accident, for example, or something that might hurt someone else.

You might wonder what this has to do with Dharma. You might think, "He didn't tell me to recite or chant anything. He told me to lose weight, that's not Dharma!" That is very narrow thinking.

All of it is Dharma. Whatever a real Guru with compassion and skill tells us will be Dharma. If we trust the Guru, we will not see a distinction between "simple" non-Dharma instructions and higher-level Dharma instructions. We will have realised the nature of the Guru and the nature of his instructions, the nature of our relationship with him and the nature of our submission to him. We will realise that our submission is not to make us lose freedom; it is to help us gain it.

5) When carrying out activities on behalf of the Guru, perform them with an attitude like a worldly servant: Who accomplishes everything without hesitation even if it means taking on all of the worst jobs.

We should do our best to fulfil the tasks our Guru gives us. We push ourselves and we get it done. We should be very conscientious about whatever we promise or say to our Guru. This is not a person who just benefits us for something small in this life. If we do what he has told us to do, our work could lead to benefiting many people later; and we can collect merit. We can then rejoice – we have done something beautiful, we gain self-confidence, and we grow.

If we are always giving 101 reasons why we cannot do what he has told us to do, we must realise that everyone also has the same reasons – all of us are lazy, want more money, want to take care of our family, want to take care of ourselves and have investments. If we say that we do not want to do Dharma work because we have to work and make money or because we have "responsibilities", then we will be doing that for the rest of our lives. We will never, ever be free.

When do we ever become free of responsibilities? When one responsibility ends, another one starts. You get married, and then you have kids, which is when another responsibility comes. If your kids do not make it in life, they fall back on you. If they have grandkids, you have extra responsibilities again. It never ends.

We all have excuses that we have commitments. When will our commitments ever finish? We are going to be working forever to support ourselves one way or another. Even if we are very rich people, we still have to do a lot of things to maintain our money. We may have to make our family or the people in our company happy, for example. If we are not rich, we have to work for an employer throughout our life. If we live off the state or government, or if we have social security, we have to follow their rules, and fill out their forms and conventions to get that money.

The thing is not to abandon boyfriends, girlfriends, family or parents. No. We should find the middle way, which is to take care of them and do Dharma together. Real Dharma practitioners forsake this life to become a Buddha but because we are not at that level yet, we find a middle way. His Holiness the Dalai Lama has advised us to split our worldly responsibilities and Dharma practice into a fifty-fifty percentage. He acknowledges that we definitely cannot practise Dharma 100% of the time but we can split our time: 50% for our future lives and 50% for this life. I never forgot him saying that at a teaching in Washington, New Jersey, 25 years ago. I remember thinking it was so practical. As a kid, I had to go to school and do my homework which took up 50% of my day and for the other half of the day, I would do my *mantras*, study, practise and attend my teacher's talks.

We have to make the leeway to do Dharma because it is for our own welfare on an ultimate, long-term basis. If we always make the excuse that we have children, then by the time our children grow up we might not be able to do Dharma anymore because we would already be too wrinkled, old, tired or sick. If we are already stuck in that position – of having children, family and commitments – then we apply the wisdom someone is telling us now. We realise that if we have put ourselves in that situation, then we work with it.

We do it the middle way and split our time equally between our commitments and Dharma. We must realise and remember that we are not doing Dharma a favour. We are doing ourselves a favour. If we think we are too young now, then one day we will think we are too old; if we think we are too busy, then one day we will not even be capable of doing it. There is no young or old. If we hear the Dharma now, our karma has ripened – now is the time.

6) When carrying out activities on behalf of the Guru, perform them with an attitude like a sweeper: Abandoning pride and feelings of superiority, and holding oneself lower than the Guru.

When we are with our Guru, the sixth attitude advises us to abandon pride. We explain to and tell our Guru all the reasons why we cannot do what he tells us to do and we make up all kinds of excuses. If, in front of our Guru, we cannot abandon our pride, then why are we studying with him?

The whole purpose of having a Guru is to help us cut our pride, which is one of the main causes of taking rebirth in *samsara*. The Guru is a person who loves and cares for us from compassion, and takes care of us. Even if we never give to the Guru, the Guru gives to us; some students never give the Guru anything. Instead, they give the Guru arrogance and pride.

This does not mean that we should just give little gifts; it means that we should really help – take care of the household, clean, wash, supply or sponsor his works. Some people give a lot of material things to the Guru and if we examine what the Guru does with them, we will see that he usually uses them to benefit other people. Giving to the Guru is not just giving to the Guru – we actually give to sentient beings. The Guru disseminates our offerings to benefit others, so we can collect merit.

7) When carrying out activities on behalf of the Guru, perform them with an attitude like a vehicle: That carries out even the most difficult and heaviest work of the Guru joyfully.

The minute things get difficult, we give it up and forget it – isn't that so typical of us? We have to realise that we will never have this chance again. This work is given by someone who has pure intention towards us. (There are other people who also have pure intention towards us but it remains as a worldly intention because they are at that level. Our parents can have pure intention towards us but it stops at worldly comfort.) By being persistent, consistent and enthusiastic towards our Guru's work, we fulfil three of the *paramitas* – giving, joyous effort and patience.

In response to whatever the Guru has assigned us, we might give up after a while because we let all our attachments or laziness take over. Our Guru may be telling us that we need to improve, he shouts and he tells us off. Our Gurus will always love us and is always in loving care of us. But the Guru manifests certain ways to tell us about ourselves and what we are doing because our attachment to laziness, for example, has prompted that. In future, this lack of awareness and lack of care might manifest as an employer telling us to leave and us suffering from financial problems. It might manifest as someone whom we love very much or who benefits us very much saying goodbye because they cannot take our behaviour anymore.

8) When carrying out activities on behalf of the Guru, perform them with an attitude like a dog: Not being upset with the Guru even if the Guru criticises, belittles, or denies you.

When we have a little pet dog, no matter how we hit it and scream at it, it never bites back, it never fights back. The Guru is not asking us to be a dog. It is not some kind of sex game, where we have to get on all fours! The Guru is not asking you to get on your hands and knees!

This phrase reminds us of how loving and loyal a dog is. No matter how much we hit it, beat it or hurt it, it remains very, very loyal. We should be very loyal and without anger like that towards our Guru.

We have to think: Is the Guru really provoking us? Is the Guru really angry with us? Is the Guru really mistreating us? If we react in anger, we must first consider whether what he has said to us is justified or not. It will show us the level we are at. If we cannot even hold back our anger or push ourselves towards something better for our own Guru, who compassionately teaches us the path, then who can we hold back our anger from?

The whole purpose of the Guru provoking us is to train us to cut down our anger. There is no other reason. The Guru will sometimes deliberately put us in no-win situations because we may have a big ego – it is a way for him to check on our anger. If our anger is getting less, that means our compassion is growing and we are getting closer to higher practice. The Guru checks, the Guru watches.

9) When carrying out activities on behalf of the Guru, perform them with an attitude like a ferry boat: Not getting tired no matter how much one goes back and forth in service of the Guru.

A boat supports passengers, it supports people. If the Guru tells us to stay late, we should stay late. If the Guru tells us to arrive somewhere early, we should arrive early. We should not go to the Guru and complain that something is too early or too late. That will show what kind of person we really are.

If it was about money or getting *boobali*[16], we would be alert! For that, we could go to a club, dance all night and not get tired. We would be very friendly with the bartender, very nice to the doorman, very cour-

---

16 As it is sometimes regarded as improper for a Guru to talk openly about sex, Rinpoche made up the word "boobali" as a replacement.

teous with our friends and very, very nice to the new person we just picked up, no matter how tired we may be. Why are we able to push ourselves in that situation?

We should reflect and think about how nice we were the first time we courted our lovers, how much effort we made, how we showed them our best side. We were very nice to them – we were groomed, very sweet and talked pleasantly. Why are we able to push ourselves for something that brings us only a little bit of pleasure? Husbands, wives, partners and lovers only bring us pleasure and company for a few years, if it lasts.

Why can't we do that for our Guru? For supreme Enlightenment – learning how to control our anger and learning the science of transforming our minds – we do not do this for our Guru. We make him kiss our rear-end!

When we do not give up, we push ourselves and we keep doing it, we will develop the six *paramitas* within us, which will be a very great tool when we practise higher teachings to cut away our anger, ego and self-grasping. It will be very, very powerful that way.

SAMAYA

> *Samaya* is about having an honest, pure, real relationship with the Guru.

The outer actions that are necessary in a Dharma student are embodied within the *Fifty Verses on Guru Devotion*. The inner qualities are embodied in the *Nine Attitudes*.

These guidelines do not need to be fulfilled to the T. Who can fulfil all that to a T, perfectly with body, speech and mind? It is more about practical thinking, consideration and logical thinking. What is more important is for the students to have consistency. We should be consistent in our Dharma practice, commitments, what we promise and what we are supposed to do. Consistency is very important.

One day our work will be finished, we will retire, our kids will grow up, and if we have not trained in consistency all these years, it is going to be impossible to do deeper practice later. Consistency is not determined by our mood, time, if someone chases us, if we are in a good mood or because we are being watched. Consistency comes from commitment. Commitment comes from care. Care comes from understanding that this is really important. It is almost like a last stop.

It is also about having very clean *samaya*. *Samaya* is big fancy word in Sanskrit for relationship, and having a good relationship with our teacher. If we are supposed to give money to our teacher and we do not give, and our teacher is upset with us, it could be that a) the teacher is a monster, or b) the teacher knows that we could have given that money but we did not because we are hiding from something again.

Having clean *samaya* or a good relationship with our Guru is very, very important because our relationship is a spiritual relationship, for spiritual attainments of something very high.

The guidelines for maintaining clean samaya with the Guru is within the *Fifty Verses on Guru Devotion* and the *Nine Attitudes*. If we condense the *Fifty Verses* and the *Nine Attitudes*, it is more about having an

> "We help him to do Dharma work to benefit others; he helps us to do Dharma work to benefit ourselves and others."

honest, pure, real relationship with the Guru. It is about getting into a relationship where he helps us and we help him. We help him to do Dharma work to benefit others; he helps us to do Dharma work to benefit ourselves and others.

On a deeper level, those 59 verses help us overcome the emotional problems that we all have so that we can be free and avoid complications, suffering and emotional problems that we may have created for ourselves without meaning to.

Having a clean *samaya* means to be honest with our teacher, to be forthright, earnest and sincere. It is our chance to train in acquiring those qualities; if we already have those qualities, the relationship helps us to increase those qualities. There is no limit to how much we can increase our good qualities since we are trying to achieve Buddhahood!

Showing respect to our Guru is not some slavish, Eastern, fanatical, the Guru-can-never-be-wrong trip. It has never, ever been about that. We are devoted to our Gurus because we realise that they have given us something that no one else can give us, not even our parents. They have given us the wisdom, path and method that no one else could have given us. They have put liberation in our palms, in return for nothing! How kind is that?

They are able to do all this for us because they spent 20 to 30 years working very hard, listening to the teachings, doing their retreats and holding their vows. They have committed to their practice, and to themselves and their transformation. Because they have committed and spent so much time in this, when they share this with us and they expect nothing back in return, we feel indebted. When we are overwhelmed with the kindness of all they have placed in our hands, we are moved by devotion for them. We are touched to the core of our heart by their kindness. Naturally we become polite, we become honest, we become direct and we carry out the assignments that our Gurus have given us.

In the beginning, when people offer their services to the Guru, it will be seen as if they are very kind for doing this or giving that. But when we understand the Guru and the nature of the relationship very well, it is not the sponsors, attendants or students who are very kind to the

Guru. It is the Guru who is very kind to them. The Guru gives them an opportunity to develop their mind and to do things with their resources and funds that they would never have done if they were left to their own devices.

Within the Tibetan tradition, where they understand the Dharma, people clamour and push to do work for the master or teacher, and they do it very well. The sponsors all fight to sponsor because it is an honour. I have sponsored my Gurus before. I have built houses for my Gurus and sponsored their long-life *pujas*, robes and medicines. I even gave my centres to some of them. I still never think I did them a favour. I always think of it as having had an opportunity to make offerings to my Gurus which is worth more than making offerings to statues.

Whenever I go to meet my Gurus, I will buy offerings from whatever personal funds I have or whatever I can squeeze out of. Then I go to see them, reverently fold my hands and make offerings to them because I believe 100% that they are doing me a favour. I make the offerings to them in a manner that reflects that they are doing me a favour. I never arrogantly give it to them, make them remember what I have done for them or make them owe me something for what I have done.

I offer everything to my Gurus. It is a perfect object for me to let go, to collect merit, to practise generosity and I know they will do good things with it. I know they will. Even if they throw my gifts down the toilet, even if they burn the money I have given to them, I have still done the right thing. They may have thrown the gift down the toilet or burnt my money to check my mind.

There was a story of a *Mahasiddha* who went to his Guru for teachings. He was a beggar and had nothing, but when he went up to his Guru for teachings, the Guru asked him what he had brought to him.

He said, "I don't have anything of value on me at all but I want the teachings."

The Guru said, "No, you have to give me something."

The guy thought and thought and thought. He realised that the only thing he had were his teeth. He had nothing else. So he hit his jaws together very hard, and his teeth fell out. He cleaned his teeth, put them on his hand and offered them to his Guru.

His Guru said, "What a wonderful offering. Thank you." The Guru taught him the Dharma and gave him initiation, practice and *sadhana*. The *Mahasiddha* became enlightened in one lifetime because his giving was so sincere.

There is another story of a *Mahasiddha* who was wandering through the forest when he met a dark, black lady with long hair, wearing very little clothes. She was actually a *dakini*. He recognised that she was something special, that she was not an ordinary person. He made three prostrations and asked her to please confer initiation and practice on him.

She said, "No, you have to give me something."

He asked her what she wanted.

She said, "I want gold."

The *Mahasiddha* somehow obtained the gold. He went around and begged, and through a lot of work, he finally got the gold which he went back to offer to this black lady.

When he offered up the gold to her, with no attachment whatsoever, she took the gold and asked, "For me?" He said yes.

"What do you want?" she asked.

He said, "I want Dharma."

"Okay!" She said as she took the gold and threw it out! "Very good. Now I'll give you the Dharma." He also became attained in that lifetime. He got all the gold he wanted after that!

When we reach a higher stage in Dharma and we offer our service to the Guru – through work, sponsorship, writing, cleaning, taking care of younger students – it no longer becomes an attitude of "doing the Guru a service" anymore. The attitude will completely change.

The qualities of a student are very simple: to be honest with our teachers, to be consistent, to have care, to have clean *samaya*, to create harmony and have clean *samaya* with fellow students and to contribute to our Guru's work.

Some people have known their Guru or teacher for many years but have done very little or nothing. We should begin to contribute and give time to our Guru's work. Our Guru has been consistent for many years, teaching, explaining and talking to us and others. We need to be consistent now.

SPIRITUAL CONVICTION, SPIRITUAL COMMITMENT

> Commitment is not how many obstacles you face. Commitment is how much you want it.

If our attitude toward everything in life is flippant and easy, then it will definitely be the same in our spiritual practice. We should not do that with our spiritual practice because that is the most important practice that we can do for ourselves.

If our Guru gives us something that is not complicated or difficult and we still cannot do it, we still find it difficult, we still find so many reasons not to do it, that itself is an obstacle arising. If we cannot even recite a few words, then we should not even think about meditation, contemplation or higher practices that bring bigger results.

A person who acknowledges a practice from a Guru, says "yes" and does not do it, definitely cannot advance spiritually; he will also not be able to advance in material, worldly, normal daily situations. It is like not caring about losing $100 – if you just stuff the pile of money in your pocket and it falls out while you run around, then why would you worry about losing one or two dollars?

In the same way, we have our Guru and spiritual commitment. However, when our Guru gives us something and we do not care, or it is according to our mood or how we feel; it is according to our lack of priorities and we throw those practices aside; we promise, we do, we do not do, then everything else in our life will be exactly the same and our projects or endeavours will not reach fruition and completion. If we promise our Guru something and we do not do it, that will also be how we treat everything in life. We can check someone's conviction in his life, in himself and in other things by his spiritual practice. When you give someone a practice, you can see their personality very clearly.

If we are like this and we look carefully at what we are focused on in our lives, we will see that our minds are not on big, important things. Instead, we spend a lot of time explaining ourselves and focusing on very small things. We cannot do bigger things because we do not focus and we do not push ourselves.

You might think that the instructions you are getting are not from your Guru. That may be true. But Buddha Shakyamuni is also not your Guru – if you take the *Bodhisattva* vows in front of an image of him and you do not keep them, does it not matter because he is not your Guru? In fact, he is just a statue, he is not even there. We might choose to take a vow of vegetarianism for 15 days a month in front of a Kuan Yin statue. But that is not your Guru! Is it a real living Buddha according to your visualisation or is it just a statue?

Similarly, if the instructions we get are not from our Guru but they are from a teacher, the teacher must have good motivation towards us. If the teacher is an advanced being, and the teacher has some sort of *Bodhicitta*, compassion or love, and holds his or her vows well, they are a proper object of devotion. Even those beings have more power than normal beings for blessings and inspiration.

When we make a promise to them – whether they are our Gurus or not – and we break our promise to them, there will be repercussions. Lying to our mother, lying to our friend or lying to someone we just met on the street has different repercussions in society. Someone who lies to his mother is considered very bad. Someone who lies to his friend is pretty bad. Someone who lies to a stranger on the street is not a good person but it is still "acceptable". So, if we break our commitment to our Gurus, or we break our commitment to a being with good intention towards us, there will be different degrees of repercussions. The karma comes very differently. The object, the action and the motivation create the karma and its intensity.

It is unimaginable for me that someone can make a commitment and not fulfil it. I remember that in the last 25 years that I have been doing my daily *sadhana*, I have only missed doing it twice. Once was when I was in Thubten Dhargye Ling Centre in Los Angeles. I had been working very hard during the day, so I laid down for a few minutes and fell asleep. When I woke up the next day, the scariest feeling overcame me – I had forgotten to do my *sadhana* before I went to sleep! I could not stop crying because I had received it from Zong Rinpoche and I was very worried. I did not know how to repair it or what to do.

I could not go to work, I was trembling and thinking, "What happens the next time I do retreats? Zong Rinpoche is not around anymore for me to repair this commitment." I went to see Geshe-la. I was hysterical. Geshe-la just looked at me and said, "Do it twice."

A few months ago, I overslept because I was very exhausted. I woke up the next day and I had that horrible feeling again. But I did my *sadhana* twice the next day. Sometimes I do my *mantras* twice if I am not sure if I have already done it.

It is not like it is now – people just do their *mantras* a little bit and they start to not feel good. The air conditioner is on, they are in their own homes, they have a refrigerator, they are comfortable and there are no mosquitoes but they cannot do the mantras because they have 108 mental problems, obstacles, "cannots" and fears. They create the obstacles for themselves.

I was doing my *mantras* on the streets. I was doing *mantras* walking back and forth to school. Whether we do it or not is not because of our obstacles. It is our commitment. If we are not committed people, we will allow ourselves to say, "No, I won't."

How strong our commitment is, is how much we want it. How much we want it depends on us realising the value of what we are doing. Understanding the value of what we are doing is dependent on knowledge. Knowledge is dependent on listening; listening is dependent on patience; patience is dependent on compassion; compassion is dependent on knowing that if we do not do this, we and others that we love will suffer. It all comes back to the self-cherishing mind.

Commitment is not about how many obstacles we face. Commitment is how much we want it. All of us have gone through very difficult situations for something we wanted. We go to extensive lengths to connect with a boyfriend or a girlfriend, to be with them, to impress them, to sweet talk them, to take a shower, to look good, to be alert and quick, to get a car and pay exorbitant amounts to impress them. We go through a lot and we are willing to suffer all those obstacles to get to that person that we want, because *we want it*. That applies to everything else.

If you think you have never had commitments and you cannot fulfil your commitments, you are absolutely wrong. Even the person with the easiest life in the world, born with a golden spoon in his mouth, has chased for things or faced difficulties (according to his own degree) to get what he wanted. It is just about whether he wanted it or not.

We have to think very, very carefully: what is the purpose of a commitment? If we do not want it, we call it an obstacle and we stop. That is actually an excuse and we should not make that excuse – we have to get our priorities straight. Everything that we do, except for Dharma practice, will bear little or no positive results and will not be continuous. They are just distractions and things that we have self-created, a web into which we have tangled ourselves. Dharma practice is very different. It looks like a tangled web but actually it is an exit, a way out.

DOUBTING THE GURU

"In the future, the Buddhas will appear in ordinary form, in the form of our Gurus."

I refer to the Kalachakra Tantra, the Kalachakra short treatises. If we observe something in our Guru that we do not understand, which we do not have the wisdom to understand, or which we do not agree with, we should just quietly stay away, not say anything and not criticise. In our meditations, we see our Guru as a Buddha.

His Holiness the 14th Dalai Lama said he had no problems with that and he gave an example. He had two regents when he was a child. One regent, Reting Rinpoche, was in power when he first assumed his position. Reting Rinpoche had the power taken away from him and another regent came into power after that. The second regent found out that there was a plot, so he had the first regent, Reting Rinpoche, imprisoned in the Potala and executed. The Dalai Lama was living upstairs and in the dungeons of the Potala was his Guru, Reting Rinpoche.

The Dalai Lama said that in his meditations he saw Reting Rinpoche as being very kind to him. He was the one who went all over Tibet to find him, who went to Palden Lhamo's lake to receive the visions to see him.[17] He was the one who was running the country when the Dalai Lama was still very young. Reting Rinpoche was the one who exchanged his clothes for lay clothes and went to the Dalai Lama's house to see if the Dalai Lama could recognise him, he was the one who brought the items for him to recognise. Reting Rinpoche was the one who gave him his vows and refuge vows, who became his first Guru and gave him teachings.

At the same time, when there was political intrigue, this same Rinpoche, the Dalai Lama's Guru, was put in the dungeon, in a holding cell in the Potala, and executed by the second regent who came into power.

---

17 A special lake associated with the Dharma Protectoress Palden Lhamo where on various occasions (for various Dalai Lamas), images foretelling circumstance, place and time of the Dalai Lama's next incarnation actually appeared on the surface of the lake.

His Holiness said in his writings that in his meditations he had no problems seeing Reting Rinpoche as his Guru, but on an ordinary, normal level, he saw him involved in political intrigue and there were consequences which had to be carried out. He said he did not see any difficulty in that.

On one level, His Holiness can meditate on his Guru being a Buddha, and on another level, he acknowledges that his Guru had committed a crime. I am not at that level, I cannot do that. If I found out that my Guru was a mass murderer, the reincarnation of Jack the Ripper and has been killing monks and nuns, it is going to be pretty hard for me to visualise him as a Buddha! I feel that what the Dalai Lama says can only apply to His Holiness, it cannot apply to us because he is forced into the position of a political king or leader and a high spiritual teacher – he has no choice and has to play two roles. That is the way he had to come to terms with what happened to his Guru.

But do we want to go in that direction, to think that our Gurus can be wrong? Do we want to listen when another Guru says that our Guru is wrong, or when our Guru says another Guru is wrong? When a Guru is dead, do we start saying that whatever he taught us was wrong? Do we want to break our *samaya*? Do we want to make people lose confidence? Then it will not end. I will not do that and this is why I choose the middle path.

Sometimes, we do find ourselves in difficult situations with the Guru. He may tell us to do something and even if we do it the way he has instructed, he then says no and tells us to do it differently. It is so difficult to please him. We work hard in the hot sun or in the cold, while we are thirsty or hungry, and for years we bear criticism from people who complain about us, from the East, the West and all ten directions. On top of that, after we have explained our work to our Guru and we expect a compliment for our good work, we get a scolding instead. It is difficult to do work and not know exactly what to do or exactly what the Guru wants.

However, we have to learn to see the scolding of the Guru like a wrathful *mantra*, purifying our hindrances and negative karma. Eventually, all the hardships and criticism become incredibly worthwhile because he is destroying our ego and our attachments. We have to ask ourselves if we did the work to get a compliment. If we get angry when our Guru tells us that we did our work wrongly, or when he tells us to do it again, we must consider that he may be mirroring our feelings and our mind. He shows us how attached, how angry and how impatient we are.

How kind that person is to put up with that kind of action. In the *Lamrim Chenmo*, it says that if the Guru shows he is pleased, it does not mean that he is really pleased. Or if the Guru shows that he is displeased, it does not mean that he is really displeased. His mind may actually be pleased but outwardly he may have to show displeasure for a purpose. Perhaps he is testing us. This is what a skilful, perfect, real Guru does.

How can we know if his actions are not a reflection of our own actions? We cannot judge our faulty eyes, our faulty mind and faulty decisions. How many faulty decisions do we make from morning to night? How can we trust ourselves?

In the first place, how do we know that what we are seeing is reliable? How do we know that we are reliable? Even when we meet an ordinary person, we cannot really trust our judgment of what he is doing, and whether it is right or wrong. We have met many people who are not at all like what we first thought they were. So how can we judge a Guru, who may be very advanced in his meditations and deliberately shows different aspects to us? How can we know if our Guru is not enlightened, manifesting in an ordinary way? How do we know if our Guru has or has not the best intentions for us? How can we make that differentiation? How can we *judge*?

If we look at ourselves honestly, we will know that we have oceans and oceans of weaknesses and very few good qualities. Yet our minds have been trained to always see ourselves in a good way, even with all our negative qualities, negative traits, and delusions. If we can learn to look at the Guru in the same way, our mind can be trained to develop Guru devotion. I am sure our personal Gurus have many more good qualities than us, for us to base our training on. It would be better to assume that our Guru is a Buddha than to make the drastic mistake to think he is not the Buddha.

> **"We need to check and meditate on the good qualities of our Guru to override the bad qualities that we think of or perceive."**

We need to check and meditate on the good qualities of our Guru to override the bad qualities that we think of or perceive. The more we train ourselves to think of the good qualities, the more our wrong thoughts are cut down. As the great Lama Tsongkhapa said, "The more we see good qualities, the less we see mistakes in others; the smaller and weaker their faults become."

It is the *Kadam*[18] way of Guru devotion to look at the good qualities our Guru has, because objectively, many Dharma teachers are not Buddhas. And unless our Guru is running around murdering people, nitpicking the bad qualities of our teacher all the time will not encourage our practice, our faith, or our spiritual quest.

The Guru is made up of four elements: water, air, earth and fire. The statues are also made up of four elements but they are not Buddha, they are a representation of a Buddha. This Buddha cannot eat, move, teach, feel, or console us. He just sits there stiff, staring at us, waiting for more offerings.

If we can visualise this as the Buddha, why can't we visualise our Gurus as the actual living Buddha? They are made of the same materials. In fact, our Guru would be a much better visualisation because he can actually eat what we offer to him, thereby giving us the opportunity to collect merits. He can actually console us. When we request for Dharma, he can actually teach, guide and help us. The Guru is none other than Buddha.

We should not run away from our responsibilities or escape his instructions. We should not avoid him because we cannot do it out of our laziness or any of the delusions. Also, if our Guru tells us something, we should not do it just because we are scared that we will be punished if we don't, and that there will be bad karma. We should try to understand and think about his intention for giving us these instructions.

---

18 The Kadam lineage of Buddhism was founded by the Indian Buddhist master Atisha in the 10th Century and passed down through an illustrious line of teachers to Lama Tsongkhapa. Lama Tsongkhapa then founded the Gelug school of Buddhism in the 14th Century. Tsem Rinpoche is of the Gelug lineage and has received teachings from an unbroken lineage of teachers, tracing back to Lama Tsongkhapa himself.

If, with our limited wisdom, we cannot understand his intention, we should go ahead and do what he has instructed, be patient and not make all sorts of comments. What he asks may be difficult and his immediate purpose may not be obvious but our teachers only tell us to do what is beneficial for ourselves and others. We should not fight him once we have accepted him as our Guru. We should receive his advice joyfully and with deep gratitude for the great concern he has for our welfare.

Sometimes, our Guru may ask us to do something and we sincerely cannot do it (not because we are stingy, lazy or just do not want to do it). If we sincerely cannot do it and we explain the situation to him, the Guru will of course say it is okay. If we really cannot comply, we should not be rude or arrogant. We should explain politely and with extreme humility what the difficulty is; the teacher will not be unreasonable as a Buddha is filled with great compassion.

In Manjushri's Tantras he quotes, "In the future, the Buddhas will appear in ordinary form, in the form of our Gurus." If the Buddhas appear to us in their regular form, how will we see them? Can you see Shakyamuni or Kuan Yin or Manjushri? If we cannot see and hear them, how will we get the teachings? If the Buddhas manifest in a very high form, we cannot see them. If they manifest in a very low form – like a dog – it is of no benefit to us. They do, of course, have the power to manifest to benefit us but they manifest in a medium form – a form of an ordinary human being with supposed problems, delusions and faults. This way, they can be closer to us, so we can relate to them easier and they can use themselves as an example to show us how we can also improve.

If a Guru manifested perfectly, does not touch the ground, walks by floating three inches off from the ground, has a halo around him, never smells, does not have to take a bath, we would all think that is too far away and that we would not be able to accomplish that. But if an enlightened being manifests in an ordinary, simple way that we can relate to, with all the same supposed problems that we have, and we learn that he started off just like us and gradually improved, then it is inspiring, it is moving. It is excellent for us. It is exemplary.

SWITCHING GURUS

> All Gurus can promise you the
> same thing – Enlightenment.
> It's up to you to pick and to do.

Once we meet our Guru, we should stick to our Guru. We should be loyal in the spiritual sense to our Guru. All Gurus can promise us the same thing – Enlightenment. All Gurus can give us different practices that lead to the same thing – Enlightenment. It is up to us to pick and to do.

It is not good if we go to this Guru and that Guru, and run here and there. The Guru does not know if we have been to 20 other Gurus. But we know. It is a spiritual supermarket but we pick the "item" we want. We do not cook steak, lamb, chicken and pork for dinner, do we?

Once we have picked our Guru, once we are certain about our lineage and our Guru, we commit. If we commit to one thing – just like a job or a relationship – it will grow. The relationship with our Guru will help our relationship with Dharma to grow. The relationship with our spouses makes our love grow and makes our loneliness go away (supposedly). Maintaining a good relationship at work – where we spend time in one job, and not flit here and there – will make us grow in prestige and earning power. Everybody looks at our portfolio and sees how long we have been at our last job. If we have been switching every month, they probably would not hire us!

People who run to this or that centre, carry politics and negative talk back and forth, and make comparisons are very damaging for other people at the centre. People who run to different centres are very damaging for any centre they go to. They set a bad example to others and they are not loyal to any centre.

There are people who go to two or three centres. They say they are involved with one centre, then they join another centre; when they are not happy, they go back to the first centre. This is a very, very bad example. Because they are not happy with one centre, they had a fight with their Guru or with someone there, they cannot deal with their anger, their shame or their ego, so they escape to another centre where nobody knows what has happened.

There are some people who are easily influenced by what other people tell them. For example, for the last 20 years, I may have been following my lineage, my practice and my Gurus, and practising yellow. All of a sudden, someone comes up to me and says, "Yellow is not good! You have to practise beige!" and indirectly insinuate that my Guru was wrong. I go ballistic because my ego lets me think that I have picked the wrong Guru. It is not even about the Guru anymore, it is about my ego. I may even go as far as to think my Guru is wrong, after I have received so much Dharma, love, care, compassion, gifts and teachings from him.

So although I have been practising yellow for the past 20 years and my Guru has been practising yellow all the way back to Lama Tsongkhapa's time, I switch to beige because someone told me yellow was wrong. What happens if, 10 years down the line, someone else comes along and says, "Beige is not right. We found out that gold is right"? I am not traumatised anymore because I have switched once, so I will just switch again and keep switching. Why not? I change my clothes, my lovers, my food, my glasses, so I will also change my beliefs, my Buddhas, my *yidams*, my practices. "Change is good," I tell myself but the only thing that is not changing is my attitude. The only fact that is not changing is that I am coming back to *samsara*! I bought myself a one way ticket.

That is how people act. They have received so much from their Guru and when they just hear one bit of gossip, one tiny little rumour from another side, they really believe it and they jump to that side. What does that tell you about the person?

Let's say we are at X Rinpoche's centre. We have been getting Dharma from X Rinpoche every day, we have been hanging out at her centre, we are all committed and doing things with X Rinpoche. Three years ago, before we met X Rinpoche, we were with Y Rinpoche. Y Rinpoche flies into town and we go to the centre and say, "Guess what?! Y Rinpoche's here" and we tell X Rinpoche's students all about Y Rinpoche. We put posters all over X Rinpoche's centres about Y Rinpoche coming to town.

We may have a great heart and good motivation for doing that but when Y Rinpoche leaves, how do the students deal with X Rinpoche?

We make them confused. It is not saying that Y Rinpoche is better than X Rinpoche, but X Rinpoche is giving this much love, care and time to the students and when we hype up Y Rinpoche, new people will, of course, feel excited.

When we take them there, do another ceremony, get another initiation or teaching, they get all hyped up and we make them confused. If they are new in the Dharma and they run to several Gurus, they will get very confused. Different Gurus are all wonderful but they have different techniques and different ways and if someone is not learned or stable in the Dharma or in his practice, it will serve to confuse him, not enhance him.

When I was young, my Gurus never let me go to other teachings anywhere. They would say outright, "No. You don't need to go. Have you learnt everything I taught you?"

If we had commitments or a Guru before we joined a centre, then of course we have to keep a relationship with them. I have that too. My Guru is Zong Rinpoche but I have Gurus from other traditions also; I have to go and see them and meet them. But if I go to the other centres and to other Gurus, I do not go to their centres and tell them, "My Guru is Zong Rinpoche. He's wonderful." I do not hang out at one centre and then go to another centre and put up pamphlets, pass out things and advertise one centre to another. That is unethical. We confuse people this way.

There are special cases where we may have met other teachers from whom we received teachings before we met our root Guru or resident teacher at the centre. When they come to town, we can quietly go, receive teachings and come back – that is very good, that is alright. It is not like once we meet our teacher, we are not allowed to meet any other teacher. If we do have three or four other teachers, we should, by all means, go to see them when they are in town. But we do not go to the centre and say, "Guess what?! My Guru who I met the first time is here!"

If we have a prior commitment to another centre and we have to be there when something is happening, we go off gently, quietly; we do not advertise and make a big fanfare about it. There is nothing wrong with that – we do need to keep our commitments. If one of our previous Gurus shows up once in a while and we do not go, that would actually be wrong. We should go. We should pay our respects but do it with the right motivation.

Some people might have an advanced mind and they have been in Dharma long enough to be able to have a few Gurus. That is okay but not everybody is like that. Each Guru will have different methods for teaching and the differences will confuse people. Lama Tsongkhapa had over 60 Gurus. Do you think he ran around putting posters of each Guru in the other Gurus' centres?

> **"Each Guru will have different methods for teaching and the differences will confuse people."**

QUESTIONS AND ANSWERS

Editor's note: At all teachings, His Eminence invites questions from the audience and will address them, often with provocative questions to the student to encourage deeper contemplation and higher realisations.

Q: How do you reconcile Guru devotion with faiths (for example Zen Buddhism) where the masters tell you to go figure it out on your own?
A: It took a teacher to say to them, "Go figure it out." The teacher gave them one-liners, or things to think about and "figure out." You definitely still need a teacher. Even in the paths that say you do not need a teacher, and tell you to do it on your own, somebody tells you to go do it on your own: a teacher!

There are some paths where you need less time with the teacher but the time you are with the teacher is still quality time. Those paths lead to a higher path, where you will definitely need a teacher.

Going off, finding, thinking and figuring it out yourself is Guru devotion to your teacher because you are doing what that person told you do to. In fact, it is harsher and more severe – you are on your own, kiddo!

Q: How do you strike that balance between a Guru telling you not to do something, and you still wanting to do it? Do you still request?
A: You check the situation. If it is something you cannot gauge at all, it would be better to trust and just do as he has instructed. Sometimes it is something you can gauge – for example, if you are going down to a dangerous part of town to give food to the homeless, the Guru might say, "No, you better not go, I don't want anything to happen to you."

You could then say politely, "May I please explain? Four other people will be going with me, and there are three guys. We will be in a car and we will all be going together."

Then the Guru would say, "I see. Okay, you can go."

You might have made plans three weeks ahead of time to have dinner with your mother for her birthday and that night, there is a special *puja* which your teacher says you have to attend. But if you explain the situation, of course the teacher will be alright. It is not fanatical. It is based on circumstances at the time. There are no hard and fast rules for this.

There will be a lot of times when the teacher tells you do something that you feel is impossible. The whole purpose is to make it possible, to push yourself until you can do it. But you have to take that with clarity, with thinking, with sensibility.

The most important thing is our attitude. Are we arrogantly telling our Guru that we can or we cannot do something? Or are we humbly explaining our reasons to him? It is the attitude behind what we say or do, not so much the words.

Q: At what point does someone become your Guru?
A: When the student, in his heart, thinks, "This is my Guru."

Q: You spoke earlier about the Guru also checking out the student. What if the Guru doesn't accept the student as his student?
A: My dear! Do you need Buddha Shakyamuni to talk from a statue and say, "I accept you?" Or do you just think, "I believe in you, I'm a Buddhist"? Do you think the Dalai Lama has to tell hundreds of thousands of people every year, "Yes, you're my student. Yes, you're my student"? Or do you think people in the audience think, "This is Avalokiteshvara, you're my Guru"?[19] There are thousands of people running around the world who have never had a private audience with him or talked to him but consider him their root Guru.

It is from your side, whether you believe it. The important thing is that you yourself think, "I am your student" and once you commit to that, you commit to that. Whether your Guru accepts you or not, does not really matter. If you are under a popular Guru who has thousands of students, it would be impossible for each student to get an affirmation from the teacher: "Yes, you're my student from now on!" Naropa ran around as a student serving his Guru Tilopa for 12 years before Tilopa even asked him what his name was!

Whether the Guru verbally, openly, directly or personally accepts you or not, or affirms your tutorship, you still have a responsibility, from your side. It is your attitude, from your side. This attitude from your side will flow into the Guru-disciple relationship automatically.

19 Millions of Buddhists believe that His Holiness the Dalai Lama is a direct incarnation of Avalokiteshvara, the Buddha of Compassion, here on earth.

The whole thing about the Guru checking out the student is because you may think he is your Guru but he may not think you are a student, so if there are higher initiations or dangerous practices that he knows you cannot make, he will not invite you.

Whether the Guru accepts you as his student or not, do you not still benefit when he gives you a teaching and if you practise his teachings? The Guru-disciple relationship is definitely defined by the student. Then, when the teacher gives you higher practices, it is a clear sign that you have been accepted as a student. There is no confusion.

If, in your mind, you have thought, "This is my Guru," the relationship is already sealed. Whether people know it or not, whether you verbalise it or not, you have thought, "This is my Guru and these teachings benefit me." Then, if you have an opportunity to say, "Will you accept me?" and the Guru says yes, it is okay!

And just because the Guru has not accepted you officially as his student, please do not think you can abuse him, beat him up and be disrespectful! Of course not! Even if someone is not your Guru but you have received Dharma from him, it is still very nice to be respectful.

Q: Do you have to take refuge with every Guru?
A: Taking refuge with someone does not mean he is your Guru. And it does not mean that the person who gives you your refuge is your root Guru. Taking refuge means you have entered and started on the path of practice to become a Buddha. To fulfil that refuge, if necessary, you might have 14 Gurus who give you knowledge, that will be very vast and wide, to help you fulfil your refuge commitments. But to take refuge with 14 Gurus is unnecessary. It is like saying that you want coffee and you get a cup from each Guru so you have 14 cups. It would be impossible to drink all that! One cup serves the purpose. You do not have to take refuge with 14 Gurus; you take refuge with just one Guru.

Even without taking refuge, your Guru can still be your root Guru, just by you simply saying, "I request you to be my Guru, please may I be your student." Even before he has accepted, if you think you are his student, you will become his student.

As I said, Naropa thought of himself as Tilopa's student for 12 years but when he mentioned that to Tilopa, he got a bashing. Tilopa said, "I'm not your Guru! And you're not my student! I've never seen you before and I hope never to see you again!" He gave him another bashing with his walking stick and walked away.

Naropa was like, "Oh! He likes me!" You should read the story! It's so funny, but that is what really happened.

Q: Could your root Guru be the author of a book that you've read, even though you've never met him?
A: Yes, he could be. But if he has great writers around them (like me!), then he might be taking refuge in the writers!

Q: Can you have two root Gurus?
A: Sure you can. But you should not differentiate between "Guru" and "root Guru." Just think that they are all your Gurus. When we do Lama Tsongkhapa's practice, we think that all our Gurus have dissolved into Lama Tsongkhapa; when we take refuge in Lama Tsongkhapa, he is all our Gurus. That is why the *Guru Yoga* of Lama Tsongkhapa is wonderful.

Q: Is it wrong to go for teachings with another Guru if you've already taken someone as your Guru?
A: If your Guru does not have the knowledge to teach you what another Guru is teaching, then you may request permission to go. If your Guru has the knowledge to give you that teaching, then you do not need to go to the other Guru's teachings. If you have parents, why would you look for step-parents?

If you are sure that your Guru does not have that knowledge, and you want to get those teachings, he will definitely not be jealous if he is a real Guru. He would say, "Yes, I don't know that. Please go and learn from that Guru, and come and tell me." But if your Guru has the knowledge and you ask him, "Can I go to another Guru for teachings?" it would be like looking for step-parents when you have parents!

Q: What if you just go to see another Guru out of curiosity?
A: Curious about what? If you have taken refuge and you have a Guru, there is no curiosity, there is practice.

Are you going there to be a spectator? Are you going there to be a spy? Are you going there to get ideas? Are you going there to compare your Guru? Or are you going there because you like watching another exotic ritual?

Q: I would be going for entertainment...
A: Then I would not go! I would really not recommend going for entertainment. If you are going there to increase your knowledge and learning, to see a different approach, and your mind is strong and stable, then when you ask your Guru, he will say yes.

According to the scriptures, the main reason why we go to another Guru while our Guru is present is if he cannot accommodate what we need to know. That is the main reason. Not all Gurus will know everything, so they will recommend and send you to another Guru to learn certain things they cannot teach you. But I would not recommend going for entertainment.

Centre

> WHEN GADEN MONASTERY'S PRAYER HALL OPENED ITS DOORS FOR THE FIRST TIME, COUNTLESS DAKINIS WERE HEARD, SINGING CELESTIAL SONGS OF JOY...
>
> – TSEM TULKU RINPOCHE

MILAREPA

> The best retreat place
> is near our Guru.

The best retreat place is near our Guru. Milarepa had a student, Rechungpa, who wanted to go to India for a pilgrimage. He went to Milarepa and said, "I would like to stop my retreats and some of the things I'm doing here, because I'd like to go with my monk friend to India for a pilgrimage. May I?"

Milarepa said, "You wish to stop your retreats and your practices so you can go on pilgrimage. Why?"

Rechungpa said, "To collect merit, to see where our Lord Buddha founder was."

Milarepa said, "That's very good but I can give you something more effective. Wherever your Guru resides, wherever your Guru lives is the holiest pilgrimage and that is the best place to practise. If you look for any place else, and at the same time you say that your Guru is Buddha, then your actions contradict what you say."

That is what Milarepa teaches.

THE PHENOMENON OF DHARMA CENTRES

The Dharma centre is there out of compassion.

Dharma Centres

In traditional Buddhist countries where Buddhism has a strong hold, the practices and institutions are supported by the government, a bastion of wealthy people or business people because the consciousness of supporting the Dharma is there.

There are countries like Malaysia, where the government is not Buddhist but they allow Buddhism to grow and that is wonderful. It is like a Buddhist country, where the government supports Buddhism but does not really support other religions. We are fortunate to live in a country where the government is very kind – they give us total freedom to practise and we can do as we like. All we have to do is follow the law. How fortunate is that?[20] We look at Malaysia as a beautiful country, not just as a geographical beauty. I call it beautiful because we have the freedom to do what we want. We can practise Dharma here.

To me, there is no home except a place where I can practise Dharma. I have given up attachment to home and place. What is home? A place where I can lounge, kick back, do nothing and become more selfish, more into myself and more into doing nothing? Or a place where I can actually expand? Home is a place where you can find home, yourself.

However, there is no mass Buddhist consciousness in countries like Malaysia. To build a temple is very hard, because you have to explain the benefits from A to Z. How do we start in countries like this where we do not have mass consciousness? How do we build a temple? How do we support monks? How do we develop Dharma activities? These countries do not have the support of the mass consciousness of the people to do these things yet. It is not something that is bad or good, it is just a statement.

---

[20] In this chapter, Rinpoche talks about the experiences of Dharma centres in non-Buddhist countries as a whole, drawn mostly from his own experiences in America, Malaysia and Singapore.

Hence, we need Dharma centres in countries where there is no mass consciousness of Buddhism. They are called Dharma centres because they are not full-fledged temples or monasteries. They are centres where people can gather to learn, study, practise and meditate.

Dharma centres everywhere start off under very difficult circumstances and struggle a lot because they are not dealing with a mass consciousness. In getting sponsorship together, Dharma centres struggle tremendously.

They start out in tiny, little shop-lots or tiny, little rented houses where they cannot do much. The place cannot be built according to traditional specifications or in a way that is conducive for meditation or for the practitioners. Traditionally, a temple is built according to specific measurements and set-up.

The worst place for a Dharma centre is a rented place because we cannot do what we want there, we are restricted, we have neighbours and there are limitations to how we can fix or decorate the place. It is very uncomfortable. When the centre is in a residential area, there are laws and rules to contend with. That is a lot of suffering because we put all this money and energy into a place we cannot even keep and there is no continuity. Parking is also a big issue. If the centre is in a commercial area, parking is a nightmare and crime sometimes makes the surroundings dangerous.

But where else can it start? Dharma centres turn into temples. The Tzu Chi Foundation[21] started in a little house in the Taiwanese hills. I heard Reverend Cheng Yen and a few disciples meditated on Manjushri, did their practices and prayers, and it has grown to what it is now. I am sure Kek Lok Si[22] did not start out huge in Penang, Malaysia. I am sure it was just a few monks who started out with something small. Look at how big the Bright Hill Temple[23] in Singapore is now. It is huge but it just started out with Venerable Zhuan Dao giving teachings and meeting people in a little house.

21 The Tzu Chi Foundation is a very large and renowned Buddhist organisation that was founded in Taiwan by the nun, Reverend Cheng Yen. It is especially well-known for its extensive welfare and charitable work, and large network of volunteers in countries all over the world.
22 Kek Lok Si is a popular Mahayana Buddhist temple in Penang, an island city in the north of Malaysia. Founded in the early 1900s, it has become one of Malaysia's largest temples.
23 Bright Hill Temple (also known as Kong Meng San Phor Kark See Monastery) began as the first traditional Chinese forest monastery in Singapore, founded by Venerable Zhuan Dao. It has grown to be one of the country's most famous temples.

Dharma centres are mushrooming all over the world by the hundreds. Some Gurus have hundreds of Dharma centres. Do you think the Guru ran around opening them? It was possible because their students were very hardworking and very organised. I do not think one Guru can run five hundred Dharma centres!

The Dharma centre phenomenon is going to continue because Dharma is growing and increasing. It benefits society – any society, any group, any country. It makes people harmonious. The first thing Dharma does is to bring people together. You will see that effect on you and your families all the more deeply when you enter the Dharma; the effects are immediate. Dharma creates cohesion and therefore, Dharma centres will grow and become bigger and bigger until a mass consciousness grows in the future. Then, there will be bigger support where the centres turn into bigger places. It is not to make other citizens Buddhists but to make the Buddhists of the country better citizens.

Dharma centres are going to grow, and get bigger and bigger. They serve as places of worship and as places to get education because for now, we do not have Dharma schools, colleges or institutions here. If we do, they are very few and far between.

They are also places for people to meditate – to find themselves. They are places for people to do rituals to avert problems and difficulties. They are places where people who have commitments can gather and do their commitments and prayers. The centre is a place where people can find a spiritual home. They can go there to listen to the truth, listen to something good and practise. That is the purpose of Dharma centres everywhere.

The Dharma centre building

If possible, the Dharma centre should be in a place that does not disturb the neighbours and residents. Sometimes, after you move in, pay your rental, do the renovations and spend all this money that has been hard-earned by fundraising, the neighbours complain and they report you. That happened to a centre of mine in the past where the neighbours complained tremendously. It made it very uncomfortable to congregate there. It is also very important that the centre should be in a place that has ample parking or easy public parking.

Make the centre accessible by making sure that directions are given clearly – pass out flyers, advertise, put a map up on your websites.

Then, we should be very, very conscientious of people who come to the centre because they may not have gone for meditation sessions before and it may be very painful for them to sit on the floor for hours and hours. Whether they want to sit on the floor or not is up to them but we should also provide chairs and comfortable seats for them.

Within the centre, we need to have good representations of the Three Jewels – the Buddha, the Dharma and the *Sangha* – which is what we are sharing with other people.

We should have a very good image of the Buddha. If we want to encourage other people to have beautiful images of the Buddha, we should have something to show. A centre's Buddha image and *stupa* should be as big as possible for many, many reasons. If we want to have big aspirations, we need to make merit and having or creating large statues helps us to collect that merit.

Some people only come to the centre once, some come again and again – it is the only place where they can seek refuge and help. If your image is very big, it has beautiful *mantras* inside and a lot of holy images inside, it will accelerate the Dharma growth of these people who come to the centre. They collect more merit by prostrating, praying and making offerings to something so vast and holy. A Dharma centre – and the offerings and prayers we make within – is not just for one person, it is for the whole community and surrounding areas.

Even in our homes, we should make our Buddha images as big as possible. We should ask ourselves how much Dharma we do. If our images are large, and filled with many more holy images or statues inside, then when we make offerings, we would, for example, be making offerings to one thousand Tsongkhapas (or however many images of Tsongkhapa there are inside), instead of just to one Tsongkhapa.

The bigger the statue, the better and more virtuous it is. That is not something of the Tibetan tradition; that is in all Buddhist traditions. Anywhere in the world, all Buddhist traditions make huge statues for their temples or build Buddhist statues into mountains. The money or sponsorship for these statues should be offered happily because it is towards something for people to worship and pray to. It is something that represents the Three Jewels manifesting to us in that form because we cannot see them directly yet.

The Buddha images in the centre should be iconographically correct because people are going to use those images as visualisation for their meditation and prayers. Having correct images will require less explanation.

The offerings in front of the Buddha images should be as beautiful, rich and as abundant as possible. When we make beautiful, grand, large offerings of silver, gold and precious items, and the offerings are clean and well made, it represents our spiritual practice.

We should know the right technique of offering – how to set up, clear and purify the offerings. People will come to our Dharma centre and see that. Dharma is not based on that but it starts somewhere – the philosophy and rituals go hand-in-hand. According to His Holiness the 13th Dalai Lama, abandoning or neglecting spiritual offerings indicates that one does not have strong spiritual conviction.

The centre could have an option for people to come and create merit by making offerings. They could offer a stone or a pearl to the images and the centre; by that, they are not just making offerings to one image but to all the images and representations of the Three Jewels that have been put inside and consecrated within the large statues. By that, we can help them to accelerate their Dharma practice and the collection of merit.

A centre should be a place that is a haven for others, where we can also give things to others; where, when people come to visit, they can get beautiful books, *tsa tsas*, statues, malas and items for their practice. When you go to a traditional temple, you usually give. Nobody thinks they will get something back when they go to the temple or a church. They think they should give. Our centre, Kechara, is different – we give things out to people and I want to continue that tradition, to show practice of the six *paramitas* with people and to never be tired of giving. Give from compassion.

The centre should be a place of creating merit. It should be a fountain in the middle of a desert, so when people come, we give to them instead of expecting them to give to us. That is why I tell people to sponsor books, *tsa tsas* and statues to be given away to others.

The Dharma centre should be in a place that is clean and well maintained. We should not wait for another committee member to clean up. We should make sure the walls and floors are clean. Cleanliness is part of the practice before we engage in meditation, and cleaning Dharma centres is a way of purifying our karma.

There was a monk during Buddha's time that was very slow. He would memorise one thing and then forget. When he went back to memorising the first thing, he would forget the second thing he had memorised. He really worked very hard but was very sad that he was so slow at his studies. He went to the Buddha, crying, and explained his situation.

The Buddha Shakyamuni, in his omniscience, told him to clean the temple, the courtyard and the shoes of the monks and *Sangha*. The Buddha told him to visualise this as his mind when he was cleaning, visualising the dirt as his delusions and illusions; he also gave him some recitations to do alongside the cleaning.

The monk had a lot of faith in his Guru, Shakyamuni, and followed the instructions. And he did it not as a job, not as a put-down. He cleaned the temple very well. All the other monks were scholars and masters, they were teaching and travelling around the villages, and people would throw flowers on them because they were so in awe of their knowledge. This monk did not have that but he did not care because the Guru had given him instructions and he followed them carefully.

He cleaned, he wiped and recited the *mantra* as Buddha had taught him. He purified a lot of negative karma by the power of cleaning the temple and in that very life, he attained arhatship which meant he did not have to return to *samsara*.

Cleaning Dharma centres or temples is a practice that came from the Buddha. You sweat, it is hard and it is difficult but it is to provide a place for people to meditate and pray – there is a purpose in your blood, sweat and tears.

Be organised with the centre. It should look very nice. Be very particular and make sure everything is set up well. Everything in your Dharma centre is an example to new people, so everything should be kept well and nice. Even holy images and holy items you have in the centre should be objects that accelerate people's spiritual practice, by giving them the chance to collect merit, and to give them an example of how they can do things at home.

We do all this with a two-fold motivation of compassion for others and for collecting merit for all people – past, present and future – who are helping the centre and who need help from the centre.

The Dharma centre is there out of compassion. We volunteer, we work, and we give our time for the Dharma out of compassion. Therefore, it becomes Dharma practice.

Retreat centres

A Dharma centre is a place which is very accessible and easy to get to in busy city life. A Dharma centre is a gateway in the city for people to enter the Dharma.

A retreat centre provides a place for deeper practice. It is a place we go to for a longer period, to retreat from the hassles of city life, to go for a retreat or to fulfil our commitments.

"A retreat centre provides a place for deeper practice."

The retreat centre should also be accessible though, because we would not want to have to drive to a retreat centre so far away that by the time we finish travelling, we need to go to another retreat centre to recover!

Preferably, the retreat centre needs to be in a place that is spacious, for us to build what we want; it should be a little quiet. It should be pleasant, green and have some nature, since all we see in the city are walls!

There needs to be a big prayer hall in the retreat centre too, so we can make all the noise we want and not worry about the neighbours. We can have Dharma parties up there!

We do not necessarily go to our retreat centre to do meditation or enter a retreat. It should be a place where we can go just to spend a weekend, walk in the forest and relax. We can join prayer sessions, or stay there long-term to do retreats.

THE DIFFERENCE BETWEEN A CENTRE RELATED TO A MOTHER MONASTERY AND ONE THAT IS NOT

Follow your centre, be loyal to your lineage, your Guru, your practice and you will be loyal to yourself.

Centres that operate on their own have their own benefits and disadvantages, as do centres that operate on the basis of belonging to a larger institution.

Centres that operate on their own have the freedom to do and practise as they like – such as to take teachings from here and there as they like. It could be right, it could be wrong, it could be great. They are not stifled by an older, bigger tradition that they might find outdated.

However, in general, centres that are founded with the inspiration of a Guru or a Dharma teacher will usually follow the traditions and practices of that Dharma teacher, and the monastery or institution that he comes from.

For centres that are under the flagship, direction, inspiration and blessings of a big institution (such as ours, being related to Gaden Monastery), there are rules and regulations we must follow or apply that may not always be applicable for laypeople because the rules are more suited to monks and the *Sangha*. The rules may be a little difficult and stricter. Sometimes, it can be a bit overwhelming and daunting. The rich tradition of such a large institution may have benefited many in the past but may not be applicable now.

Having said that, the benefit of following the traditions and the teachings of those traditions is that we will have full confidence that we are on the right path and right direction. We have no fear about the practices because we have plenty of proof from the mother monastery and the practitioners there that the practices bring results. Even if it takes us longer when we do certain practices, or if there are initially no results, we will not have any fear because we are basing our practices on something that has been proven correct through time, again and again.

If we follow a traditional monastery or are under the flagship of one, it is very beneficial. It also has its disadvantages but I feel that its benefits are more. If we follow a centre that is not under the flagship of any traditional monastery, there are benefits and disadvantages also.

The bottom line is there is no better or worse. Follow your centre, be loyal to your lineage, your Guru, your practice and you will be loyal to yourself. There is not much difference.

THE CHALLENGES

Have compassion for your Dharma teacher. Think of what your Dharma teacher goes through.

Before, in Buddhist countries, teachings were not really available for laypeople. During British colonial rule in Burma, there was a very big vacuum of Buddhist monks and teachers because the missionaries were very fervent in stamping down on Buddhism and it was against the law to practise at that time. A lot of laypeople who wanted to learn the Dharma manifested then but they could not find any qualified or available monks. A phenomenon of lay teachers appeared in Burma who gave teachings to the crowd but they were not treated as Gurus, or divine masters, more as Dharma instructors.

This phenomenon of laypeople teaching did not take off in other countries because Buddhism and the *Sangha* were quite strong there. For example, it was previously very rare or unheard of in China to have laypeople teaching the Dharma. In the Tibetan tradition, teachings were mostly given by ordained members of the *Sangha* or lay practitioners, or passed down by lineage.

It was even rarer that these institutions catered to laypeople because it was assumed that laypeople's minds would not be focused and that they would not make the time to practise or meditate. It was very rare that laypeople advanced in their spiritual practice because they were very, very caught up in their worldly affairs. A lot of the ordinary laypeople were also illiterate. Basic Dharma was already hard for them to grasp, so the deeper teachings would have been even harder for them to absorb.

However, when we look at other countries that are not of a mass Buddhist consciousness, the majority of the people there that receive Dharma teachings are laypeople. In those places, taking ordination is not encouraged. It is, in fact, looked down upon. It is something you do if you are a loser or if you cannot make it in life. In contrast, having a child in the family become a monk or nun in Buddhist countries like Thailand, Tibet, Cambodia or Burma is an honour.

(Actually, Buddha's intention of having people take ordination was for them to focus their mind solely on liberation, so that living simply and not having attachments became a tool for advancing in Dharma practice.)

Dharma teachers in countries where Buddhist consciousness is not prevalent have a double challenge. Firstly, the students do not have a Buddhist base or Buddhist consciousness. They do not understand anything, so you have to teach them everything from the basics, all the way up. A lot of very basic problems we experience in Dharma centres – such as people breaking their vows – do not happen in monasteries. All the monks I met had no problem holding their vows! Secondly, when you teach non-*Sangha* members, they come with a lot of emotional baggage, more than monks and nuns.

Dharma centres teach only laypeople. Very rarely are there *Sangha*, and even if there are, there are very few and the *Sangha* are very new. They are wearing robes, they are doing their best but the Dharma has not gone in fully yet. There are incredible obstacles, problems and difficulties in teaching laypeople. Any Dharma teacher will find that a tremendous challenge and almost daunting. Some Dharma teachers go back to their monasteries because it is too much for them to handle.

Teaching laypeople is a very difficult phenomenon and that is part of the reason Dharma centres have problems raising funds and getting people to abide by rules. This is why there are so many laypeople who pretend to be in the Dharma but who still find it difficult to attend *pujas* and classes after 10 or 20 years of being in the Dharma centre!

When they go home, even when they want to meditate or practise, they have screaming kids, wives who tell them they are freaks, husbands who tell them they are cultists! Then they have to hide their practice. There are all these obstacles for laypeople.

It is monumental for a layperson to come to a Dharma talk because of the obstacles they create for themselves. There is not that phenomenon within the *Sangha* community. If there is a Dharma talk, everybody flocks there because they are in the monastery for that reason!

Laypeople have so many distractions and emotional baggage. Sometimes they can come to a Dharma gathering, sometimes they cannot – it all depends on their schedule, their kids, attachments, entertainment, business, money. It depends on so many factors. Sometimes they just create the obstacles for themselves, because they are always immersed in themselves.

Some laypeople take a little bit of what they want from the Dharma but when they go back home, they have no support for them to do more Dharma than the little bit they are doing. Their family usually does not understand it, does not like it or are against it. Once a layperson leaves the Dharma centre, he goes back to whatever he was; whereas when a monk (or a nun) goes back to his room, he goes back to himself, his altars, texts and teachers. Monks and nuns are in the Dharma 24/7 so they always have support.

If you tell traditional *Sangha* members to go to teachings at a certain time, they are there, even if the teaching goes on for one month! I have even attended teachings in the monastery that lasted for six months. In the monasteries, we do not miss even one day or one hour of the teachings; we do not dare sleep for even a minute because we are thirsting for the Dharma. Within the *Sangha*, the monks and nuns are really motivated and dedicated to receive the Dharma.

All this is not because laypeople are bad. It is because it is assumed that they will not practise or push themselves, and that even if they wanted to do Dharma, they have so many self-created obstacles that stop them from practising. If we look at the historical facts of every country, teaching in a Dharma centre actually seems unnatural!

This is what all Dharma centres go through around the world. When His Holiness the 14th Dalai Lama is giving a discourse, prior, in between, and after the Kalachakra initiation and teachings, we see Tibetan laypeople on the outskirts attending the teachings, having tea, taking a nap, talking, listening to the news when the Kalachakra is going on right there! It is something that happens with laypeople in Dharma centres everywhere.

When the teacher has to deal with laypeople from a different culture, it is another whole new challenge. They do not understand a simple thing like offering khatas, they question and they want a three-hour explanation about *khatas*![24]

So the teacher explains, "To receive Dharma, we need to make merit. In order to make merit, we need to offer up something. By offering something, we create and receive the merit."

Then they ask, "What's merit? Why create merit? I've already got merit!"

Then the teacher gives another three-hour explanation on why they need to create merit so they can buy *khatas* so they can offer it back to the teacher! After the students offer the *khata* to the teacher and the teacher puts it back around their head, it starts again! "Why did you put it back on my head? I already offered it to you!"

After the teacher explains things to them for six hours, they leave the room all happy and floating on a cloud with a halo. Then the next clown walks in, and asks, "Why do I need to offer a *khata*?"

In Tibet, the sponsors take care of everything and the sponsors encourage other sponsors. It is a well-known fact in the Buddhist world that to sponsor a Guru (especially a teaching Guru) is very meritorious because the best, most supreme Dharma action we can do is giving and receiving teachings as it brings Dharma to other people.

The sponsors in traditional Buddhist societies donate because they know they cannot do as much or spread the Dharma as much as the Guru, so they sponsor the Guru to teach and do because they believe in him. They understand the merit of sponsoring. Sponsorship does not just mean to help with money – they help with their knowledge, their time, their energy; statue-makers or *thangka* painters may offer their services because they do not have money. There, the Gurus do not have to say anything to the sponsors.

---

[24] It is a Tibetan custom to offer a white silk scarf to our Gurus, elders or people we respect, as a symbolic representation of our respect to them. Khatas also symbolise our prayers which we offer to the Gurus or Buddhas. When the Guru places the khata back around our necks, it symbolises that he has accepted our prayers and blesses us to fulfil them.

In non-Buddhist countries, the Gurus have to beg, "Please sponsor me! Please!" and the Guru has to do what the sponsors say. You have to make the sponsors happy – entertain them, tell them they are beautiful and handsome (although they may be grotesque!) and say they are wonderful Dharma practitioners.

Sometimes, if you do something that the sponsors do not like (heaven forbid!), they suddenly become very "honest", "direct", wonderful people, and say that they are not giving you any money anymore. Sometimes they send you long, nasty faxes to tell you off, to tell you what a rotten, spoilt Guru you are. If other sponsors want to sponsor you, they make sure they go away because they are afraid that you will become "spoilt". I have encountered that.

They will physically threaten you, tell you off, take things away, cancel your permits, run around to other Dharma centres and say very nasty things about you. If they are not happy with you, they do not want anybody else to come close to you or talk to you, just to prove their point. That has not only happened to me but to many other Dharma teachers.

Convincing laypeople to help and do things for the Dharma is met with a lot of mistrust. The mistrust is correct because the people do not have this cultural background and they do not know what it is about. For example, a lot of the Chinese here in Malaysia like to sponsor the Dharma but it is more with an attitude that they will only come back to say thank you and make an offering if and when they win the lottery.

Getting and maintaining sponsorship is one of the biggest fears and challenges of teaching. That was one of my reasons for not wanting to go out to teach because raising funds is scary. You are basically a car salesman, convincing people how wonderful Dharma is. It is good if you convince them and they remain that way; but sometimes their mind goes up and down and you have to keep talking and convincing. Sponsors are not bad if they lose confidence or faith, or feel down and depressed – they do not have the culture, people, friends or a whole lifetime to support them. The few sponsors who come out of the woodwork and help with no mind games are exceptional.

I am not saying this is bad, I am telling you the facts. That is how it is. This is what Gurus go through in non-Buddhist countries to teach the Dharma and tell you about being compassionate. Have compassion for your Dharma teacher. Think of what your Dharma teacher goes through.

THE "ROLES" OF THE GURU

> Pick what kind of Guru you want
> – one who tells you nice things or one who tells you the truth.

You have to expect that when you teach Dharma in countries that do not have mass Buddhist consciousness, the group will be smaller, it will need longer periods of training and you will expect students who fight back, students with anger.

Students may think negative things about the Guru because the Guru has to tell them what is wrong, tell them the truth, encourage them to do their practice, encourage them to attend *pujas* and go to Dharma classes, encourage them to be kind to each other, encourage them not to use each other for money or other gains, and encourage them to keep their promises and commitments. The Guru has to tell them to please study, read, try to do meditation and retreats. That, of course, attracts a smaller crowd and the crowd comes and goes because it is not what they want to hear.

The Guru has to experience students fighting with him, telling him off, accusing and threatening him, running away, ignoring him. Some students have the audacity to say negative things to other students – nicely and indirectly – to influence them away from the teachers, to validate their wrong, so it looks right.

It will be tougher to get sponsorship in non-Buddhist countries. The Guru will do his best not to cheat, lie and to use all types of nice stories to attract people and sponsors. That will take a longer time to attract sponsors, people and resources because the people who do turn up to sponsor are arrogant to him, think negative thoughts about him and parasite off him. The Guru will get people who cheat him, fight him, curse him, ignore and avoid him and who are influenced by other negative students. All this because a Guru dares tell them the truth!

You have to pick what kind of Guru you want – one who tells you all the nice things that you want to hear, so you never advance in your practice; or one who tells you the truth, and in whom you may initially doubt but come to understand in time.

His Holiness 101st Gaden Tri Rinpoche has told us that teachers who teach the Dharma today are very brave, very courageous and have compassion for the world because they dare tell the truth, kindly, without harming.

If you want to hear nice words, you can get that anywhere. You can pay a nice pretty girl to tell you all types of nice things. If you shout loud enough, you can get your partners to tell you nice things too, because they want you to stop shouting.

If I were really interested in just extorting things from you, if I were the type of person that was here solely for the motivation of getting material gains, finances and self-gratification, then I would never scold anyone, never tell anyone off, not criticise, not ostracise, not ignore; if students missed a commitment, I would not say a word. I would say it is okay. Let them think that they are doing Dharma and never say anything if they are not.

Some students complain, "Rinpoche's not compassionate, he doesn't talk to me!" If I wanted things from you, wouldn't I talk to you? I want those cheques! I want the nice things, I want more cars, I want more buildings, I want another diamond ring!!! So wouldn't it behove me to be nice to you? To write you nice e-mails that say you are wonderful, you are fabulous, you are reaching third level *Bodhisattvahood*?

If you want to extort money from your students, here's the recipe: do not shout at them, do not tell them they are going the wrong way, do not slap them, do not scream at them and do not ignore them for more than one hour. Tell them they are fabulous and they are advanced. The biggest secret is to tell people that they are a reincarnation of something. That is the secret ingredient to becoming a high, famous Rinpoche anywhere in the world!

Why would I tell you to do your *sadhana* if you did not want to do it? Why would I criticise people, tell them off, give them dirty looks if they do not come for teachings or force them to go to prayers? Why should I (or any Guru) do that to you if I wanted money, respect and help from you?

If a Guru has big sponsors and he ignores them, he does not see them, call them, talk to them or eat with them, is that the right way to get more money from his big sponsors? Or is it that he is trying to impart the Dharma to them? You must check if it matches.

Also, to talk nicely and eloquently in a class situation is great but I believe in "after-sales service"! This is to make sure the students are doing their *mantras* and their visualisations, to make sure the students are holding their commitments and vows, to make sure that when they slip I can get them back on the path, be it by jokes, fun, scolding, fears, wrath, peace or any other way.

A lot of people find that to be very comforting, caring and very nice. One or two people feel that the after-sales service is pressure, that it is focusing on them, nitpicking or pointing out their mistakes but that is not my intention. We can soothe people's minds and teach their minds, but we have to realise their level, understand their minds and where they are right now. Then we slowly take care of them, nurture them, give them love and care.

Sometimes love and care can be wrathful and fierce. Sometimes I run the risk that the people to whom I am wrathful, fierce and direct with will retaliate, fight back, ignore, avoid, or dislike me. I feel very sorry if they do that but if I have used a fierce and wrathful method, it means that I must have used the peaceful method many times and it did not work.

If you are hanging off the edge of a cliff and I need help to get you off, I will need to scream very loudly for help. In that way, if you are breaking your commitments, your *samaya* or your practices, of course I will "scream", I will intervene and intercede. If I do not, do not call me a Guru, a teacher or a Dharma instructor. Do not even call me a human being.

I need to intercede, I need to talk, I need to say things and because you do not have a Buddhist-conscious background – where the Guru just needs to say one sentence or one word – saying it simply and gently is probably not going to work. Students around the world, outside of Buddhist countries, require tremendous explanation, cajoling, jokes and a tremendous number of methods to educate their minds about Buddhist culture – which took millenniums to be established – within a few years.

The bottom line is if people are not doing their commitments, then whether they belong to another Guru or not, if they are in my territory, in my centre, I will tell them what is right and what is wrong, with respect to their Dharma practice and their Gurus.

My teachers have told me that there will always be one or two people who feel dissatisfied and unhappy. When you go on your teaching career, some will come, some will go, some will come back, some will not come back, some will stay – all of it is okay. Look at them with compassion and let it be. I realised that all this happened to my teachers too.

As a Dharma teacher, I am in a precarious situation because I also have to take on the role of disciplinarian within the centre. There are disciplinarian monks and head household monks in the monasteries who instil discipline and remind us of what we are supposed to do. Then, the Gurus, the Rinpoches, the teachers and the abbots simply teach; everything else is taken care of.

> **"The situation in Dharma centres outside is completely different because the Guru has to do everything and play many roles."**

The situation in Dharma centres outside is completely different because the Guru has to do everything and play many roles: The Guru has to be in front of you in robes, trying to look like a Dharma teacher, give Dharma teachings, remember what he has learned, go through notes, information, and the scriptures, to ensure that what he teaches you has a valid scriptural source. He has to stay up extra late at night to make sure of valid scriptural sources; if any of you asks him anything, he can tell you where it is and advise you where you can refer to it.

On top of being a Dharma teacher, the Guru also has to be a disciplinarian. When things are not right in the centre, he has to be the one that speaks up, scolds, cajoles and rewards the students. That is quite a hard job because on one hand the Guru is sitting on the throne screaming compassion, compassion, compassion; and on the other, he manifests as this watchdog barking at you all the time.

When students are not happy with each other, the Guru also has to be the mediator sometimes, to intercede when there are catfights, dogfights, revenge fights, ignore fights, and all the different types of mind games that students have with each other. In the monastery, it is the disciplinarian monks who would act as mediator. They do not just come round with big sticks and hit you on the head, they actually sit down and talk, and enforce the discipline. They are charged to do that by the monastic institution because these situations do arise.

The Guru has to be the cultural instructor. If you have a Dharma instructor among your midst, you have to know where he comes from, the lineage and practices of his teachings, how to do things, receive or make offerings, teach and practise Dharma according to a certain tradition. Gurus will not just make up teachings out of the air so they would usually follow a particular tradition. Since I am Tibetan, the most convenient tradition to follow is the Tibetan Buddhist one. So, as both Dharma teacher and cultural instructor, I have to talk to students about the nuances and differences in culture and explain what everything means – for example, the significance of *khatas*, prostrations, *mandala* offerings and religious culture.

When people want to do certain *pujas* and rituals in Buddhist countries, no explanation is needed. In Tibet, for example, we have ritual and *puja* houses which have been there for a thousand years, where the Tibetans go to for *pujas*. Here, we have to explain everything, in full detail again and again – when they do their *pujas*, how much, where, how. It is almost like a business deal, like a convincing game!

The senior students forget, do not practise, or are not interested in the Dharma teachings that the Guru has taught. Some do not push themselves to talk, suffer a lack of confidence or feel that since their Guru is around, they should just let him do the talking! For many reasons (both good and bad), it is always left to the Guru to repeat the preliminary teachings and practical things (such as taking refuge, becoming a member of the centre, Guru devotion, karma, *pujas* etc.) over and over again.

All these things are very preliminary and basic but the Guru does have to speak about it again and again and again because he is there in the centre and people rely on him to explain these things. In centres that do not have resident Gurus, the students will learn. It is a matter of their centre's survival because new people will come and the students have to give the explanations because there is no Guru to depend on.

There, the students come up with the course, the curriculum, they go to

India, learn the *pujas*, come back and carry it out in their own centres. The students actively engage, look for and talk to the new students or sponsors – they have to do that, if not their centre closes down. They keep it going for their Gurus. This is devotion to the Dharma.

The Guru also has to be the fundraiser. In the monastery, the abbots and Gurus do not do all that but as some teachers are not in their traditional societies, they have to go out and do the fundraising. He has to talk endlessly, tirelessly, again and again about money, raising funds, what the centre needs, and even take loans out under his own name; this is unheard of in Buddhist societies.

The Guru has to be the one that appeases the sponsors, the people who donate and give, and make sure they get something back. In the beginning that is what is necessary for people who donate – there is a consciousness in many non-Buddhist countries that if they donate something to the centre, they would like to get something back as a blessing or a token.

The Guru also has to appear as a gift-giver – to personally get gifts for the students. In the past, I have also had to be my own secretary, write my own letters and cards, stamp it, seal it, send it and reply the hundreds of e-mails, letters and correspondences.

On top of that, the Guru also has to be the intermediary for the centre and the monastery for whatever needs to be done because the monastery does not speak English well enough, the centre members do not speak Tibetan and there are differences in thought. He also has to be the tour guide whenever he brings students to visit the mother monastery.

Some people want to teach Dharma. They send out eloquent text messages or e-mails about Dharma, or sit in a small room with one or two people teaching, sharing and talking about their spiritual knowledge but they do not want to take the responsibility behind it.

There is a responsibility behind teaching Dharma to others. You have to practise. You have to hold your vows. You have to fulfil your commitments and keep your *samaya*. You have to have after-sales service to take care of the people you teach Dharma to. You cannot just talk to them and then ignore them when the questions get difficult, when you do not have the answers, or when you are not available.

If you want to teach Dharma, there are responsibilities. It does not start when you open your mouth and start talking. It starts right now. You have to have the personal characteristics to do that. You have to have perseverance. If you are always fumbling, bumbling, messing up things, dropping things, ruining things, but yet talk so eloquently about the Dharma, it will not move, change or bring anybody to the Dharma.

> "If you want to teach Dharma, there are responsibilities. It does not start when you open your mouth and start talking. It starts right now."

SERVING THE DHARMA CENTRE

> In Dharma, we suffer for a reason
> – we suffer to get happiness, to bring happiness to others.

I have done everything – a little bit of acting and commercials in America, worked in retail, secretarial jobs, gardening, cooking, dish-washing. I know what it is to have to survive. I went through a lot of ups and downs. Please do not think that I have been sitting in the mountains meditating and that I know nothing about work. I know more than you do about work!

The most difficult industry I have seen and been in is the entertainment business. When I did those fashion catwalk shows I saw all the things that people talk about in the fashion industry[25]. The designers, the make-up artists and the coordinators actually scream and shout. Some of them are not nice. I saw models being screamed at in the back until they cried; when they went out onto the catwalk, they had to pretend that everything was alright. All we could do was to walk by and pat them on the back. I have seen it all.

What is all that suffering for? What do all these designers, models, entertainment people, retail people, business people do it all for? You make the money and then what? At least in Dharma, we suffer for a reason – we suffer to get happiness and to bring happiness to others. The suffering has a purpose.

Other jobs have a purpose but the purpose ends when we get our money. Yes, in Dharma we still fight like cats and dogs, we hate each other, we hate the Guru, we disappear, we send nasty text messages to each other, we do not like this or that sometimes. But it is like that everywhere in life.

---

25 Rinpoche did some modeling work in Malaysia for a few years, participating in some of the top catwalk fashion shows for prominent brands and the prestigious annual Kuala Lumpur Fashion Week.

People ask why there are these problems in Dharma. That's ridiculous! It is like asking why everybody is ill when you go to a hospital! Similarly, when you go into a Dharma centre everyone there is also "ill"; that is precisely why they are going to a Dharma centre, they need mental help! At least they are going for help.

The purpose of suffering, fighting, working, getting tired, pushing, putting our effort and exerting ourselves in a Dharma centre is for something higher: the happiness of ourselves and others, to gain spiritual attainments and practice.

We should never see our involvement in a Dharma centre as work because it is not work. Work is when we do things just for this life and it ends when we die. Dharma is when we do things for future lives and for Enlightenment, it does not end.

Therefore, be happy to suffer for others. Be happy to attend meetings, Dharma talks and *pujas* for others. Be happy to fight for others. Be happy to be patient for others. Be happy to participate for others. Teachings can be difficult – they are long, they make us sleepy, sometimes they criticise or hurt us, but when we attend teachings and we stay awake out of compassion, we collect merit, because we are attending the teachings for others and we are "suffering" for others.

A Dharma centre's growth depends on our individual growth. If we do not individually grow, the centre will never grow, even if we acquire a hundred buildings. It just becomes a business and we do not need to use religion as a business.

Every Dharma centre must judge its growth by the members in it, how they improve with each Dharma talk and Dharma session, and how the harmony within and between the members grows.

COMMITTEES

> When you're doing committee work, your responsibility is to sharpen your *Bodhisattva* intention and your *Bodhicitta* attainments.

Dharma centres are places for people to grow and improve and, because this is beneficial, more centres will open in the future.

Within these centres, we need committees to run them. The committees are chosen by various means – sometimes by divination,[26] sometimes by the Guru or sometimes by voting within the centre. This is needed because Dharma centres can sometimes be fronts for wrong activities or wrong people. Having committee members who are citizens of the country is very logical – they are given legally-binding positions to ensure that everybody involved is not engaged in dubious businesses or using the centre as a weird front that looks holy. Having a committee is the government's way to love and protect its people. That is in every place in the world.

When we become a committee of a centre, it is assumed we are devoted to our Guru and we are devoted to the inner and outer growth of the Dharma. Therefore, it is assumed that when we are part of the committee, we will follow the statutes that are required by the law, so the centre can thrive, grow and expand without creating any problems for the citizens of this country or breaking any laws.

When we are part of the committee, or a committee member, we are in a very special position to be an inspiration or example to others. Some of us may be put into a committee although we are not used to being an inspiration or example to others. This is our chance. We become an inspiration or example when we are put in a position where we have

---

[26] Propitiating an enlightened Being for advice that will bring long-term benefit to all involved.

to be. All the Gurus, Dharma Protectors and members are very kind – they may choose qualified people for the committee or sometimes they may choose people who will *become* qualified by serving in the committee.

The Gurus give initiations to people who are not Buddhas, for them to become a Buddha; they do not give initiations to Buddhas! Why would a Guru give a Yamantaka initiation to a Yamantaka?

Similarly, the Guru selects us for certain jobs, puts us in certain positions, committees or departments to do certain jobs because we cannot do it, because we are not good at doing it. These positions give us an opportunity to do it and to improve. That is what Dharma centres are all about – they give us the opportunities to improve spiritually, inwardly and outwardly.

If the people are qualified, devoted to the Guru and devoted to the growth of Dharma, they will carry their positions out very well according to the statutes of the country and the statutes of Lord Buddha's teachings. They will follow the rules of the country and hold their commitments. People who are new in committees and who have never done this type of work may be scared and wonder why they were picked. It may be because they have potential that they have not seen themselves. If the Guru has picked you for the committee and you say, "Well, I don't know why the Guru picked me," then you put yourself and your own potential down. If you always suppress that potential, how will you ever grow, how will you ever inspire others?

The committee would also carry out their duties because they are very devoted to the Guru. Being in a committee of a centre is equivalent to doing retreats to gain attainments because we collect merit and purify negative karma through our work in the committee.

Anyone who is elected into positions in the monastery of Gaden is praised, given gifts, and very much respected because they run the whole monastery and they make things grow for all the meditators, masters and teachers. If any monk dares talk back or be offensive to any of the administrators, liaisons[27] or committee members of the monastery, it is a very big offence. The disciplinarian or house teacher will deal with the monk and talk to him. If that cannot be resolved, it will be taken up with the abbot himself and the heads of the twelve houses

---

27 Liaisons (*changtzo*) represent Gurus or specific departments in a monastery to help to carry out work on their behalf.

within the monastery. Some monks have been expelled for that offence. Committee members and liaisons all hold very important positions because they do very important work.

We may be meditating in a forest or in Gaden monastery, but how can our meditation happen if someone is not running the monastery? It is wonderful to walk in, do retreats, recite prayers and *mantras*, learn the Dharma and make dedications but if we do not contribute to its growth, its learning, meditation and practices, how can we expect it to survive? Therefore, there is no difference between someone who meditates and someone who runs the meditation centre.

In fact, I feel that the committees and sub-committees who run the meditation centres collect more merit than the meditators because they have to deal with real life situations that challenge their spiritual growth, all the time. As a committee member, we are dealing with ourselves. We learn how we deal with ourselves by the way we react to other people.

We must deal with people who do not do their work, who are perpetually late in submitting their work, who always complain, who always look for small problems and make them big. That is a bigger challenge than being in retreat. It makes us learn.

There is a story about a meditator who was at peace, calm, happy, never got angry and who achieved whatever practice he was doing in the caves in the mountains for 12 years. When he had achieved what he thought he wanted to achieve, he left the cave. On the way, he came across a man, and though the path was small, the man did not move over for the monk. The monk felt that he was not being respected for his attainments and practice, so he got angry. He scolded the man: "You should get out of the way! I'm a hermit, a meditator; you're just a normal layperson. Get out of the way!"

The man said to him, "You're a meditator? What have you meditated on?"

That was the end of the conversation.

When we are in a cave, in the confines of our homes or our shrine rooms, sitting there all peaceful, happy and meditating on universal Buddhas, it is very easy. There is nothing to challenge us, irk us, or bring out the dirt.

When we are in a position in a centre, it is like getting an x-ray – we see all our problems and bad points. Actually, it is a blessing and it is beneficial to be in that position if we want to advance in our Dharma practice. There, we can see how strong our spiritual conviction is, in dealing with others and in overcoming problems.

A committee member, a liaison or a member of a Dharma community must also show respect to other people. Never point fingers at anyone. Nothing is accomplished by hurting or damaging people. Everybody knows who is doing nothing and who is doing something. If we point fingers and accuse people of being sneaky, lazy, selfish, we just increase their sneakiness, laziness and selfishness because they will just go deeper into their shell.

As committee members, we have to learn to talk about problems and issues in general, in a skilful manner – it is not a matter of giving people face, it is compassion. Everybody will get through a difficult stage if we give them love, patience, support and help. Everything is accomplished by giving them care and understanding, and by forgiving them and forgiving ourselves.

Be forgiving of each other. We should not wait for another person to inspire us; we should inspire each other. We should try hard, push each other in a positive way and make the centre grow. When we have arguments, we should shake hands and say we are sorry before we leave. We are all human. If we have disagreements with each other and someone says something that offends us, we should not hold it. It is not a matter of winning or losing. It is a matter of letting the other person win.

When we are doing committee work, our responsibility is also to sharpen our *Bodhisattva* intention and our *Bodhicitta* attainments by working with difficult people, with people we would not ordinarily work with and in situations that we find difficult. We overcome them and we grow. The whole situation allows us to grow, to bring attainments to other people and to collect merit.

We always recite our dedication prayers for the sake of all sentient beings, but why do we think about all sentient beings when we cannot even take care of one or two hundred sentient beings in a Dharma centre? Do we want to just sit on a cloud, give them a rain of Dharma, pour nectar on them from a vase and hope that they all become enlightened? Go back to fantasy land. That does not happen!

How do we work for all sentient beings? We start with one, two, three, four, and we dedicate our merits. From that one person or those few people, we gain the merit and experience to deal with 10, 20, 100, 200, and eventually we are able to deal with thousands. Then we can deal with all sentient beings. People like His Holiness the Dalai Lama practised over many, many lifetimes so that whatever they say now can influence 5,000 people's minds. He started with one or two people. That is a *Bodhisattva's* way of going toward Buddhahood.

If we are devoted to our Gurus, to the Dharma centre, to the growth of Dharma and to our own Dharma growth, then we will be very, very energetic in doing committee or Dharma work. If our Guru gives us a position and we happily take it, or we take it unhappily but become happy, it means we are growing. We have challenged ourselves out of devotion to our Guru and therefore, to ourselves.

VOLUNTEERS

When you volunteer, you are not doing anyone a favour. You're doing yourself a favour.

Contributing to the centre as a volunteer

Volunteers are people who take time away from work, their families and their commitments because they really believe in the Dharma, they really believe in themselves and they want to do something good. They could be volunteering for relief services, earthquake or tsunami victims, or anything meaningful. Volunteers are basically people who willingly do something without any wish to be compensated or given something back.

Those who do Dharma work are of an even higher level. They are doing work for something very supreme – the goal is supreme, the motivation is supreme and their actions will lead to supreme results. Dharma volunteers are very, very special.

Those who are volunteering – although they are very special and are doing something special – should do their work well, conscientiously and not have the attitude that they are doing someone a favour. You are not doing anyone a favour, you are doing yourself a favour – whether you volunteer for the Red Cross or a Dharma organisation, you are doing yourself a favour by giving something back for all the things you have taken. And if you are looking for somewhere to gain something, you will find it when you volunteer your free services. You gain something that can never be bought – a sense of happiness, peace and the satisfaction that comes from doing something for the good of it. All of us will feel good about that.

Inspiring and helping new volunteers

There are a lot of volunteers and a lot of people who want to do things. The problem is that they want to do things their way. They are not different from any of us and they have their own comfort zones too.

It is important for people with positions in the centre (as committee members, staff etc.) to be an example to the volunteers. Getting volunteers is quite easy but we need to be a beacon of inspiration. We cannot just sit on a lotus, wear an Amitabha Buddha Halloween costume, all red with a star and proclaim that we are Amitabha, and hope they will be inspired to join and volunteer. We inspire them by attending the classes and Dharma talks, volunteering at the different departments, going for *pujas* on a regular basis.

No one is asking us to tell them their fortune, to tell them how many fairies we have dancing round inside our head, to tell them their previous and future lives, or to blow into the sky and make the weather fabulous. What volunteers will expect from us is for us to show persistence, enthusiasm, devotion and effort – that will inspire people.

When I say "inspire", it is not a big sweeping statement that we need to be of some incredible, monumental level to be of inspiration to others. It is very basic, human qualities that will inspire volunteers – our effort, enthusiasm, patience, perseverance, trial and error. We can inspire others just by being ourselves and pushing ourselves a little bit more. It will become natural.

We need to be alert during Dharma teachings, listen to the Dharma, absorb the knowledge and practise. When we do that, people see our effort on the outside, whether we are becoming a Buddha or not on the inside. When people see our effort on the outside, they will be inspired. That is something we can all achieve and that is the first step in harnessing volunteers' help.

The whole point of having a centre is to have Dharma teachings because the achievement of Buddhahood is through the teachings. That is why in all religious or Buddhist institutions, the throne is in the centre. Therefore, we should attend Dharma teachings happily. If we attend happily and we get the feeling of happiness by going to teachings, we will inspire volunteers to go for teachings. When they learn more, it will be easier for us to tap into their help.

If we always say, "I'm lazy, I don't feel like doing it, I'm busy, I don't have time, I've got to work, I've got to survive," what is the message we send to another person? If we are always lazy, we cannot make it to teachings or *pujas*, we do not read, we have this or that appointment, people are going to look at us and think we are hogwash, we are just pretending and we are just using them for something. When we make excuses that people can see through – valid or not – we set an example for them to make excuses too. They will start to feel that they can be "busy" too or that they do not have enough time. By consistently and constantly advertising no success, failure and laziness to other people, we do not inspire other Dharma students. Instead, we might bring them down if they are not strong.

We are allowed to be down. We are not supposed to be perfect, but the key here is not to be down all the time. To always say that we are busy and we cannot make it will not inspire another person nor bring them higher attainments.

The second thing that needs to be done is for the people in positions to get organised. Identify what departments are in need of help and assistance, or which departments need to improve. Think about why they are not improving and what the weak points are.

When we have identified what needs to be done, we should make ourselves available to guide the volunteers and to divide the responsibilities between volunteers, staff and committee members.

WORKING FOR THE DHARMA

> If we are working in a Dharma institution, our attitude has to be twice as good as that of the people walking in through the door.

The staff that work in an organisation, who have a Dharma stipend, who are close to the Guru or who have been in Dharma for a long time, should be very kind to the volunteers and should set an extra special example, for more volunteers to come. It is their responsibility to make the Dharma grow. How many volunteers come will be totally dependent on the current volunteers and staff, and how they act.

If the Guru is not around anymore and we need to maintain the centre until his next incarnation comes back, who do you expect to keep the centre together? Why wait until the Guru is dead, and then get yourself together? We should start right now so the transition is very, very smooth.

We should start right now – be harmonious, set a good example, work hard, make our work not that of a volunteer's but that of devotion to spiritual growth and attainment. We have always had devotion – to our family, making money, finding a partner, having friends, perfecting some hobby. We have a lot of devotion. We are not trying to develop something we do not have. It is switching it toward something higher.

Everybody knows that Dharma centres are for the betterment of society. So if we contribute toward and help a Dharma centre, we are contributing to society. Isn't that good work? Isn't that healing? Isn't that very positive?

If we are working in a Dharma institution, our attitude has to be twice as good as that of the people walking in through the door. It has to be doubly good because we are receiving a stipend from the Dharma, which is an offering of money given by people who want solace, kindness, compassion and to be encouraged that we have become a better person. People donate for us to work for the Dharma and have purpose in our lives. They come with the expectation of becoming better, to meet better people who will inspire them to practise. So if we are just as bad as them or we are worse than them, why should they pay for our salary?

It is like donating to a monk and he does not want to meditate, study or learn, he is not kind, he is always just hanging out watching DVDs, at the movies or fixing his hair. He is not interested in anything else. Why would you want to donate to that? Why would you want to help that kind of monk? If you would not want to help a monk that does not practise Dharma, why would you want to sponsor a layperson who does not want to do the Dharma?

We should refrain from complaining just like we do with any other job. We should not say things like, "I don't like this job, I'm going to move, I'm going to quit, there are people like this, I've had enough, I can't take it anymore". If we think and talk like that in a Dharma institution, we are doing more damage, we are not collecting merit and we are directly taking from the *Sangha*. If we are miserly, selfish, greedy, calculative with money, then by doing Dharma work or by representing the Dharma, we will give a very bad face to the Dharma. If we are quarrelsome, we cannot control our anger and do not practise patience, how do we represent the Dharma? If we do not have any perseverance, we are always saying that we do not know anything and we do not try to find out, then how can we work in a Dharma institution and collect the merit or salary from a Dharma institution?

Maybe we do not do the job well, nor push ourselves to go all the way with our job; when we have free time, we are sleeping or on the phone with our friends instead of studying, reading or trying to learn more. That way, we become the cause for other people to get angry at us, and when they retaliate, we might say we cannot take it anymore and start to complain. The worst thing in a Dharma centre is to complain about other people. We should realise that we are in a Dharma institution and that should inspire us to do more!

People who act like this in a Dharma centre, and who are wrong objects of sponsorship, actually discourage sponsors very much. Sponsors will look at them and say, "Why should I sponsor this mess or these losers? Why should I sponsor people who are full of anger, who give up easily, who complain, who say nasty things, who fight, who are bitchy? Why should I sponsor them to do more negative actions?

Why should I sponsor committees who do not show up for meetings? Why should I sponsor a centre that is disorganised? Why am I giving my money away?"

I may have a 100 million dollars and whether I want to give you just five dollars or not is up to me. But if I give it, I have some expectation – we cannot deny anyone that and whether that expectation is correct or not is a different story. The fact is that the Dharma needs donations and sponsors to survive and whether a person gives five dollars, 500,000 dollars or five million dollars, they are saying they have an expectation that when they go to the Dharma centre or any of its affiliates, the people there will be a little bit better.

People who work in the Dharma centre and its departments, and even people who are not on a Dharma stipend but who work in the centre, have a special responsibility to the people who sponsor them. We may not be on a regular stipend, but we do get some kind of help or financial assistance from our Gurus – where does the money comes from? We must think.

A cheap little thank-you text message to the Guru or to the Dharma friends who gave us some help is not good enough. People sponsor and help each other in the Dharma because they are coming to look for something better. If we are worse than them, why should they sponsor us?

If we work in a posh restaurant as a waitress, we have to make sure that whatever problems we are having at home stay at home. We do not run around the restaurant throwing water at the customers and snapping at them if they want an extra napkin when we are in a bad mood, because our husband left us or is seeing a better-looking girl. We have to go to work smiling, looking professional and good, with our hair in place, even if our house has fallen down an earthquake or even if our kids have been kidnapped. We still have to do it because we have to survive.

We cannot act opposite in a Dharma situation. In fact, the Dharma is even more important. Whatever job we work in – sales, retail, business, and more so if we are in our own business – nobody cares whether we are in a good mood or not. Why should they?

STUDENTS

> You "win" people over by respecting them, giving them Dharma knowledge and being friendly with them.

A Dharma centre is a place for people to interact. A Dharma centre is not a place filled with *Bodhisattvas* and Buddhas and enlightened Beings. It should be that, but it is not that. As I said earlier, why lament and be sad when you go to the hospital and find that everybody there is sick? It is the same in a Dharma centre – there will be people who are not well.

It is totally wrong, unfounded and illogical to walk into a Dharma centre with an expectation that the committee, assistants, practitioners and students are perfect. Where in this world have we seen, encountered or had relations with people or situations that were perfect? Even though we are in full control of our body, speech and mind, we ourselves are not perfect, so to go to a Dharma centre and expect perfection is illogical.

What we should expect from a Dharma centre firstly is to see if we have affinity with the place. Affinity could be upon first sight and our first feeling about the place, or it could be from gradually listening to what is happening at the centre, looking at the activities and feeling a closeness.

New students

There are many new people who will come into the Dharma centre with a lot of questions and though their questions may seem silly or small to us, we should remember that that is how we all started out. If these people come in and we just let them float around, how would it look? If we go into a shop somewhere and there are no shop assistants or help there, how do we feel about that shop?

If any Dharma centre wants to grow, it needs to take care of the new people, have a guiding hand and be organised. If we handle the new people well in the beginning, I guarantee you, disgruntled and unhappy students will be much, much less.

When new people enter a Dharma centre, there needs to be a committee or group that can take care of them – to guide them and to answer their questions. Human love, feeling and social contact is what they are looking for. If we spend time with them, our sincerity, time and love in explaining things to them will override how much we do not know.

We should believe that how the Dharma community is represents the Dharma teachings. That reflects back to the Buddha. This means if we are kind, and we take the time and love to share, show and explain, it helps us to learn and it helps them to understand the principle of Dharma, which is compassion and care.

When people come to the Dharma centre, they will not feel the power of Tsongkhapa, or the lovely, motherly, energy of Tara. What they are going to feel is our compassion, love, energy and effort towards them. And when they feel that, they will know the teachings are good and the centre is good. Then people will feel warmth when they come to our centre.

We should start from the fundamentals and the basic questions that new people have. We could let them know about our Guru – who he is, where he comes from, what he is doing here, how long he has been here, etc. We could inform them about the centre – the history, the purpose of the centre, past events, the different departments, show them notices and articles on the bulletin boards and websites.

We need to explain things to them, and after awhile, they will feel our love and sincerity and understand what our centre is about. We should introduce them to other Dharma brothers and sisters and get closer. It is fun to meet new people, listen to their questions and help them solve their problems. It is fun to see why they are here and to see them grow; when they come up to us a few weeks or months later and say thank you, we will have received the biggest reward that nothing could ever beat.

They are like salmon swimming upstream. Some die. But if there is someone there to help them and push them along, they will all survive. Some strong new people "survive" and get stronger and stronger; they look around the centre and go deeper into it. But some do not and we need to take care of them.

Instead of just sitting in meetings and wondering how to raise funds all the time, how about doing something very useful and practical that is all within our power? Every person in the committees, every staff or volunteer can take on a few new members that come in, get their phone numbers, exchange and talk. That would be very beautiful.

We must develop good relations with new people and help them. If we let people come in and just leave them on their own or if we are not organised, then when the Guru goes out to teach and lots of new people come who we do not contact or stay in touch with, we lose the chance to benefit them.

The buddy system

Dharma centres could set up a buddy system to guide new students. There are many members and people in the centre's committee, so each person could take care of two or three people. Or centres could set up a rotation system between the "buddies", to take turns to look after each new person that comes to the centre.

Those people who volunteer time to the centre, should really volunteer. We should not just talk and not actually do anything, not show up and are always busy or unhappy with this or that. That is not a buddy system. If we do that, we bring down the new people. (Or, if we are new in Dharma and we are always hanging round so-called Dharma students who always bring us down, eventually we will go down too.)

We need to guide new people, but we also need to be firm with them. We need to let them know politely that we will be with them to help them but they also need to do their part and not just sit back and expect the centre to do everything. If we are firm and, at the same time, we take good care of new people and volunteers, they will definitely start doing things and getting involved. Getting more volunteers starts with this.

Members of Dharma centres need to make themselves accessible. It would be good to have a buddy system where these new people can meet with us once or twice a week for a coffee, or get together for a few hours and talk. We all like to socialise! What better way to socialise than with potential Dharma students who we can help so much? In the beginning, they are not going to see attainments, Buddhahood, *Bodhicitta* or saving the world; what they are going to see is a kind person who takes the time to talk to them. "Gossip" for Dharma!

Dharma centres in countries with no mass-Buddhist consciousness are filled with laypeople and there are very few *Sangha* members. In these places, instead of going to a monastery or temple, where people know what is going on, we go to a Dharma centre where people do not know what is going on! We need a counterculture and we need to start something new. There will always be a lot of young, fresh, happy people who like to run around and jump all over the place, drink coffee, have a good time. If we like to do that too, we could help new people that way.

We can introduce new people to Dharma by taking them out to the movies, or having a space in the centre where people can meet and socialise. Instead of just concentrating on having huge chapels, we should also have rooms or a space within our centre where we can spend time with new people to watch Dharma videos, relax, laugh and have fun. That is more important – from that, more people will come into the Dharma.

Make the centre a warm, happy place. Have Dharma events, karaoke sessions or picnics, gather at one of the student's houses for little Dharma potluck get-togethers and watch videos. Sometimes we could even go out to watch movies (which do not have to be Dharma movies!). Think of different programmes and activities.

Unhappy students

Dharma centres should also set up a committee or a group to deal with unhappy students or people in the centre. In every Dharma centre or Dharma teacher's organisation everywhere, there will be students who are disgruntled for right and wrong reasons. We can straighten out those with right reasons because they do want a solution; but there will also be some people who may not actually want a solution.

Gauge the person: if this person has been unhappy and complaining about the centre for the last 10 years, then never mind! They are happy being unhappy! But if there is a new person who is unhappy about someone or something, or there is a miscommunication and they do not understand something, we should call them and talk to them, ask them what is going on, give them some Dharma or something to read, or send them a nice e-mail. We should help to calm their anger. We do all this because we care.

We must realise that there will always be one or two unhappy people wherever we are and whatever we do. There are people who hate the

Buddha, past and present! There are people who hate the Dalai Lama. There are even people who shot Mahatma Gandhi – he never raised one weapon against anyone, but he freed hundreds of millions of people from colonialism in his country by starving himself. They shot him. How many assassination attempts have there been on Mother Theresa?

There are one or two people who do not like Tsem Rinpoche either! *Om Mani Peme Hung* to them. I have a closet full of kites and when these people get on my nerves, I give them a kite. When they ask me what they should do with it, I tell them to fly it. There will always be one or two disgruntled people. Whatever!

Students who take advantage of the centre

Some students come to a Dharma centre because they want to take advantage of it or of the situation there. (I am so sorry to be saying this, and I am not happy saying it, but it is the truth.) The people they connect with may not be aware of this because when people come to the centre, we automatically assume they are looking for something spiritual. People in the centre let their guard down more than usual because they automatically assume that because people are praying, chanting, meditating, taking refuge and have a Guru, they must be good. There are some people who take advantage of this. I have seen it happen a few times.

There are some people who see that the centre is full of people who they could do business with. They join the centre thinking they can sell something or get some sort of financial profit by connecting with the people there. I have seen people ask for money and loans from members of the centre but do not get involved with or help the centre at all. That hurts me very badly because I can see that it hurts them. Why does it hurt them? They have a great opportunity at hand but they use it for using people instead. We have all used people in business, relationships and our dealings in social and work situations. Must we also use people in the centre? People in the centre are more vulnerable. I have seen examples of this in America and here in Asia.

There are also people who come to the centre but do not join in the prayers or classes, do not volunteer for any of the activities, offer their time, energy or help, nor support the centre financially in any way. These people do not bring any new people to the centre nor help any new people. They perpetually have something else going on in their lives. Yet they want to connect with the Dharma students – they want their phone numbers and contacts, and they are constantly talking to the centre's members. When we ask them why they do not join in the centre's activities and events, they always have eloquent answers.

There are people who do not listen to any of the advice that the Gurus or senior students have given them. They avoid the seniors and the Gurus. They only go to the juniors and the new people who do not know anything, so they can say anything they want and influence them. I have also seen this before. They get close to the new people and when they are in a bad mood or upset about something or someone in the centre, they start saying very negative things to the new people. Then the new people start having doubts. They show a bad example to new people and it brings down the energy of the whole centre. These people do nothing and contribute nothing to the centre but they do so much damage indirectly.

For people who are not committed to their Dharma centres but keep disturbing or contacting centre members, and for people who are involved with the centre at their own convenience, my question is why? I am not saying do not go to the centre. We should go to the centre but it is to go there to pray, meditate, learn, get involved, donate and contribute our time, skills, knowledge, help, money or whatever we can to benefit others.

These people make me very sad because usually, if they do not get what they want or need from the centre, they are not the type to leave you in peace and quiet. They usually do damage. Every centre in the world has to be very wary of that and realise there are people like that. But that is where they are right now. We need to forgive them by not hurting them but we do not need to get involved either. Compassion does not mean being stupid or going along with their ways – that is not being compassionate, it is being taken advantage of. Compassion can mean saying no to them.

High-profile or well-known students and visitors

When elite, wealthy people with status or name come to our centre, we should carefully consider how we handle them.

Everyone has a different view of people who are wealthy, rich, of calibre or who are well-known celebrities, but they have all worked very hard and sacrificed countless hours, blood, sweat and tears to get to where they are. The deep fundamental respect and admiration we have for them arises because we acknowledge that they have worked hard and established themselves.

We must realise that these well-known, wealthy people of calibre, name and position get harassed by people all the time, asking them to do something for them. They have their sufferings and problems just like us. In fact, with respect to people with money, position, name and fame, they have more problems and sufferings than us. In order to get to where they are, more had to be sacrificed, there is more jealousy and higher expectations of them. Wherever they go, people expect them to dole out connections, money and help, and if they do not give freely, they are looked down upon. They need the Dharma too. Not everything is going wonderfully in wonderland all the time.

When they come to the centre and we victimise them again, expecting them to give to us, that is not very good. We should not always focus on that. **"We should have compassion for them just like we have compassion for everybody else. They are people just like us."** We should have compassion for them just like we have compassion for everybody else. They are people just like us and they have feelings. Some of them may be very well-known and keep their feelings hidden away very deeply because they have been hurt many times because of who they are. People have used them many times. We cannot use them. We have to be better than the rest.

They *can* help and do things for the centre but we must realise that they also have to deal with people who are not in the Dharma. We must understand how much others are already doing to them on the outside.

We need to respect them by not having any expectations that they will sponsor, give and do things for us. Maybe they are able to, maybe they are not. Maybe they have their hands tied by certain situations we do not know about, but we cannot assume that they are rich, well-known and can do things for us.

We must talk to them without motive. (Anyway, if they are wealthy, well-known and of a high profile, they will be smarter than us and be able to sense our motives better than ourselves! They have had experience because people approach them for these things all the time.) We should open up to them from our heart and be sincere to them. In time, when they learn the Dharma, they will see how sincere everybody is, be just like one of the group, practise and open their hearts and, when they can, they will help. We "win" people over by respecting them, giving them Dharma knowledge and being friendly with them.

Also, some people who are of a high calibre and status were born into a background of wealth and position. They may have a way of carrying themselves, talking and interacting with people as they are used to among other wealthy people. Sometimes, because of this, they might look distant, aloof or arrogant and when we meet them, they may look like they want special treatment, special status and special care. Sometimes, for some of these people, we do need to do that for them. In giving them something they are familiar with, their minds will relax. They will see who we are.

Lastly, if these people are brought in by existing members or students of the centre who they are comfortable with, then we should leave them with those people. We do not have to stick them into the buddy system! We should always respect them and the friends who brought them in. If everyone in the centre swoops down on this one person, how will he feel? If we need to contact them, we should do it through their friend or contact within the centre.

This is not an easy issue to talk about; it is a sensitive thing, but it has to be talked about because it is important in Dharma centres. All Dharma centres need high-profile people and wealthy patrons. It is on the basis of their kindness that the centre can grow and benefit everybody else. All centres need that but that need must be fulfilled with wisdom, skilful means, compassion and respect.

EFFECTIVE COMMUNICATION

> A phrase that we must always avoid in the centre is "I don't know".

A centre and its members must be confident and have knowledge of their tradition, Guru, practice, and the benefits of the practice (when I say practice, I do not mean just extensive practice in Tantra. I mean the very basic practices that we do in the centre or have in our prayer books). We should at least be familiar with it. Whether the members or new people stay or not depends on us – the committees, the senior students – and how we give information.

The committee members and centre members should sit down together and learn what is in the centre's prayer book or practices – what the deities are for, what some basic meditations are, what refuge is, how to do prostrations. Then, when new people come to the centre, we will know how to direct them to a certain prayer or practice. This is very practical, free and accomplishable.

Centre members should know what their tradition is and where they stem from. We must have grounded information on Buddha Shakyamuni's life and, for example, if we are in the Gelugpa sect, we should know and understand Lama Tsongkhapa's life. We should read Lama Tsongkhapa's stories and be familiar with them, so we can tell people who he is and talk about his teachings. Those things are very fundamental.

Instead of worrying about how to raise five billion dollars, members in the centre should gather to do readings on Lama Tsongkhapa's life, share knowledge and test each other.

When we are helping "newbies", we could tell them that we will give them little "tests" and whoever wins will get a free meal (but even if they "lose" the test, we should still treat them to a meal anyway!). Make the learning process fun, interesting.

We need to be knowledgeable. The committee should research the history of their lineage and any monastery that they may be affiliated to

(Gaden Monastery for example, in the case of our centre), and compile it into something simple and practical to read.

We should also be familiar with the centre itself – who the current members, committee members or staff are, what departments there are and who is in them. New people will need to know these things.

A phrase that we must always avoid in a centre is "I don't know". Imagine if we went to the hospital, we have pain, we are coughing, dizzy, about to puke, dragging our entrails and the doctor says, "I don't know." People are coming here for help.

Phrases like, "I don't know", "I don't understand", "I'm new" all have to stop. We should never say we do not know and leave it like that. If we do not know, we need to know, because they are asking us about Dharma. If we know, we will be able to benefit them and ourselves. We should not make up something if we do not know because we are dealing with people's spirituality. We must find out whatever we need to know from reliable sources.

"I don't know but I will find out" is a good adage to add on. Not everyone can know everything in Dharma. Even I do not know everything in Dharma! But we should try to find out. We must let people know honestly that we do not know but we will find out and let them know within a week. Then people will see that we are trying. That is a human quality.

The centre members and committee members should also set up very efficient communications systems by e-mail, text messages, word of mouth or notice boards.

If there is something extraordinary going on – such as a beautiful offering, a wedding, or a death – or if someone needs a prayer, if there are new books and teachings being produced, if there are trips being made abroad or upcoming teachings etc. there should be a good communication system to ensure everybody receives the information on time. It would be good to authorise one member of staff to compile, arrange and disseminate information to everyone.

Making a very concise, precise network of sharing information, having effective communication, notice boards, educating our members and letting them know what is going on will eliminate the "I don't knows".

ENCOURAGING PEOPLE TO JOIN THE CENTRE

We join a Dharma centre so we have support for our spiritual endeavours.

If new people come to our Dharma centres and they are not involved in other centres, we should encourage them to join. We should encourage them to come, with compassion, clarity and the understanding that any centre in the world can benefit people.

This does not mean we shove the membership form in their face and say, "Sign up now and write the cheque!" Encouraging them to join the centre means to show them the benefits of being with a centre, a spiritual community and people who can support them.

The reason we join a Dharma centre is so we have support for our spiritual endeavours. When we leave the centre, we are on our own, we are surrounded by friends who tell us we are insane and crazy, or ask us what we are doing, why we are praying or setting up an altar. We will have friends who tell us there is no karma and there is only this life, so we might as well enjoy ourselves! When we go outside the centre, we are surrounded by all types of materialistic, crazy and fun-filled friends who are going to tell us everything we are doing is wrong. When we come back to the centre, everybody there reminds us that that is materialistic and gives us encouragement for our spiritual endeavours.

If we have "worldly *Sangha*" – who encourage us to drink, to have fun, to look good, to fix our hair, to have sex – then why can't we have Dharma *Sangha*? We have so many friends who encourage us to do everything else, so why can't we have Dharma friends who encourage us to do Dharma?

We join a Dharma centre because it is a support group. When we go to the centre, the people in the centre tell us our friends are crazy. When we go outside, the people tell us our centre friends are crazy. Everybody is crazy but that is alright. Who cares? We should encourage people to join the Dharma centre – it is moral support, it supports the committee, it supports ourselves and it supports something good.

When we join and we pay membership fees for the Dharma centre, we also help the centre to survive and support its activities. Remember that most Dharma centres are not supported by a big church or organisation that funds and builds everything, and are paid back through donations. Everything is through begging in Buddhism! We should support our Dharma centre – our membership fees pay for maintaining the premises and activities of the centre so it can help more people.

PROTOCOL

> Religious protocol is about learning
> a system of creating the karmic
> causes to receive teachings.

What is protocol?

The religious protocol that we follow in a Dharma centre is not just about protocol or forcing a culture down someone's throat. It is about learning a system of creating the karmic causes to receive teachings. This system would have been long established and agreed upon by a majority – in monasteries, temples or religious institutions and traditions – as a way to help us create an affinity and bring benefit to ourselves and others. Once we learn and understand the reasoning behind the protocol, then the merit is doubled.

If there is a systematised way, we can borrow that. It is the same for all the places where people are following the teachings of Buddhism. We teach the people protocol first – such as prostrations, making offerings, serving the Guru etc. – so they will understand, as the teachings come along, how they might collect merit in very simple ways.

In time, I am sure Malaysia and other countries around the world will develop their own unique way to do the same things, with the same purpose. For example, the Tibetan tradition of offering *khatas* was not practised by the original Indian Buddhists. In India, they scattered flowers on the teachers' heads and gave flower garlands to the teachers as an offering, to show respect and love. Tibet did not have flowers because the land was dry. They could not fly in flowers from other countries, so they offered pure, white *khatas* as a replacement for flower garlands instead.

Protocol can change with culture, but the motivation and purpose stay the same. Nothing I say is hard and fast but we are now in an interim period where things are being poured out from Tibet into the world. While we are pouring it, we are using a Tibetan container. That container can change but the substance – the Dharma – stays the same.

Making offerings

Buddhism, as it has been since Buddha's time, operates on the basis that we do not teach unless requested. We do not force someone into Dharma practice or wrongly tempt them into Dharma, unless they are willing. The basic belief is that if they do not have the karmic affinity, then even if they enter the Dharma, they are not really practising Dharma. It can even be detrimental.

That formed a dilemma – during Buddha's time, before Buddha started speaking, nobody knew what to ask, what to request or what to say; they did not even know they were suffering. Following the principles of all past Buddhas where they cannot teach unless requested, the Buddha emanated into the audience. He had students who were part of him, who would request the appropriate teachings, do the prostrations and make the appropriate offerings to set an example to others.

What would a mendicant monk like Lord Buddha – who lived in the forest, wandered and begged for his food, and kept no possessions except a few monk's items – want with offerings? Why would he want to emanate as a student to make offerings to himself, to show that other people should make offerings to him? Even when Buddha received the offerings, he gave them away immediately. He has shown us therefore, that the practice of making offerings is definitely something that benefits the requester and not the recipient.

It is by Buddha's own methods during his lifetime that people are still able to make a connection with an enlightened Being, even until today. The best way is by making offerings – of flowers, rice, precious metals, precious items or whatever is within the person's capacity and means. We make offerings in order to make a connection with the enlightened Beings and to create the merit on which the teachings can be supported. And hence, one of the six *paramitas* is giving, or generosity. This is why we make offerings to the Three Jewels every single day.

Buddha predicted that, "In the future, when I am not around, making offerings to the images that represent an enlightened Being will be equivalent to making them to an enlightened Being directly. In the future, I will emanate, I will appear as your Dharma teachers. Making offerings to your Dharma teachers will be equivalent to making offerings to me."

Now that can be misconstrued. Twisted people can run around and say things like that without any explanation and trick people. However, what Buddha said can have two meanings. Firstly, it can mean that some Dharma teachers actually are enlightened, so making offerings to them automatically creates a lot of merit. Secondly, there are some teachers who look like they are not enlightened but who we are supposed to visualise as an enlightened Being in order to receive larger benefit.

We can make offerings out of appreciation, as tokens of our gratitude or for sustenance to take care of our teacher – all those motivations for making offerings are good but the real reason for making offerings is for us to create the propensity to receive the Dharma and achieve the Dharma.

Offerings should be done without expectation. Needless to say, a real Dharma Being or a Buddha would not expect offerings. They would not be excited about it, they would not look forward to it, and they would never use or enact any of their knowledge or do anything just to receive offerings. They would not see offerings as praise, gratitude or thanks. They would see it as an object to transform immediately into an offering to the Three Jewels, on behalf of the giver. There is a lot of complex meditation involved in receiving and taking offerings.

A proper object of offering – a person who does not need to make any prayers in return when they receive an offering – is a Buddha or a *Bodhisattva*. By their very being, anything positive we do towards them automatically generates merit.

When we make offerings to a fully ordained monk who keeps his vows, or to an arhat, we automatically collect merit but the recipient must do dedications and prayers in return. If not, it is equivalent to swallowing hot lava. Anyone below that, which includes us, has to be very careful with people's offerings – there are karmic repercussions.

For example, I am definitely not a qualified being. I would think I am not an object of offering in any way. But people do make offerings to me, and so that their offerings, effort, money and all the love and care that they have put into their gifts are not wasted, I make sure that I offer it up to the Three Jewels.

For me, an offering is an offering. I do not think of it as anything more. I think of it as an object to help the giver create a stronger connection to the Dharma. Sometimes I go to different stores and I meet a nice salesperson. They know nothing about Dharma but they simply like me and want to give me an extra little gift. When I receive the gift, I think of it as their only link to the Dharma. I hold on to it, take it home and make offerings to the Three Jewels for that person. I may never meet them again but at least I have something of theirs that they have given to me and I make an offering for them to have some connection to the Buddhas.

It may be subtle and small but it is better than just thinking it is for me, me, me. It is much better than me – it creates awareness and it benefits them. Even if the benefit is that small, it piles up because when we keep thinking like that, we will develop a mind that can benefit people. We will develop into a being that eventually becomes a proper object of offering when people make offerings to us.

Requesting for teachings

As *The Fifty Verses on Guru Devotion* explains, when there are specific teachings we would like to receive from our Gurus, we should make proper offerings (it is subjective how much we should offer). With great reverence and great respect, we fold our hands, make three prostrations, offer up a *khata* and request for the teachings.

Whether the Guru gives us the teachings immediately, later or he never gives them at all, we should remember that our request is not wasted. Once we make our request, we have created the karma to receive those teachings somehow, when we are ready.

We do not sit there and say, "Well, I requested for the teaching, I offered the *khata*, I gave him a bag of fruits and I'm still not getting the teachings, I'm moving to another centre, see you later!"

The most important ingredient of requesting and getting a teaching is to ask ourselves if we are practising all the teachings we have received before. If we are not practising all the other teachings that we have been getting, why are we requesting for more? If we have taken one big bite off a sandwich and we are chewing it, would we take another bite? The teacher may have given us something simple to recite every day. If we cannot even do that, how strong is our conviction? (On the other hand, it is also silly to say we are not ready to do more practice so we do not request teachings. That would be just another excuse and hideaway.)

If the committee of the Dharma centre wishes to request teachings, they should have a meeting to talk about what they need, what they are ready for and what they are not ready for. Then they request for a teaching. When they request for a teaching, it is not to request with the assumption that the Guru will give it to them. They should request with humility.

After we receive the teachings (or after we take vows of refuge), we should make three prostrations to say thank you, to collect merit and to show our submission to what we have learned. If someone has a physical disability and cannot prostrate, folding our hands is good enough.

Public teachings

When the Guru goes to other places, we should be very organised and have everything prepared for the Guru to just show up and give teachings; and he leaves when he finishes. Everything else in between should be prepared and done. We must think: what do we want our Guru to do? Give teachings or be the agent? We have to think of what impression it will leave on other people.

The Guru should never be seen or heard before and after the teachings. The Guru should never have to talk about anything other than what the Guru is talking about right now – he should only talk about the Dharma. That is how we promote our Guru.

In order for the Guru to focus on the Dharma, we must make everything else easy so he can give Dharma to the people. Then people will be attracted to the Dharma and eventually, they will also support the Guru, the Dharma centre and his work.

Everything should be well prepared for Dharma teachings. The committee or organisers must arrange the itinerary for the Guru, make arrangements, talk to other parties who are involved, let the appropriate people in the centre know what is going on and let everybody know the schedule so they can rejoice, be happy and kept up to date.

Once we have made arrangements with the other people, we should go to the venue and check it out to see what needs to be set up, what materials need to be there, what is allowed and appropriate. How we set up before the Guru comes will give others an impression of what kind of Guru is coming. How we set up for the teachings and how we treat our Guru is how much, in turn, they will respect the Dharma being taught by the Guru.

We should make sure that things like clothes, robes and the transport for our Guru is arranged, so the Guru just shows up and teaches. A driver should be provided and a place to change clothes if possible. The students, friends, supporters and sponsors should arrive before the Guru, announce his arrival and escort him in when he arrives.

If the Guru comes in and sets everything up for himself, takes the phone numbers down, has a snack and a cigarette with the people, and then comes in grandly with his robes and announces, "Hi, I'm Rinpoche!" it will look like a scam!

We should also talk very nicely about protocol to the people attending the teaching. Even if they do not fully understand the mechanics of it at first, it would still be very good to tell them about it because many people would like to respect and follow tradition. If they can follow it, that would be fabulous. If they do not, it is still okay. We did our part to explain it to them. If they do not follow protocol it does not mean they do not deserve Dharma. If they do not want to prostrate, they do not have to prostrate. If they do not want to offer a *khata* because they find it looks strange, they do not have to. If we explain, nicely and confidently, there will be no problem.

Then, after the Guru gives a Dharma discourse, what do you want him to do? a) pass out his business cards, call his assistants and hook up? b) throw his cards to the crowd and make them catch or c) the students get organised and go out to talk to people?

After the Guru gives a Dharma talk, there are all these potential Buddhas-to-be in the audience. The Dharma centre's members and committee should organise to pass out contacts and information to the audience, go up to new people and talk to them – from there, we might be able to bring the Dharma to them or they might be able to help us bring the Dharma to many other people.

Educating others on protocol

If we are in a Dharma centre, we should understand the protocol. Committee members should write it all down in a simple instruction booklet or post it on their bulletin boards and websites. This is very basic information for every Dharma centre that can be distributed for all members to have something to read and refer to.

For example, within a Tibetan Buddhist centre, explanations on protocol could include aspects such as what a *khata* is, what an altar is, how we greet the Guru, why we prostrate, what refuge is, how we ask for refuge, what the purpose of the Dharma centre is, how we should dress, how to keep Dharma books, why we keep the place clean, etc.

We should educate the people who come to our centre. The secret behind success is educating people and letting people know what should be done and what we need to do. The committee can do that. I never said any of the committee has to raise $500,000! I said try to raise whatever you can and the money will come. But I wish to advise committee members of Dharma centres (and even people who have not been selected for committees but who are members of a centre), that these are things that we can all do right now.

Once we accomplish one thing and we see other people reading it and saying that it has helped them a lot, we will feel good and happy, and know that we have accomplished something. From that one little thing we have accomplished, we can go to the next one and the next one. We begin to accomplish more and more and more, and that is how we can raise $500,000. It starts somewhere small. We can start to do a lot of things that do not require money by getting ourselves organised.

If Dharma centre committees and members do these little things that provide information to others and get organised (which is all free!) more and more people will join and want to help. That is how they do it.

PROMOTING THE GURU

If we talk about our Gurus, it is out of compassion and care for others.

The image

They make movie stars and singers look great! They promote stars! They get them in the best light, take pictures and make sure they fix up the pictures in computers to make them look even greater. They do all this so they can create more business, more people will like them and more people will see their movie or buy their CD. They do all this for stars just to do business and make money. Certainly we would like more people to listen to the Dharma so they can develop respect for our Guru and feel that Dharma is something sacred.

Secretaries and receptionists are so important for CEOs or dentists, for when we enter their offices or clinics. It leaves us with an impression. What about a Guru? The CEO just gives us a business deal; the dentist just cleans our teeth. Our Guru brings us Enlightenment!

We have to make sure our Guru does nothing but the Guru's job. We do not have to sit there on our hands and knees with our Guru all the time. We can do it in a modern way – be alert, be available, have things ready. We do not have to walk from the kitchen to the throne on our knees and then lay down on our chests to offer up a cup of tea with one finger. But make sure that during breaks, or in between the teachings, the Guru has a cup of tea before you drink *your* cup of tea!

We have to be organised. Think of it as marketing. Either the Guru is the driver, the gardener, the cook, the financier, the accountant... or the Guru is a teacher.

The Guru always attracts the people in and will always get the people in. Whether they stay or not is dependent on the students. No matter how wonderful the Guru is, new people will run away if the students are nightmarish, irresponsible, uncaring, difficult people. Those are the first people they see and the last people they see. The Guru is in between.

How will we attract other people to fulfil Dharma work? It is by our Guru giving the Dharma. It is all very logical. Therefore, we must think carefully of how we want to "promote" and "market" our Guru (I hate to use those words but we are going to have to use them in this time and age). That will be the result we get.

When we are travelling or going out with the Guru, we should always walk in front of him. We do not make the Guru wait, open the door, scream and look for us. The Guru should never look for the assistants; the assistants or students should always look for the Guru.

We must think about how it looks for our own practice of awareness. How does it reflect on us if we think that the Dharma we receive is sacred? And what is the impression it leaves on other people? If we treat our Guru badly, people are going to think, "Is this how you treat your Guru? He's nothing, certainly!" So if they think our Guru is nothing, then they will also think the Dharma they are receiving is nothing. If they do not think our Guru is anything, we have created that in their mind with our laxity, laziness, selfishness and habituations. That is the image we have portrayed to the world about our Guru. We can do incredible damage.

But why does the Guru even need this image? You might wonder why image is important for the Guru who is "not attached"? It is because he is dealing with people who are attached and who are image conscious. The first thing they will see is how we treat our Guru. When the assistants are organised and mature – not by age, but by mind – caring, conscientious, alert and ready to help, it promotes a very big image.

We might announce the arrival of our Guru with "His Royal Eminence of Tibet! His 19th incarnation, the emanation of Manjushri Buddha! His Divine Presence Tsem Tulku Rinpoche is here!" but there is a bumbling, idiotic assistant who smells, who drops things, knocks things over, forgets things, locks Rinpoche out, Rinpoche's clothes are smelly and the car he arrives in is smelly. People will wonder, "What's with His Eminence? His Eminence should go take a bath and wash his clothes! And if His Eminence is so great, why doesn't His Eminence have great liaisons, assistants or people around him?!"

Is that the image we want to give of our Guru? If we give our Guru that kind of image, we waste our Guru's time. The people he could attract, talk to, and reach; the people who could help the Dharma to grow and sponsor in any way (not just in monetary sponsorship) would be lost because those people will see the bumbling students around them, who are supposed to reflect the Guru they are serving! If these students do not care, how will they inspire other people to care? If they do not give a hoot, how are they going to inspire others?

The Guru is compassionate and he may do things for us a hundred times over. But if we make our Guru look bad, we collect the incredible negative karma that arises from the impression we leave with other people and the impact it makes on their mind on whether the teachings are valuable or not.

The Guru is highly compassionate and he has taken on a special vow to suck in all the leftover refuse of the world. That is fine, the Guru will love these bumbling students just like anybody else but new people are not going to see that. He is not going to be able to make his teachings penetrative and effective because of how the students around him treat him.

We must ask ourselves: what is the image we portray? What kind of people and assistants do we surround our Guru with? How do they dress? How do they look? Do they spit when they talk?

It would be fine in a closed environment where everybody knows that we are little loafing, loser, parasite monsters; they will accept and forgive us. But if we are out in public and we act in this way, the loafing monsters will create a horrible image for the Guru and the Dharma centre, and a horrible example in the future for people.

I am not here to tell you to treat me like royalty but I am telling you the facts. If the Guru always has to say, "Where is this? Where is that? Do this, do that" over and over again to assistants, then why does he need assistants? If we allow that to happen again and again, it reflects our insensitivity and lack of respect. For people who have the potential to receive the Dharma, we might even lead them in that direction also.

As the Dharma centre grows, what I am saying will be even more apt and important. Do we want our Dharma centre to have more students? Do we want more people to join? Do we want to expand? The Guru is already having this much difficulty maintaining a small group of students. If we cannot handle our Guru at this stage, how are we going to handle him if there are double or triple the number of students in the centre?

We need to ask ourselves why we are "advertising" our Guru or our centre. Why write about the Guru and send articles to newspapers? Why talk about the Guru? Why ask the media for interviews? Why make him grow when we do not have the foundation to grow? The foundation is not just a building being bigger. It is our attitude, responsibility and how we want to promote our Guru.

Promotion

Our behaviour, how we act and how we hold ourselves come first. Talking and promotion is secondary. How a Guru or the teachings spread is dependent on how the students speak and act. If the students know how to praise, speak and talk about the good qualities of the Guru, then people will know about him. If the students remain quiet and do not say anything, the Gurus will never grow.

And why would we want to promote our Guru? Because we are fanatical, insecure and reassuring ourselves? Those could be reasons but the real reason for promoting our Guru is that we have trust and confidence that he can help many beings. We tell other people about our Guru out of great compassion and care for others.

That is why anybody would talk about great masters like His Holiness the Dalai Lama or His Holiness Kyabje Zong Rinpoche. They hope that by recording their teachings, writing about them and by spreading this, more people will meet these Beings and get the benefits they themselves have received. That is why I talk about it. I do not talk about Zong Rinpoche and the Dalai Lama to make myself high. Their qualities did not rub off on me just because I received initiation from them. Their Enlightenment did not rub off on me just because I had the honour to serve them. I am still me. But I am concerned about a lot of people and I know that if people hear about this in the world – that these great Gurus exist and their qualities are like that – they will somehow find a way to connect with these Gurus. It is my way of "advertising". I hope that when it gets onto the Internet, and thousands and thousands of people are looking at it, they will somehow find these Gurus or similar Gurus of their calibre. Then, they can receive Dharma teachings too.

For the Gurus who grow these days, it is not just a matter of their status, attainments and who they are. These days, it is a matter of having a good publicist – people who write books about them, feature them in articles, advertise their good qualities and talk about them. It is not like it was before in Tibet. Now it is a matter of good publicists, writers, media and people who believe in their Gurus so much that they spread their Guru's kindness and Dharma through those mediums.

If we do nothing about this and just sit back, though we know our Guru's good qualities, we are being very selfish because we do not help anybody else; we are actually just keeping our Guru's potential to ourselves. When we are lazy to promote or talk about our Gurus, it shows our lack of care. If we cannot help people directly, we can still help by explaining and letting them know about our Guru's good qualities. That is our responsibility.

How did we all come to Buddhism? Did Buddha teach us about his good qualities or did his students teach us? How do we have faith in masters like Kyabje Zong Rinpoche? How do we have faith in the Dalai Lama, when we have never even met him or even if we did, only for a few brief moments? It was because someone repeatedly explained their qualities to us, again and again.

How did we ever buy anything, like our apartment, car or refrigerator? Because someone said that this location and developer was good, and this brand was good, or someone advertised, so we heard or read about it. Then we bought our apartment, car or refrigerator and enjoyed its good qualities because someone told us it would be good!

CENTRES WITH HIGH-RANKING AND WELL-KNOWN GURUS

> A sign of eminence, a sign of greatness is not competitiveness or jealousy but rejoicing in other people's wellbeing and growth.

Dharma centres that are under the patronage or the spiritual guidance of a Rinpoche or a renowned Guru or master definitely pull more weight than a centre that is under a teacher who is not as well-known.

We must realise that even the Gurus who are well-known were not well-known at one time; and Gurus who are not famous now may become famous at another time. Actually, there is no difference but within normal, worldly perceptions, we tend to think that a centre must be doing something right if the Guru has a big name, many books under his name, a great publicist, a high title and a wealthy estate with a lot of sponsors.

Some Gurus choose to be very humble, simple and not grow big. For example, there is a great master, Jangtze Geshe Yeshe of Gaden Jangtze Monastery, who has been repeatedly requested to submit his name under the candidacy for abbot of the monastery, and he has repeatedly turned it down. If his name is sent to His Holiness the 14th Dalai Lama, I believe, without being presumptuous, that His Holiness would definitely choose him. But he repeatedly says no. Although he says no, they put him on a very big throne when he attends *pujas* and ceremonies in the monastery.

Just because some centres have these elite, well-known Gurus, it does not necessarily mean their Gurus are better than the Gurus who are not well-known. The "quality" of a Guru is not reflected in his status, rank or position. The ranking of a Guru is determined by hierarchy, according to the monastic system. However, a Guru's attainments cannot be judged by a monastic system at all. There are some very famous and well-known Gurus, Geshes and Rinpoches out there who have many, many centres, but if they go to the monasteries, they actually do not have a throne, or any special seating. It does not mean they are bad. Within the monastic system, it simply means that they have been working more outside the monastery, so they have not reached a high hierarchical position gained from working within the monastery.

People realised this in Tibet, where there are Gurus with no rank or position that everybody flocks to see. Gen Nyima Rinpoche, who I had the great fortune to meet and befriend in Gaden Monastery, had no rank. If you put him into Gaden's prayer hall, he would have no throne; he would just have an ordinary, normal cushion with every other monk. It does not mean he was not spiritually attained. Monks and laypeople from all over Mundgod[28] flocked to see him, all the time.

However, there are people in other countries who, when they have high ranking Gurus, teachers or Rinpoches in their centres, use that to press down other centres, to validate their centre and practice as good. They sometimes try to take members, influence members and steal members by saying, "Our Guru is so-and-so. Our Guru has this many centres. Our Guru has very well-known students. Our Guru travels to so many countries a year. Our Guru is good, so come to our centre!" What they do not understand is that maybe 10 years ago nobody had even heard of their Guru!

Actually, when they do that, they are the worst reflection of their high-ranking Guru and his lineage. If their Guru is high-ranking, we would assume that he must also be highly attained (it is not necessarily so but we would assume that). If their Guru is highly attained, then he would advise the students not to do things like that.

Those of us who hear those things may wonder if the Guru really is like that or if those people are really sincere. The Guru may be good but we wonder why his students practise and behave like that. If we cannot think any deeper or higher, we will be attracted to that name, position and status. We will not be attracted to the Dharma practice. Then it is not a Dharma practice and we are not going there for Dharma. We are going there for the reputation we have heard people talk about, for the famous people, the big centre and the big people.

---

28 Mundgod is a village in the southern Indian state of Karnataka, an hour away from Hubli, which is a Tibetan settlement. Gaden Monastery and Drepung Monastery are located here, among many other lay settlements.

The people who are under the patronage of, and have the luck and merit to be under a high Guru, must be even humbler, kinder, more down to earth and diligent in their practice; their behaviour should be very ethical. They have an extraordinary, special responsibility to be even more committed, to have very strong Guru devotion, and to be very, very nice to everybody else. That would reflect the high status of their Guru. If they do not do that, it will not reflect his greatness. A great person is not petty. A great person is not focused on minor issues. A great person is focused on big issues.

We must think: if our Guru is His Holiness So-and-So and we run around putting down other Gurus, criticising their lineage, practice and traditions, did our Guru teach us that? If our Guru taught us that, is our Guru high? If our Guru did not teach us to do that but we are doing it anyway, are we making our Guru look high? Is talking and acting like that the result of hanging around our high Guru? People who belong to high-ranking Gurus must be very, very careful and aware in their practice because they love their Guru, they have Guru devotion and they have faith. That is how I think it should be.

Members and students in the Dharma centres of high, well-known, famous Gurus also have a special responsibility to be more encouraging to other centres. If their Guru is very eminent and well-known, it is very easy for them to get sponsors, centres, members, assistance and resources. So why do they need to squash another centre that may not have a Guru – well-known or not – to guide them? Instead of being greedy and taking everybody else's members, they should encourage other centres' activities and growth.

A sign of eminence and greatness is not competitiveness or jealousy, but rejoicing in other people's well-being and growth. Because they are doing so well and because they are kind, these centres under a high, famous Guru should be the ones to encourage other people to their Guru. They should be the ones giving donations to encourage other people's centres to grow and to give discounts to members and students of other centres. The extension of their kindness is to help other centres and their members, and to encourage them.

The smaller centres or centres that do not have high-ranking, well-known Gurus will find it difficult to get sponsorship, members and people because outwardly they do not have anything to attract those things yet. They do not have the resources to get their books everywhere or to distribute flyers and advertisements; they do not have resources to make their centre big, they do not have beautiful statues or even a place to house a lot of people. It does not mean their Gurus are not good.

The responsibility will fall more on the well-known Gurus' students and centres to help everybody else and not to suppress other centres, other sects or other lineages.

CENTRE-BASHING

If we generate compassion to hungry ghosts but we're mean to people, isn't there some kind of contradiction?

The phenomenon of centre-bashing

Sometimes, when one centre is doing good things – such as attracting many people and students and having lots of activities and events – students from another centre can feel jealous, threatened and uncomfortable and they will centre-bash.

They will try to increase the number of their centres and membership at the cost of another centre's membership and they do not care about the consequences. They will go to other centres and say they are practising bad things, their Guru is evil, a fake and has no basis. They will say all kinds of nasty things at the expense of one centre. They do not realise that they are creating extreme disharmony.

It is very bad but there is a trend of centres doing that. Increasing membership in one centre at the expense of other centres is the biggest problem suffered by centres in the world now. It is dangerous and it is very detrimental. It is self-destructive. I have seen in both the West and the East centres that criticise other centres, their ceremonies, their rituals and their traditions. They even dare criticise the Gurus.

For example, a group of people may be doing something for a particular centre. Instead of rejoicing for those people and their centre, another centre immediately targets them and says, "Hey, come to our centre, we have so-and-so. We have this and that. We are doing this and this." They never encourage people towards their own centres or towards their own Gurus.

Some centres are sometimes economically forced or pressured to do that; they want to impress their Gurus or their members and students, or they are losing students and they want to keep them. Centres are in competition to get members – they need to pay their bills or they need to prove their lineage is good. Some people in these centres have a small identity crisis or an inferiority complex. If fewer people practise what they practise, they feel that they may be on the wrong path because they do not have confidence in themselves. They need to make the group bigger, advertise and talk more to prove that they are on the right path. Numbers mean authenticity to them.

They have many, many sociological pressures to make them do things like this. They do not want to but they are forced to because they do not know enough Dharma or they have not practised enough Dharma to control themselves.

Fanatical Buddhism – when they put everybody down and increase their centre at the expense of another centre – is very bad. Get your own members! You go stand on the street, talk to everybody and pass out "You want to be saved?" flyers. Why do you not want to put effort into nurturing new students? Why is it that another centre nurtures them, takes care of them, teaches them everything and you just snatch them away by saying something evil? Some people then join those centres out of fear, through lies, coercion and manipulation or through the centre's members' negative motivation to defame their practice, their Guru and their lineage.

The damage

It is a heinous crime for one centre to put another centre down in order to get membership. Centres should never criticise another centre, even if we think that that centre is not good at all. Societies, organisations and all this should not be set up to judge Gurus, centres, students and practices. No one has that authority.

Within the tradition of Tibetan Buddhism, one head of a religious school has no authority over another. His Holiness Gaden Tri Rinpoche has no say over the other three schools of Buddhism. The other three schools of Buddhism have no say over each other.

If these great enlightened Beings have no say over the other schools, how can anybody, anywhere else, anywhere in the world have any say over any lineage or any practice? How can laypeople, who have not studied and practised, have that authority to say anything about the *Sangha*, practices or lineages that have been existent for hundreds and thousands of years? They are not even learned monks or *Sangha* and yet they want to control and protect, when it is actually a guise to be "politically correct" to get members.

A head of state disparaging another head of state is very bad. That is not decorum or good manners, that is not diplomatic and that is not the way to win people over. If one head of state criticising another is bad, one spiritual teacher criticising another is also very bad! It will look like jealousy and competition; if the spiritual teacher has jealousy and is competitive, is that being spiritual? If they have fanatical, crazy students running around carrying out this un-spiritual attitude, it will not make the Dharma grow.

One should never, ever criticise another centre, another Guru, another lineage or another tradition. The minute another so-called Dharma student tells us that "that lineage" or "that Guru" is bad, that we went to the wrong place or that we are doing the wrong practice, we should regard them as very dangerous people. Let's say hypothetically that our Guru is bad but the person who tells us our Guru is bad, actually destroys his own – and our – spiritual evolution.

I am sorry to say that any Dharma centre who would stoop to such low levels to criticise another person's Guru, lineage and practice to get members will not gain any attainments from their practice. There will be no attainments, unless there is something contradictory in the Buddha's teachings.

These people might go to another centre to get people for their centre, but once they destroy a person's faith, confidence, and loyalty, what kind of person does that turn out to be? Even if they manage to convince people to join them, do they even want these kinds of people, who are so light-eared, in their centre?

Anybody who would resort to that level of saying negative things to bring us to their centre will destroy us and make us look stupid. They destroy themselves and they are a bad representation of the Buddha, Dharma, their Guru and their lineage. It reflects on the person and sometimes, without wanting to, it also reflects their Guru. Do we want to reflect our Guru that way, by putting down other people, their lineage, their practice and what they are doing?

When we make people lose faith in the Guru that they have taken refuge with, or who they believe in, it is equivalent to sending them and ourselves to hell! Isn't Guru devotion the top of the list?

Guru devotion is not criticising another centre so they come to our centre and our centre grows. That is Guru destruction because that is the face we show other people – we show others that that is what our Guru has "taught" us. Our Gurus did not teach us that and we have misinterpreted his teachings if we do those things. If the Guru is genuine, he will never teach his students to disparage another centre, lineage or teacher.

We are supposed to be nice to spirits and to generate compassion to hungry ghosts. If we generate compassion to hungry ghosts but we are mean to people, isn't there a contradiction?

There are enough outer enemies; we make inner enemies by our ignorance, greed, desires and passions. That is why people steal members from other centres to their own centres. But is that how Buddhists act? Is that how people who have taken refuge act? To disparage another centre? To put down another Guru, another practice and another lineage due to rumours, hearsay, personal likes and dislikes?

How to handle it

If someone is saying things to us about our centre or our Guru, we need to check their motivation. Do they help our centre? Do they donate to our centre? Do they become close and try to share in our activities? Do we celebrate together? Do we combine prayers? Do we share? If they do that and then advise us, there may be a chance that their motivation is good. But if they know nothing about our centre, do not contribute or get involved in the activities, yet start to criticise our practice, lineage and Guru, they definitely have an ulterior motive.

If anybody says to us, "Your Dharma centre is not good, your Dharma centre is not valid, your Guru is not good," we should run away immediately! We should not even talk. We should not even try unless we are advanced in Dharma, and we can debate. If we cannot, their talk will influence our minds.

We should stop criticism, and not increase it or listen to it. If we are in a position where we are able to convince them (and not have them convince us), then we can begin to talk. If we know we cannot talk, then we should not listen. Do not stoop to their level and do not encourage them to do what they are doing.

The minute someone tells us that our Guru is bad and our lineage is bad, and we listen to the rumours, then firstly, we are a flippant, very light-eared, silly person who is not able to use logic or who does not have any logic; and secondly, those people who said that to us are not nice people and not spiritual aspirants. Spiritual aspirants do not talk like that. If we can listen to rumours about our Guru, have doubts and run away at the drop of a hat, we will do that everywhere we go, with everything, all the time.

It also shows us clearly that our spiritual endeavour was not really a spiritual endeavour. It was more like going to a movie and seeing what it is about or trying a new restaurant. We are definitely not spiritual if we can give up things at the drop of hat like that.

What we should say to people from other centres is something like, "You've started studying Dharma? I rejoice! If there are any books or anything you need, let me know. What Guru are you studying with? You're studying with X Rinpoche? I rejoice! I'm so happy! Please go to your centre, please be loyal, please follow your Guru and practise Dharma, do retreats, you'll get a lot of benefit."

When we talk to other people like that, we will respect their centre, we will respect their students, we will respect their Guru, we will respect their lineage. That is what we are supposed to say.

If these people really cared about other students from other centres, their centres, practice and well-being, they should say, "If your centre needs help, statues or books, we will help to sponsor you." If they really cared about other students and their centres, and it was not for other motives, they would help these centres.

(They might question why they should help a centre that is doing something wrong... but how do you know they are doing something wrong? What right does one Guru have to say another Guru is wrong? Can ordinary people judge and tell? Wouldn't it be better to respect all Gurus?)

Let me make one logical point: In big cities, anywhere in the world, we do not need to steal and kidnap Dharma students from another Dharma centre. The more centres there are in any one place in the world, the better it will be because there are plenty of people to go around!

Malaysia, for example, has 27 million people. Kuala Lumpur has about 1.5 million people. If we had about 10 Dharma centres, each one would take about 150,000 people. So we take 150,000 people into our centre, make them sit on the roof or outside on the parking lot, set up tents outside and put speakers up all over the place! 150,000 people are more than enough!! Why should we have everybody else? Share. Let everybody go around. Why should everybody be attracted to just one centre?

Some people may walk into a centre and not like it because it is not their lineage or their practice. Some people may have followed the same traditions in their previous lives so they have greater affinity; others might not have that affinity. Either way is okay! We should not be offended if other people do not like our Guru or our centre. Everybody has his own affinity. What's the big deal!? There is no big deal at all.

When I went to India and Nepal, I used to go to many centres that belonged to different Gurus because I took initiations and practices from those Gurus. I went, but I did not talk about this and that at all. I just went there and quietly followed what they did there. It was not because I was restricted or scared; there was simply nothing to talk about.

A real spiritual teacher or one aspiring to be one will not criticise another spiritual teacher and will not put another Dharma centre down. If we hear a person putting our centre or any centre down, we should immediately advise them, "Please show a good reflection of your teacher, don't do that."

In my Dharma centre, I disparage people who criticise other lineages, Gurus and centres. I stop them immediately. I cut down and stamp down on sectarianism. I have never at any time taught any of my friends or students anything about politics. I have never, ever told anyone in our centre or in any place to take sides or to criticise another side. I have always critically and openly given my students both sides of the coin, explained things to them and let them decide for themselves.

I ran away and I slept on the streets for the Dharma. I would not, at this age and level, sink myself to this low level of playing politics for Dharma, the thing that I treasure and love the most. If I could give up everything in the United States – my worldly dreams and aspirations – because of my promise to my Guru, His Holiness Zong Rinpoche, I would surely not give up my promise to him to practise and to keep my spiritual commitments.

That is what I expect of my spiritual friends and students – to be loyal to their Guru and the practices he has given them, not to criticise others, to be non-political. Just practise. That is what I expect from my people. If they do not follow that, I come down very harshly.

If people hear things and they have so much doubt, and they still do not believe me after I talk to them, I just tell them to go. If they are like that now, they are going to be like that all the time. They are just a disruption to themselves and the people around them. I do not care if they are rich or poor, or if we depend on them. I am not saying this to be mean; I am saying we should be straightforward and we have to have principles. There are some things we have to stand up for, which is our spiritual Enlightenment.

The important thing is that whatever centre we are at, we should put our energy into that centre to make it grow; not dispel or disperse the energy. Our allegiance should be to our Guru who is teaching us the Dharma, to the Dharma, the centre, and to the Dharma students and staff working in the centre. I am not trying to start some kind of warfare here. That is the truth. If someone says something about our parents – whether it is right or wrong – our allegiance is to our parents because they are kind to us! Similarly, our allegiance should be to the people who run the centre, who give time, energy, resources, help, work and effort to the centre for many years. Without them there would be no centre.

GURU BASHING

> The whole respect for the Three Jewels is disintegrating due to politics.

The phenomenon of Guru bashing

In the past, Dharma was not really taught to laypeople. It was always *Sangha* teaching the *Sangha*. Now there is a phenomenon in Dharma centres where Dharma is being taught to laypeople that just walk into the centre looking for spiritual happiness and peace.

However, these people listen to all kinds of words and politics, and they start criticising and bashing other Gurus, monks and traditions. Nowadays, there are ordinary laypeople running around criticising other lineages. There are housewives, businessmen and salesgirls who join a Dharma centre, hear some rumours and run around on a rampage criticising high Gurus, reincarnated Gurus, Tulkus and Geshes. But they have not held their vows for even one day and they will not even consider taking ordination vows. They have zero compassion, their refuge vows are in tatters, they do not know what the cause and effect theory is, they have no knowledge or fear of karma and its effects.

These are laypeople that have been running around chasing money, fun, entertainment, position and titles their whole lives. They come into Dharma for one or two years and all of a sudden, they think they are higher than every Guru in Tibet!

Laypeople should show respect to the *Sangha* and not criticise the *Sangha*. Even members of the Sangha do not criticise other *Sangha* or the Gurus! There are laypeople that do not know anything, or know very little about the Dharma and do wooden mechanical practices. And yet, they criticise the people who have given up their worldly life many years ago, studied, practised and listened to thousands of hours of teachings, stayed in thousands of hours of retreats, and out of compassion are forced or requested to go to other countries to teach. The whole respect for the Three Jewels is disintegrating due to politics.

If we criticise a Guru or monks, we should remove the third refuge – *"Namo Sangha Ya"* – from our recitations and prayers. Yes, not all *Sangha* members are the real refuge, who are *arya* Beings (beings who are out of *samsara*), but they represent the *arya* Beings. There may be some *Sangha* members who do not show a good example but there are more *Sangha* members who *do* show a good example. There are certainly more *Sangha* members that show a good example than laypeople.

The Gurus are not above criticism but certainly not from a layperson who has not studied any Dharma and knows nothing. The Gurus are not above reproach. I am not above reproach but I certainly will not accept reproach about a Dharma doctrine from a person who has not studied, practised, kept his commitments, taken any vows or done anything for himself or others. I will take it from my seniors, my elders and other members of my community who I know have the authority – due to their many years of study and practice – to let me know the right thing. It is not a matter of pride.

Can a student of biophysics criticise the professor and tell him his theory is wrong when he just entered the class today? He can question as a matter of debate, conjecture or learning but he would say it with respect, in a way which indicates that he knows the professor is right but that he is questioning to understand the theory better.

There are also some people who like to align themselves with high, famous Gurus and say they are connected with them in order to validate their greed, ego or jealousy. They align themselves with these high Gurus' views and thoughts, compare it to other Gurus and judge. They say, "We're following His Holiness' or His Eminence's sect or views, so we are good."

Just because someone follows one view of that high, eminent Guru, it does not mean he is following all the views. All high Gurus tell us not to criticise, to scorn, hurt or disparage other traditions and Gurus. Why do they not listen to that?

There are cases where people align their centre with one view of a Guru that is very high and put it on their bulletin board. When people come to their centre, they interrogate them, "Where are you from? Who's your Guru? What's your lineage?" If they find them to be opposite of what their view is, they point to the signboard and say, "You're not allowed in!"

Even spirits are allowed into the Dharma centres, to receive blessings from the Guru! But some people are not allowed in because their view does not match what is on their bulletin board. Is that because they are trying to market and cash in on the high Guru's name so they can look good, holy and better to get more members and sponsors for their centre?

These people align themselves to this or that Guru not out of faith, love and Guru devotion. Their intention is not to help or benefit others. Their intention arises from politics – to get others to their centre and to make their centre grow in membership, money and resources. If they followed everything their high Guru had said, they would be a Buddha, a *Bodhisattva*, a *Mahasiddha*, or a very gentle, wonderful citizen of this world emanating compassion.

If they are going to align themselves with a high Guru's name, they should not put up political statements. They should put Dharma statements on their bulletin boards instead, such as the *Eight Verses of Thought Transformation*[29] or something which their high Guru has taught.

There are also some people who are not fanatical and who do not criticise and say things against other Gurus because of greed. They do it because everybody else does it and they do not know any better, they just follow along. Their allegiance switches back and forth. When they hear one Guru talk in one way, they think it makes sense and they go that way. When they hear another Guru saying something else, they go another way. These people accomplish nothing in their lives or in anything they do because they are not stable in their thought, they are not committed to anything and they can never think on their own or take responsibility.

If a centre, a Guru or a group of people say, "That group or that Guru is wrong," then they or their Guru also has the potential to be wrong. If we want to start going down that road to say, "This Guru is right, this Guru is wrong," then we have to realise that our Guru could therefore also be wrong, because who or what is to say which Guru is right or wrong? The higher their thrones? The bigger their status? The greater their following? Their name? What makes them the highest? Their *ladrang*? The number of students they have?

---

29 A prayer written by the Buddhist master Geshe Langri Tangpa. For a more extensive commentary on this prayer, please refer to H.E. Tsem Tulku Rinpoche's book, *Compassion Conquers All*.

If we criticise our own Gurus and say our Gurus are wrong, we could be wrong too. If we want to say another Guru is wrong, then we could be wrong too. Then Buddhism is finished because the outside world (which is much larger than the Buddhists) will question, "Well, who is right then?"

Then, what happens if these high Gurus were to pass away? There are many other Gurus who are not as eminent but who are still high, and who may start factional fighting. One will say that Guru X is wrong; another will start quoting, "He's right, he said he's wrong, that Rinpoche said they're right, that Rinpoche said they're wrong." They go back and forth. There will be no end and soon, people will say we do not need to practise Buddhism because we start questioning who's right and who's wrong. How do we even judge who's right and who's wrong, and on what basis?

Someone of authority, power, eminence and spiritual background has recognised and made this person a Rinpoche, Tulku, Geshe or Dharma teacher. When we put that person down and we say he is doing a bad practice, we must think: how can that Rinpoche or Geshe do bad practice, and still be a Rinpoche or a Geshe?

Some people were recognised by His Holiness the Dalai Lama. When we criticise them, we also criticise the Dalai Lama. Some people are recognised by the abbots of the monasteries, so if we criticise them, does that mean the abbots of the monasteries are all wrong? Can the oracles that recognised these Rinpoches and Tulkus all be wrong? Can those people who have been practising for years and who recognise these people always be wrong? If they are always wrong, then everything is wrong. There is no end to what is wrong.

If this person is a so-called Rinpoche or a so-called teacher and he is doing "bad practices" that we do not agree with, that is just our view. We may like what some Gurus do and not like what other Gurus do but who are we to judge? When we think negative things, we train our mind to think negative things again about the next Guru and the next one... Then it does not end!

We should not jump on the band wagon. The minute we take sides with one group, no matter how holier-than-thou we think we are, we have already become political. Therefore, it is not Dharma.

How to handle it

There are Gurus out there who I would not take teachings from and whose practices I have issues about. But when their students come to me, I will never say one word about their Gurus to them. The minute we make another person lose faith in his Gurus, we are not practising Dharma.

If someone is saying things about his own Guru, we should be very, very skilful with them and say, "No, don't think that about your Guru. How has your Guru helped you? What have they done for you? Think about the good things. Remember that they have benefited you somehow, and don't think negative things."

The minute another person tells us our Guru is bad and wrong, our lineage is bad, our practices are wrong, our deities are bad and our particular style is bad, we should run away! We should cut them off immediately, and say very nicely, "Please don't criticise my Guru, please don't criticise my lineage. I choose and do what I want. You choose and do what you want. We will all get to Enlightenment together."

No matter what others say about our Guru, we need to be sure about our Guru. People have many things to say about every one of us too! Who cares? We have to be confident about our Guru. Does our Guru benefit us? Does our teacher give us Dharma? Does our teacher care? Does our teacher have kindness? Do we learn from our teacher? Do we benefit from our teacher? If the answer is yes, then that is all there is. The end. We do not need to be concerned about anything else.

I have had people tell me that my Guru, Geshe Tsultim Gyeltsen, was like this or like that.

I said, "Really? I hope he does more!"

They told me, "Geshe-la likes women you know, he likes the nun."

I said, "Oh, really, which one? Do you think she's cute?" I could not care less because I was sure about my Guru.

I am not a Guru police to record what Gurus can and cannot do. So I choose to keep quiet. I do not care what this top-ranking, high Rinpoche says about this teacher or that teacher. I have eyes, I have ears, and I have a brain and it works! So I look, I listen and I think. If I like it, I say thank you. If I do not like it, I say thank you. If they continue, I say to them, "See that place that sells kites? Buy one!"

THE OTHER TACTIC: ENCOURAGING OTHERS IN THEIR PRACTICE

*Before being spiritual,
we should be ethical.*

"Encourage people toward their Gurus, even if their Gurus are far away or they do not get to see their Gurus often." Encourage people toward their Gurus, even if their Gurus are far away or they do not get to see their Gurus often. When they come to our centre because they have nowhere else to go, always respect their lineage, their practice and their Gurus. Always make sure their faith in their Guru is firm. Then when we teach them the Dharma, it will add to what they already have.

This is us truly wanting them to become enlightened. For them to become enlightened, they must have clean, pure *samaya* with their Guru. If we wish them to gain spiritual attainments, they will get spiritual attainments because we have helped them towards that. Is that not the job of a spiritual teacher and practitioner – to encourage others towards Guru devotion, towards their Guru?

If, for any reason, they cannot be with their Guru or study and learn from him, they have their reasons. We do not have to dig, ask and say, "Well, aren't you glad you're with us now?" because that is damaging their faith and we cannot do that. That is not spiritual practice.

When anyone is a confirmed member with a centre and with their Guru, do not encourage them to go to other centres or to go to other Gurus. Perhaps we are at a very high level and we can go to a few Gurus because we have been requesting them for Dharma and our minds are stable. There are people like that who can have several Gurus, and there is no conflict because they know how to think above it. However, not all of us are at that level.

We should encourage people towards whatever they have done, encourage their practice and not take their practice away. We should encourage them towards whatever practice they have received, help them and teach them if we know. Our purpose is to bring people to Enlightenment. Once they are enlightened, it does not matter what colour hat – yellow, red or black – they wear![30]

We do not bash other centres. If someone has committed and signed up with a centre, we do not encourage them to leave or come to our centre. That is totally contradictory to Dharma. We want peace in the centre, so why would we create disharmony in the minds of people who come to the centre looking for peace, by bashing other lineages and practices?

If we encourage people to our centre, and it becomes filled with people who have broken *samaya* with their centre and Guru, how will our centre grow? How can a centre, filled with broken *samaya*, be able to advance? How can broken *samaya* grow? Won't our centre then have controversy?

If we think advancing is about getting a bigger building and a lot of money, we have to realise that businessmen, swindlers and liars can do that. The growth of a centre and being full of money does not validate our practice. Swindlers, liars and cheaters can make their empire grow, it is nothing impressive. Broken *samaya* cannot grow. As a spiritual advisor and teacher, I am telling you that straight.

We must never, ever increase the members at our Dharma centre at the cost of another centre. It is bad karma, it is unethical, it is un-Buddhist, we represent our Guru badly and we fill our centre with people who have broken their *samaya* and who will never advance. They will be filled with confusion again and again and again. Before being spiritual, we should be ethical.

If another Dharma centre is starting out, we should rejoice, in order to get over our bias, prejudices and wrong views. We should give donations to other centres, big or small. If we give donations to another centre, it should be done via our own centre – that creates unity.

Let other Dharma centres grow. Whether they remember us, care about us, think that we have helped them or not, does not matter. We have to ask ourselves what our purpose is – to gain recognition or to make the Dharma grow.

---

[30] The different coloured hats worn in the Tibetan Buddhist tradition are an indication of which school or lineage that practitioner is from. Yellow is Gelugpa, red is Sakya and black is Kagyu.

OTHER STUDENTS, YOUR CENTRE

We must never bring people to our centre by hurting their past.

If other students from other centres have some problems in their centre, we should encourage them back gently to make peace and create harmony with their centre. We should advise and help them. In the interim, they can use our centre as something like a spiritual hospital to heal, but we should encourage them to go back to their centre and not just happily say, "Welcome! You've come to the right place, because you've been in the wrong place" (because that is basically what we are telling them when we welcome them).

If there is something going on in their centre that is really irreparable and not helping their spiritual progress, then we let them rest in our centre, observe and watch in such a way that never hurts them, their spiritual practice, their background, their Guru or their lineage.

If students from other centres come to my centre, I would encourage them and talk to them about their Guru, their lineage and their practice and never take away their practice. Who am I to override their Guru's practice? In time I might become their second Guru, or their Dharma friend or teacher, but I should always encourage their existing practice.

If they have completed their existing practice, I can replace it or recommend another practice. For example, their Guru may have recommended that they do 400,000 prostrations. If they have finished the practice but are not able to reach their Guru or he has passed away, then I could advise, "It is wonderful that you have finished what your Guru said. Since you've finished your commitment, may I suggest you now do *mandala* offerings?" But I do not say, "Hey! Your Guru said to do prostrations. Stop that immediately and do *mandala* offerings instead." That is not a sign of a spiritual teacher, compassion, care or skilful means.

Never hurt them. We must never bring people to our centre by hurting their past. We cannot do that. If you make them mistrust their lineage, they will never gain attainments from the new lineage we give them. The karma that comes from disparaging one's Guru cannot be overridden by just having another Guru.

Do not think that just because a person's Guru is an ordinary monk or nun, another top-notch, highly-incarnated Guru who we introduce them to can erase their negative thoughts about what happened before. If high incarnations and high-ranking Gurus could erase all this, they would also be able to erase our negative karma and make us a Buddha overnight. If the Buddha cannot take away our broken *samaya* and broken karma, how can a Guru do it? He cannot. In any case, why would introducing them to a high-ranking, famous, popular Guru be better than their "unknown" Guru?

SECTARIANISM

A Buddha is a Buddha, without any lineage.

What it means to be sectarian

If you are a member of the royalty of one country and you criticise your own royalty, it is okay because inadvertently, you include yourself. For example, if I were in the royal family of a certain country and I criticised the royalty of my country, some people in our country or in the royal house may be a little unhappy, but it is generally acceptable, because I have included myself in the criticism. I am showing humility and not pointing fingers at other people.

However, it would not be acceptable if I started saying that our royalty was very good, but the royalty of another country was excessive, stupid, not educated, spoiled and did not do anything for their country. Some people who are fanatical in our country might agree but the people who can think will see that it is not a very good policy and not very diplomatic. They will say that we do not have the full information, that we are just looking at things in the media and that we do not know the inside story. They will question our right to criticise another royal family of another country that people respect. Once we start saying those kinds of things, we invite criticism of our own royal family and we open the doors for other people to criticise us also.

Similarly, we have four sects of Buddhism in Tibet. Each sect has its own head but the four sects have the same goal, priorities and requirements for Enlightenment. All their teachings are textually and scripturally sound, based on reliable sources that come from India, stemming back to Lord Buddha himself.

I have not studied the other lineages. I have read a little here and there but I can never claim to know anything about the other lineages. However, I can tell you from observing the other lineages and erudite Gurus that I do not see a difference between them and the erudite masters of my lineage. They are compassionate, just as the ones in my lineage are. If a master of another lineage becomes a Buddha or becomes highly attained, I do not see them as different from a master of my lineage. Once he attains Enlightenment, a Buddha is a Buddha, without any lineage. Once we climb to the top of a mountain, it is what flag we put on the top of that mountain that identifies who we are. Actually, the person who climbs to the top is just a mountain climber who got to the top!

I can only say that the other lineages (besides Gelugpa) are definitely valid because I have checked out their masters, their students and disciples. I can say they are good because I look at the results. Just as in my own lineage (Gelugpa), they also have great practitioners and practitioners who do not really practise. It is the same. (I do not say this politically. If I say this politically, I can see through my motive and so can you.)

His Holiness the 14th Dalai Lama has mentioned this during teachings. What His Holiness says is correct. I believe it, but I am a critical person and will still check it out and think about it.

When one sect criticises another sect, it is very, very serious. One sect has no right to criticise another sect. One sect has not fully studied another sect's or another school's tenets in order to have the knowledge to criticise or to say anything. That is why I would not ever criticise, even if I had studied it; and dare not since I have never studied it. I would not even go in that direction.

Prejudice and bias toward another sect or another form of Buddhism is dangerous, as explained in the *Lamrim Chenmo*. The karmic effect of saying negative things about other lineages is very damaging.

Let's consider how dangerous it is to kill an animal; how bad the karma is to kill a person or a monk. We cannot kill a Buddha because a Buddha does not have the karma to be killed; but if we could kill a Buddha, imagine the incredible amount of negative karma that would arise from that action. The *Lamrim* says that if we spread sectarian views, it is understood, the other person accepts and we rejoice, the four completing actions or the four factors of intention[31] are complete: the demerit of spreading sectarian views is equivalent to killing 1,000 Buddhas. That is what His Holiness Pabongkha Rinpoche explained in the *Lamrim Chenmo*.

---

31 The four completing actions or the four factors of intention are: 1) having the intent for the action 2) doing the action 3) completing the action and 4) rejoicing in the action.

If other people dare spread sectarian views, we should have great compassion for them, never listen and just cut their talk off. We should not entertain or listen to them. Remember, we are trying to gain merit! If the demerit of spreading sectarian views is equivalent to killing 1,000 Buddhas, then all the merit we create from doing prostrations, making offerings and meditating will go down the drain! Symbolically, the amount of practice we do can fill up one bathtub. If we were to put that bathtub into the ocean, it becomes nothing. The karma of killing 1,000 Buddhas is like the ocean. When we engage in sectarian talk, it is like putting our little bathtub of merit into the ocean and wondering what happened!

If we were to judge another school or sect of Buddhism and say they are not as good as ours, then we are also presupposing that no attainments can be gained from their practice. It is saying that in their lineage, there are no enlightened Gurus, no high-level, attained teachers or practitioners. It is impossible. It cannot be!

Every lineage and every school of Buddhism in every country, everywhere, has elite, erudite, practised masters who prove to us that if we practise each school individually and correctly, we will get the results. The techniques and the way the different schools are formed may differ a little bit due to time, place, geography and culture but that does not mean they are not complete paths in themselves.

It is sectarianism to have biased views against another lineage, another school or another form, based on prejudice, ego, self-centredness, insecurity, fear and ignorance; or to think that it might not be good if someone is not practising what we are practising.

You will never see, feel, hear or sense one bit of sectarianism in a real practitioner of Buddhism who wishes to become a fully enlightened Buddha for the benefit of others. Why would a real Dharma practitioner speak about something that was never on their mind? Why would they dwell on or express things that are not true? Real Buddhist practitioners do not lie or have a baseless bias.

We cannot even be biased against other religions, as spoken by the perfect Buddha and as taught by the perfect Dalai Lama. If we cannot be biased against other religions, how can we be biased against different sects within our own religion?

THE NEW "SECTARIANISM"

A new phenomenon is emerging in cities where Dharma centres belonging to the same lineage are criticising and saying things about each other.

They dare not criticise another lineage because that would be like one royal house criticising another royal house and they have no right to say anything. But they criticise each other within their own sect or lineage. If they say something about their own lineage and their own centres, it looks like they are being very brave and honest to criticise themselves, their lineage and their practice.

Some Dharma centres, unfortunately, are in heavy competition and they are dying to get more members. Their members will go all out to criticise another centre of their own school of Buddhism, say all types of negative things and make up all types of stories. Some of the members are well-known, so people think they must be right and they listen.

What they are really doing when they compete with each other, criticise or put down another centre or Guru from their own lineage is trying to steal or influence members from other centres away. If there are two, three or four Gelugpa centres in the city, for example, their practices would be very similar, and their lineage would stem back to the same Guru and the same traditions, so it would be "easier" for them to make the switch and assimilate students into their centre.

If they get rid of all the other centres that belong to their same school of Buddhism and they are the only one left, there would be no more competition, would there? Certainly they do not have competition from the other schools of Buddhism. For example, there may be five Gelugpa centres in the city, which then dissolves into one because one centre has said nasty things about the other four centres and destroyed them. Now there is only one Gelugpa centre in the whole city, so everybody who is attracted to Lama Tsongkhapa would go to them. Doesn't that sound suspicious? The bottom line is their motivation for taking away members for their own personal and financial gain. It is very sensitive, but that is what is happening.

That is very bad. They are not thinking of the bigger picture, where they are going against Guru devotion or breaking their *samaya*. What they are doing is making themselves look very, very bad – they bring their prestige down and they bring the prestige of their Guru down, because one day they will be proven wrong.

When they are proven wrong, they look ridiculous; whatever they are promoting is not a promotion anymore. They make their Gurus look very bad, they make the lineage look very bad because to other lineages and to new people it looks like there is no cohesion or harmony within their own lineage. It is like five kids from the same family fighting with each other – that family would not look cohesive or harmonious at all.

Criticising other sects is a heinous crime. Criticising our own sect can be considered heinous also. It destroys Dharma from the inside; it gives others an impression that it is not stable. When people can argue and hurt each other for philosophical differences, it is horrible. When people argue about the right incarnation of this Guru or that Guru (because they do not know which one is "right") or when they fight about certain practices within the lineage (where one side says it is good and another side says it is bad) and they call the police on each other, it gives a very bad image.

People think it is safer to criticise within their own lineage because it will not look sectarian. We cannot put the label "sectarian" on it but it is actually worse than being sectarian – it is cutting off our own fingers! Killing an enemy is already very bad. Killing ourselves is worse! Why would we want to kill ourselves?

When we destroy our own school of Buddhism and criticise it, are we helping our school or are we destroying it? When we destroy one school of Buddhism, how can our school grow bigger in prestige? Or are we building our foundation on the ashes of another destroyed group of Buddhists from our own school?

We have enough obstacles from fanatical, insecure practitioners of other faiths whose mission in life is to tell us we are doing the wrong thing, and they are doing the right thing. If we tell them the opposite, they become really, really unhappy. They are a very bad representation of their faith because they do not respect anyone else at all. When they try to convert others or they say negative things about other faiths, it is tantamount and equivalent to insulting and putting other people's intelligence down. They are saying, "You're stupid, I'm smart. You're in the wrong way, I'm in the right way."

We already have that obstacle. We do not need to create a further obstacle from within our own faith, and then from within our own lineage. If we continue to do this, we are going to be the only one practising our lineage, standing on the top of a hill by ourselves!

How to handle it

Sometimes there are some political issues within our religion. Among the religious groups in Tibetan Buddhism for example, there are some issues with practices or not being able to know or decide which Guru's incarnation is the "right" one. Leave it to the Gurus to take care of it! Why do we need to bring those issues here to Kuala Lumpur and add it to our *samsara*? Don't we have enough *samsara*? Why would we want to add the Tibetan *samsara* to our *samsara* here?

One faction might say, "This practice is good," and another faction might say, "This practice is not good". If we are in the faction that says it is good, we do it; if we are in the faction that says it is not good, we do not do it. Just keep quiet! Once we take sides, it does not end. Ego gets involved and we have to protect the side we have taken.

"Just keep quiet! Once we take sides, it does not end. Ego gets involved and we have to protect the side we have taken."

A lot of politics does go on. We might ask why this happens within Buddhism. It is because the people we hear about all the time are the ones who create the politics, under the guise of Buddhism. There are people who really practise but we do not hear from them because they do not create politics. There are hundreds of great practitioners in the monasteries who we never hear or know about because they just quietly practise Dharma.

My stance is not to take any side. We remain quiet. If I take either side, I will be political. If I go on this side, these people will hate me; if I go on that side, those people will hate me. If I go on this side, I hate myself; if I go on that side, I also hate myself because I constantly have to speak for this side or against that side. Then I do not speak about Dharma at all. So, I choose to remain quiet.

We should make our centre and our lineage grow with the correct motivation. Most importantly, we should make our centre and lineage grow not at the expense of another centre and lineage. Isn't that ethical? Isn't that human? Isn't that compassion? Isn't that kindness? Isn't that Dharma? I think it is.

If, for example, there are three or four Nyingma centres in a city, Nyingma practitioners should have pride in their own lineage, not at the expense of others. They should make their Nyingma centres expand, become bigger and better and grow to show that their lineage is unified and good, and project a good face of the Nyingma lineage. Why should they fight among themselves?

For us, within the Gelugpa sect, if we all pray to Lama Tsongkhapa, we must embody Lama Tsongkhapa's qualities. It is okay and acceptable if we do not want to be involved with the other sects because we have our own traditions, but we should never criticise. If other centres have events and activities, we should, if we can, give a donation or offer help, show harmony and love. There is nothing wrong in making our own school of Buddhism grow, as long as it is *not at the expense* of another school of Buddhism. Buddhism is Buddhism.

ORDINATION VOWS

A monk is a state of his mind, not what he wears.

Why there are vows (or not)

In the *Vinaya* (the rules and regulations for monks) Buddha mentioned that women who become ordained should be on a lower status than men who become ordained. For the last 2,000 years, it was fine, but people who hear that today would say that is wrong. We now know that is wrong but historically, there was a reason for Buddha to say that.

During his time, Buddha was introducing a whole new faith to society. He may have been a Buddha but everybody else who was receiving the teachings was not a Buddha and the ancient Indian society at the time had very strict rules for women. Women were not of equal status to men then. The women never had the freedom that the men had. A woman running around with another male who was not her relative was very bad, for the man and the woman, because it was considered bad manners and meant something not good.

Buddha had to be very sensitive to the place, the people and the culture. He was starting a new order with monks, within a society where women were second-class citizens. If he was to ordain women and put them on the same level as men (with the same monasteries and the same dwelling places), it would have been very scandalous, society would not have accepted it and they would have stopped the movement of Buddhism.

So Buddha separated the women into nunneries. They were not allowed to live together or sit together. In ancient Indian society, men sat in front and women sat at the back; so monks also sat in front and nuns sat at the back to reflect the order of society then. This was done to help the Buddha's teachings gain adherence and acceptance. It was a cultural move of acceptance that Buddha had to implement.

It is not like that anymore; now monks and nuns sit equally, which is the way it should be. Buddha has compassion and all beings are the same but he had to work with the society then, he had no choice. Buddha would have known if something was wrong or right, but he could not fight the whole society at that time if they did not have the karma to receive the truth then. In time, people would understand Dharma, and then wrong would become right.

> **"Buddha had said that although rules were made up for the *Sangha*, the 249 auxiliary vows could be changed in the future, according to time and place."**

The major root vows of the *Vinaya* cannot be manipulated, moved or changed, but Buddha had said that although rules (253 vows) were made for the *Sangha*, the 249 auxiliary (minor) vows could be changed in the future, according to time and place. For example, monks were not allowed to wear a cloth between their thighs, from the front of their genitalia to the back. The reason for that was to avoid stimulation. But if you have a bunch of monks running around now with nothing there, it would be very questionable!

Also, the monks used to bathe in the river naked. They had very little clothes, they did not have underwear and, because it was hot, they would take off their robes to bathe. Problems arose from that – the village people would get a free show (some of the monks were tall, dark and handsome!) and that created problems. So Buddha said, "You cannot go into lakes and rivers, and bathe naked." But these things can change; these kinds of rules do not apply anymore because who goes to bathe in a river naked now?

Monks are not allowed to work in the fields because they might kill insects, but when Gaden monks from Tibet fled to south India, they had to work in the fields or the whole religious tradition would die. They either had to break a minor rule and confess it, or let the Dharma die because they sat in the jungle waiting for someone else to clear the forest for them! Those things can be "broken" and with the right intent (if I dare say so), I do not think the repercussion is that horrible.

The minor rules are more cultural and can be changed, but it must be by a council of *Sangha* members. Buddha specifically advised that a council of elders must convene, talk and decide together in order for minor rules to be changed. The major rules however, cannot be changed.

In a tradition like Dharma that has been around for such a long time, it cannot be just one person changing the rules, even if he is famous, well-known, big or powerful. Even if he had the power to change things, someone else could change it again when he dies. When he is alive, he might say, "White, no black". When he dies, someone else might say, "Black, no white," and it goes back and forth. One generation says yes, another generation says no. It creates confusion on the whole *samsaric* level.

If we want to go down that road, to say our Gurus are wrong and our practice is wrong; if we want to set a precedent where eminent people can change things just like that, we will start a trend. Other eminent people will arise and change things again and again and again.

Disrobement – what it means

When a monk takes ordination, he has four root vows that cannot be broken and another 249 auxiliary vows that he must hold. These vows are on the basis of the refuge vows which he would have already taken. A monk can be a *Mahayana* monk or a *Hinayana* monk but both the vows are exactly the same. It is the motivation that makes it different.

The vows of a monk are called *Pratimoksha* vows. *Moksha* is a Sanskrit word meaning the end of suffering, *nirvana*. *Prati* means self. *Pratimoksha* means self-liberating vows. Lama Tsongkhapa's *Guru Yoga* mentions three sets of vows. The first set is *Pratimoksha*, the second is *Bodhisattv*a and the third is *Tantrayana* (tantric) vows. (For laypeople, *Pratimoksha* vows are likened to refuge vows. The three sets of vows can also be refuge, *Bodhisattva* and tantric.)

For a monk to disrobe, he has to be in front of at least four people who are sound in mind and knowledge, who are alert and awake, and who understand the significance of what is going on. He has to pronounce three times to them, "I give up my vows" and think that he has no more vows. Then he has no more vows. Or he can go to his Guru and offer the vows back in the same manner.

The second way is if any of the four root vows are broken – for example, stealing with intention and completion of the act; killing with intention and completion of the act, etc. If any one of the four root vows is broken with the four factors of intention – he wants it, he does it, the act is completed and he is happy – then although only one was broken, all is lost and he is disrobed. The four transgressions which would cause a monk to be disrobed are lying, killing, stealing and sexual misconduct.

An example of lying is talking about attainments that you do not have and the person you lied to believes you.

For killing, there must be intent, the object must be a human, the action is completed (the person actually dies) and we rejoice. If a monk kills someone by accident – for example, he accidentally runs him over and the person dies – then he is not disrobed. He has the karma of killing that person, of course, and he has to purify that karma but he is not disrobed.

If a monk steals, he takes an object, he keeps it, and has the feeling that it is his (whether the other person knows or not), he is disrobed.

The last is sexual intercourse in any of the orifices, which means the monk's genitalia is inserted into the orifice, he performs the action and completes it inside the orifice. Then the monk is disrobed.

During Buddha's time there was a nun who attended Buddha's teachings. When she attended the teachings, the monks made a lot of noise and told her she could not sit with the *Sangha*. She was told she must sit with the laypeople because she had broken her vows. When asked why, it was revealed that she was raped by bandits while meditating in her cave.

The Buddha asked her, "Did you invite that? She said no.

"When they were doing the act, did you rejoice?" She said no.

"And when they finished, were you happy? Did you think this was a good experience?" She said no.

Then Buddha said, "You are not disrobed, please sit with the *Sangha*." Even though she was in full intercourse, she was not disrobed because the intent was not there. Some of the petty monks who did not know better accused her of being disrobed simply because she was raped and was in full sexual intercourse. But the Buddha said no – intent is very important.

If any of the 249 auxiliary vows are broken, a monk is not disrobed. He can repair infractions of those during monk confessionals held once a month, where the *Sangha* confess any minor infractions to the abbot. Any of the minor infractions that are broken – such as eating after noon, not meditating, wearing underwear, having hair longer than two fingers' span – can be repaired. Those do not constitute breaking your vow because those depend on the situation or circumstances. In extreme cases, in certain environmental conditions monks may have to wear lay clothes, grow their hair long or carry weapons. If it is for a purpose, then it is an infringement of the vows but not a broken vow. It does not mean he is disrobed.

For example, when His Holiness the 14th Dalai Lama escaped from Tibet, he wore a layperson's outfit, with a sling and a rifle, because if he wore his robes, they would have found him and captured him. Did he break his monk vows? No. There was a reason for him doing that.

In some places, it is not appropriate to wear monk robes because if they do, they will be scorned, or there will be danger or difficulty in entering the place. They do not wear or reside in monk robes for the sake of being able to disseminate the Dharma. A monk who is not wearing monk robes or who has his hair longer than two fingers' width is not breaking his vows; this does not merit being disrobed.

Giving and taking back robes

If a monk or nun breaks any of the four root vows, he or she can never take robes in this life again. They are disrobed.

A good thing for a monk or a nun to do is to go back and offer the remaining vows that are not broken to their Guru. That is very important. He may have broken one vow and become disrobed but he still has three other vows and he would not want to break those also. It is better to repair the vows and give them back intact.

That means that even if a monk killed someone out of anger (I have not heard this happen), he has not stolen, lied or committed sexual misconduct. Once he becomes a layperson, there might be a danger that he would steal or lie, so he would break the remaining vows. He is not a monk anymore but the vows are still there, and he has to return those vows so he does not commit more error.

When monks or nuns declare they are giving their vows back in front of four people or more, or to the abbot, they may take the robes again when they are ready. They can give back and take their robes seven times in one lifetime.

For example, a monk at the monastery may find out that his parents are dying and suffering very much. He may need to go back to his family's hometown to work and support his parents for a few years. He can give his robes and vows back and go to work as a layperson (since he cannot work as a monk), to support his family. After he has taken care of his family, he can go back to the abbot and retake his vows again.

I have seen holy monks give their vows back because they were in other countries and had to work to support themselves, and take the vows back later. My holy *Mahasiddha* master, Geshe Tsultim Gyeltsen did that. He gave his vows back properly in the 1980s because he had to support himself and had to work. About 10 years later, he went to His Holiness and received his vows back again. It is allowed, as long as the vows are given back intact.

There were monks in prison in Tibet who were not allowed to wear their robes or cut their hair for 20 or 30 years. The minute they got out of prison, they put their robes back on. Does this mean they are disrobed? Absolutely not. A monk is a state of his mind, not what he wears.

There are other minor rules like monks not being allowed to wear sleeves and having to cover the left side of their body. But what are the monks supposed to do if they are travelling to freezing, cold places? His Holiness Kyabje Zong Rinpoche wore sleeves when he travelled in America, because it was very cold; then his *zen* would be folded and put on top.

The sixth Dalai Lama, Tsangyang Gyatso, gave his vows back. He was a layperson, he had consorts and he hung around in Lhasa. It was no problem at all. The previous Panchen Lama was a layperson for the last 30 to 40 years of his life and wore yellow *chubas* (traditional Tibetan clothes) all the time. The Communists forced him to take a wife, so he took a wife to make them happy. It did not affect his attainments and his incarnation came back.

In the Tibetan tradition, no layperson can disrobe a monk or a nun. No layperson can touch or pull their robes off, and say they are disrobed. The layperson does not have any authority to say anything to a monk.

Laypeople who do not understand the monk vows or never studied the monk vows will say, "He's disrobed and now he's robed again." When they talk like that, they reveal their ignorance and lack of knowledge. It is laypeople pointing fingers at the *Sangha* and not knowing the consequences. It is very derogatory and very dangerous because they spread very, very unhealthy rumours which have repercussions.

SUPERNATURAL PHENOMENA

There were no shortcuts even for Lama Tsongkhapa.

When new people come to the centre and they talk about supernatural phenomenon, I would not recommend talking to them about those things.

I know there is this thing in Malaysia where people say, "The Guru read my mind. The Guru knew the future!" Everybody runs to the centre to check it out, but how long does that last? I do not encourage that. Maybe it was coincidence, maybe the Guru really is psychic, but that is not what we are in the centre to learn. We are not here to see things or get psychic powers from our Guru. We are here to develop compassion and to develop forgiveness.

Psychic and mysterious phenomena do exist and there are people who see things or have experiences. I do not deny that there are mysterious phenomena. There are spirits and ghosts, good and bad. Some people claim that they can see the Buddha. Maybe they can or maybe they cannot – either way, it is not a very good idea to talk about it or express it to new people. It is not that these people are wrong, bad, liars or fakes but it does not help new people. What they need is to hear something different, something that gives them relief and hope, something that teaches non-materialism, an end to hate, anti-war. They need to hear something that creates harmony and gives them a new perspective towards that goal.

"I could teach you how to attain psychic powers but you still have to start with *Bodhicitta*, compassion and renunciation."

After all, what are we here to promote? What am I here to promote? I could teach psychic powers but you still have to start with *Bodhicitta*, compassion and renunciation. In order for us to gain psychic powers from one of the higher-level deities and psychic powers to stay with us in every lifetime, we have to generate those qualities first as a prerequisite. We still have to be nice. Which Buddhist psychic monk is not nice?

If we want psychic powers, we should aim to achieve psychic powers that are not going to be at the expense of any damage to ourselves. When we seek psychic abilities and powers through the wrong avenues or the wrong beings, we will get those powers but we will also have to pay dearly. Once they give us what we want, they are going to be hanging around wanting something too. Nothing is for free.

We are in Buddhism and nothing is for free either! We have to give up our ego, our hatred, our attachment, our unforgiving nature and our anger. We have to give all that up to replace it with compassion, love, gentleness, skilful means and wisdom. Then we will get psychic powers.

Some people say they see Buddha Shakyamuni. When we have coffee with them and the bill comes, they look the other way. What kind of Buddha Shakyamuni vision is that!? They are stingy, greedy, they do not even want to pay for their own coffee and yet they claim they have visions of Shakyamuni?!

If we claim to have visions of the Buddha, we have to think if we are actually seeing a ghost behind a Halloween costume, dressed up as Tara or Manjushri. These spirits can tell us things and they come true. Then they tell us another thing and it also comes true... and after a while, we depend on them. Behind their mask, they are laughing at us! Spirits are very tricky.

Highly realised Gurus will tell you they are ordinary, simple human beings and they do not see anything. There is a reason for them to say that. Lama Tsongkhapa had visions of Manjushri for many, many years. He denied it and told Manjushri to go away. The only time he believed it was Manjushri was when Manjushri talked to his Guru and the Guru told Tsongkhapa, "You've got to acknowledge your vision, it's Manjushri!"

Tsongkhapa said, "If my Guru said so, then it is Manjushri". He then started talking to Manjushri. But in the beginning, Tsongkhapa had ignored him! Tsongkhapa felt he was not attained or learned, that he was not a good monk and that he was very simple. He wondered why someone like him would have the power to see Manjushri.

Even after Guru Umapa told him and he acknowledged his visions, Manjushri told him what texts to check and study. Lama Tsongkhapa did not tell people he had a vision, that Manjushri dictated something to him, and that we had better study this because it came from Manjushri. He would say that this great master or Shakyamuni wrote this teaching, that it is in this particular commentary and that Manjushri indicated to study this to get a better view.

He validated everything he taught by scriptural knowledge and not by visions, although he did have visions. The visions did not give him the knowledge. It is not that when you see Manjushri, you have achieved! The visions directed him to where to study, how to study and what retreats to do. Manjushri told him what to study, and what teachers to go to, to get what type of knowledge. Manjushri could have taught it himself to Tsongkhapa but he did not. How would that validate anything to Tsongkhapa's students? The people who lived closely with Tsongkhapa may have believed that he had visions and believed that it was good but what about people today, 600 years later, who would wonder if it was true?

I am not saying that people who have visions are making invalid claims. I am saying that for today's world, Tsongkhapa's method works very well because even when he had visions, the visions directed him to what Guru, what practice and what text to study. There were no shortcuts, even for Lama Tsongkhapa.

SUCCESSION

> Holding our commitments will be a hook to draw our Guru's incarnation back.

The *samaya* that hooks the Guru back

If I make good prayers, I make a good motivation and I do my practice well, then even if I do not have the power to reincarnate, I will reincarnate into a good situation. Do you have the power to reincarnate?[32] But you have reincarnated into a nice situation and country, and you can listen to the Dharma. This is a result of your good prayers from your previous lives that have brought you back to a place where you are able to practise the Dharma.

I do not have that power to reincarnate but I make good prayers, collect good merit, control my mind, do not harm others, push myself and keep my commitment to my root Guru. The karma I create should make me take another good rebirth, to practise again, learn and maybe even teach the Dharma.

There are many types and levels of Gurus. There are many levels from the generation stage of Tantra all the way up to full Buddhahood. Within each level and in between each level, there are many Gurus. We cannot see what level our Guru is at; even if he explains it to us, we cannot perceive it. Even if our Guru is not at a level between the generation stage of *Tantra* to the full steps of Buddhahood or tenth stage *Bodhisattva*,[33] he will still reincarnate back and fulfil the prayers he has made if he does good things, has good motivation, does good prayers and collects merit.

In this life, I am a Dharma teacher. Maybe that was what I was in my previous lives. That does not mean I have the power to reincarnate; but whether I do or not, I am back and teaching, so that must come from

---

[32] Rinpoche refers here to the power or ability to control the specific situations and conditions into which we reincarnate.
[33] Highly advanced level of spiritual attainment.

something. That must come from the good imprints of my previous lives, so if I continue what I am doing, it will probably be the same in my next lives.

That is from my side. From the side of the students or friends who believe that a reincarnation or a succession of their Guru will come back, they must hold the commitments their Guru has given them. If we hold those commitments, it will be like a hook drawing back our Guru's incarnation.

If we want a successor, or we want our Guru to come back, then while our Guru is here, we have to make him want to stay – by organising ourselves, having harmony, getting work done on time, not saying, "I don't know, I forgot, I can't stay awake, I don't understand," making Dharma a priority, not making our Guru repeat to us over and over and over again the same thing, everyday, not making our Guru talk about money and not visualising our Guru as an ATM machine!

If we do that now, everything will be good now and we create the causes for the institution to continue. Then, when our Guru comes back, we can continue our work.

There are many institutions in the West now where their Gurus have passed away but they manage their Dharma institutions, wait for the incarnations and the incarnations do come back. The great Lama Yeshe has hundreds of centres throughout the world. His incarnation has come back in the form of a Spanish boy who is in his twenties now. There is a Hong Kong incarnation, a Taiwanese incarnation, a New Zealander incarnation. The Gurus are appearing all over the world to continue and fulfil what they have left off in their previous lives.

What takes our Guru away, creates the karma for him to stay away and for us not to receive the Dharma is us always breaking our promises to our Guru. Observe people who break their promises, fall asleep during class, do not go to Dharma class and constantly have obstacles: even when they are close to the Guru, they cannot stay close, they have to run away or leave because they break their commitments to their Guru all the time. Even when the Guru compassionately takes care of them and helps them, they still cannot stay nearby; they still run away and do something else that brings more harm to themselves.

Their broken commitments and broken *samaya* will not allow them to be around. Keeping *samaya* with our Guru is not just showing respect and giving him offerings. It is about keeping our promises to him. If we keep our promise not to scream at someone and we hold that promise every day, we are changing our whole mind. When we change our whole mind, that practice fulfils the purpose of him teaching us in the first place. And if we fulfil the purpose he taught us, doesn't that create the merit for him to come back and continue to teach us? That is called *samaya*.

Whether the Guru comes back and is installed in the same organisation is not dependent on the Guru. If the Guru is going to come back, he will come back – whether it is to the same organisation or anywhere else. If the Guru has the motivation to benefit others, he will come back to benefit, whether the organisation is ready, doing its job or is responsible or not.

The Guru does not get lost. The Guru will find his way, do the Dharma again and benefit others again because his motivation to benefit others does not depend on the student. The student meeting the Guru and continuing the relationship is dependent on the student.

You may think that the Guru should have compassion. He does, but he will go to people who want the Dharma. If we do not want the Dharma, why should he come back to us? We should not say we want the Dharma but we do not change ourselves.

If we request him to come back, we say prayers and recite *mantras*, but we lie, play mind games and power games, harass our Guru, always argue and fight against whatever little instruction we get from him, how can we create the karma to be back with the Guru? If we are always fighting, we should not think about the Guru reincarnating back; he would not even want to be with us now if we fight! Why would he want to come back to that? If we always forget things, knock things over, say we are sorry, disappoint him, lie to him and to other Dharma friends, how does that create the causes for our Guru to come back?

The Guru may be saying, "Let's do this project, and this project" but because it is hard, we abandon it. Why would the Guru come back and continue another project with us? It is not that he does not want to. *We* don't want to.

The Guru has to die, go to the *bardo*, visit his friends in Vajrayogini heaven. Then it is a tearful goodbye and he has to go back to *samsara*. He has to find the right woman, go inside of her and hope she is not a fruitcake. He has to come out after nine months of being stuffed in a claustrophobic little space. He has to be pushed out, if he's lucky, head-first. When he comes out, he gets a slap. He gets pillows and cushions, which feel like sandpaper, rubbed against his skin.

Then he is forced to go through all the little political games the parents may or may not have. He has to watch his parents fight, maybe die early, get sick, contract some disease from his lineage. He has to go to that rotten school and study all that stuff all over again. He has to grow up and if he's unlucky, have one or two kids. Or he has to go back to the monastery and memorise all those texts again! He has to get his visa and permits, come back to the organisation, fly back to sit on the throne at the Dharma centre to hear people say, "I can't make it to the Dharma talk." The Guru came all the way back through time, space, *bardo* and a womb, and we can't make it to a Dharma talk?

But we say, "Please come back and teach us the Dharma!" Teach who?

The Gurus can come back. As I said, we do not have to be highly attained to control our rebirth to come back. I am not but look! I am back! I made it back – it took a little longer, but I made it back, 3,000 miles across the USA. When I come back, I hear, "I can't make it to the teachings, I have an appointment."

"I'm going to another centre."

"But my other Guru's in town… who should I go to? Eenie meenie miney mo."

"Rinpoche, I didn't eat my dinner and I don't have energy."

"Rinpoche, I have a slight headache."

"Rinpoche, I'm slightly sleepy."

After that long journey, I want to go back to the USA! That is what the Gurus have to hear all the time. The students say, "Please return to this planet to teach the world" and the Gurus just wish they were an alien so they could get off this planet, go to the moon and retreat there.

Centres around the world should stay around their Guru, keep their commitments, do their work and follow their advice because their advice only benefits. If we are benefited, we do the practice our Guru has given us and we fulfil whatever we have promised him, isn't that the ultimate hook that brings the Guru back?

The preparation, the commitment

What are we doing now to make sure the organisation, the Guru and all that we have started will survive into the future? That is not up to the Guru to plan, it is up to us. If we want our Gurus to come back, we have to do it right now. We have to ensure that the organisation continues. We have to make sure the centre is firm and running efficiently, ensure the rules hold and the teachings are carried out. We should make sure the institution is financially sound such that even if we are not around when the Guru comes back, there will be funds available to help him. All that should be done according to the law in our country.

Whatever position we hold in the organisation, we should carry it out 100% with our heart; and if we face any difficulties or problems, we should suffer it through for the Dharma.

Serving a Guru and making sure things are running well, doing the secretarial work and administrative work, being organised, talking to the students, having the committee help each other, giving out information, creating systems that work and not leaving it all to the Guru are all part of Guru devotion. If we make a commitment to our Guru and we keep it, that is Guru devotion. If we do not have that Guru devotion, why would it create the causes for our Guru to come back and for there to be a succession?

Most importantly, the people in positions who can do things should do things, train new people to continue the work in the organisation in case the Guru comes back after we have died. Then those people will also train new people and start a system.

We need to get organised and ensure the older students take on real commitment and do not just do things halfway. We must push ourselves to do more, to do things we normally could not do and that we are afraid of. Do it! Nothing bad can happen. Even if something bad happens, something good will happen from it. Do not be afraid.

We will definitely benefit from that, if we really believe that the Guru's teachings will benefit others. And after we die, our foundation will continue to benefit people. There are many beautiful philanthropists in the world who give to many causes and when they die, their hospitals and museums continue to educate and help people. This is like a philanthropist project.

The pujas

The *pujas* for the Guru to come back are very simple. The Guru gives instructions to one or two people and the *pujas* are carried out for his "journey" back. That has nothing to do with our organisational skills in the Dharma institution. The *pujas* are for him to come back, to make the journey easier, to remove obstacles for the Guru to come back and for the students to collect merit.

However, our responsibility is not just to do a few *pujas* in the monasteries, sit back, watch TV and say, "When you get back, let me know!" We have to get organised – if we are working for the organisation or we are a committee member, we should do what is difficult for us, sacrifice what is difficult for us and push ourselves a little further. The purpose is great. Set an example. Then the Guru will be back.

While the Guru is alive, the real *puja* is listening to the Guru, practising the Dharma, holding our commitments – that is the real *puja*. Instead of worrying about what we will do when the Guru is dead, it would be more important to start worrying about what we are going to do while he is still alive. That goes for every Guru around the world. We should take care of our Gurus and listen to their instructions while they are alive. We should do what they say, practise the Dharma and hold our commitments while they are alive. We should transform our mind while they are alive. We should not just sit there and cry when our Guru is dead and say we have Guru devotion when we do not do what they have told us to do.

If we want our Guru to come back, we must get organised now. Even if our Guru does not come back, we still need to get organised. If for some reason the incarnation does not come back and we find out from the high Gurus that there is no incarnation, we have to get ready for another Guru of the same lineage, practice, background and teachings to take over. (We are not betraying our Guru in this case. We need to continue the teachings and our Guru will understand because he is not ego-centric.) We create that karma. All comes from keeping our commitments.

When the Guru returns

Once the Guru comes back, we have to have a place where we can either invite an eminent teacher to train him (he should learn and master things very fast because it is just a recollection of something in his memory) or put him back in his great monastery.

The responsibility of the centre would be to build his house in the monastery, make sure they find good attendants to take care of him and train him in the various languages he will need when he grows up in the modern world.

There are organisations in America that take care of their Guru's young reincarnations and put him back in some of the great monasteries such as Gaden, Sera or Drepung to study. The minute the incarnation is discovered, the students from the American organisation would go to the monastery, build up his *ladrang*, find the students and assistants, put everything in place and invite the Rinpoche back.

Every few months or every year, they would go to the monastery in India or Tibet, check on their Guru and make sure he is alright. They would occasionally bring their Guru to America for him to reconnect with his old students, and then bring him back to the monastery. They go back and forth between the monastery and their centre in America until the Guru is of a ripened age to teach.

We should keep all of the Guru's items and his throne very sacred, as if he was still living there. We should keep his items very well and show them reverence and care. Having his throne and items there are symbolic of him coming back. It creates a connection.

> **"We should keep all of the Guru's items and his throne very sacred, as if he was still living there."**

For example, when His Holiness Zong Rinpoche left Thubten Dhargye Ling centre in Los Angeles, he left his shoes for us. They were brown boots that he wore all the time. Geshe Tsultim Gyeltsen put the shoes on the steps of the throne and explained that because they were Zong Rinpoche's shoes, it was a sign that he would be back and he was leaving us a message in his own way. When I was studying and working at the centre, I remember always cleaning the shoes, wiping them, putting them to my head and placing them back on the throne to wait for Rinpoche to come back. And he came back; he visited the centre (where he left his shoes!).

QUESTIONS AND ANSWERS

Q: If we come across people whose Gurus are not here, would inviting them to our centre conflict with inter-centre harmony?
A: If their Gurus are not in the area and they do not have a centre to go to, it would not be a conflict. If they never see their Gurus and they do not get much Dharma, we can help. There is no conflict. It would only be a conflict if they are going to a regular centre.

Q: If a monk is disrobed by the breaking of his vows, what happens to the Guru-disciple relationship?
A: Nothing. The vows related to a monk have nothing to do with Guru *samaya*. If that was the case then laypeople cannot have a Guru because they have never been robed. If we take refuge vows from our Guru and we lie, does that mean we hate our Gurus? No. There is no connection.

For highly incarnate Gurus, disrobing or giving back their robes for any reason does not take away from their attainments at all. In Tibet, there are a few, very well-known lay Gurus. Serkong Dorje Chang's previous incarnations were lay Gurus. Milarepa was a lay Guru.

Disrobing or having robes has nothing to do with a person's status, who he is or his attainments. We take vows, we do not "take" our attainments. So if a monk removes his vows, it just means his work will manifest in another way.

For example, Chogyam Trungpa Rinpoche gave his robes back in England. It did not affect his work at all in America and it continues to grow very big. His Eminence Gehlek Rinpoche gave his vows back many years ago and took on a consort. It did not affect his teachings or his abilities at all; nor does it affect his relationship with his Guru at all.

Each Guru may have a personal liking and disliking – he may prefer a particular person to remain a monk or not, but it would not affect their relationship.

Q: If I take ordination as damage control, would that be a valid reason?
A: Yes, because you want self-liberation, you want to help and free yourself, it is still okay. If you take the vows and you hold them every day, you collect the merit. A year later, you may learn even more Dharma and begin to think, "It can benefit my parents." From then on, you bring even more benefit to your parents if you hold the vows, as long as they are not broken.

This is why I always say that holding vows and taking vows is from compassion, practising Dharma is from compassion. The real reason is from compassion.

To take ordination, we must have renunciation or refuge. It is not necessary to have *Bodhicitta* or a *Mahayana* motivation. If would be better if we did have *Bodhicitta* or a *Mahayana* motivation but it is not a requirement.

It would, however, be a requirement to have *Bodhicitta* or a *Mahayana* motivation if we wished to take tantric initiation. Tantric vows are much higher than ordination vows.

Q: If, for example, a monk grew long hair and had a consort, how would we explain that to others?
A: That is why when we listen to Dharma teachings and we gain knowledge, it will be easy to quell rumours when we hear them on the outside. When we do not listen to teachings or read, we will immediately run off and go here and there when people spread rumours on the outside.

With regard to the monk with long hair and a consort, firstly it is none of our business. However, if people ask us about it, we do have to give them an answer. They would have to ask the monk if any of his four root vows are broken. He could be with a consort but does not engage in full sexual intercourse that would cause him to break his vows. But this is not something we can say and judge without asking the person himself. It is impossible.

Q: Are the four factors of intention the same for monks as they are for laypeople?
A: They are exactly the same. Intent, action, completion of the act and rejoicing in the act are the same four factors that determine whether we have broken a vow. Those are not rules determined for either laypeople or monks. They are rules for karma. It has nothing to do with whether someone is a layperson or a monk.

Q: Can the bad seeds (negative dispositions) in our mind be eradicated? How do purification practices help this? Do they eradicate bad seeds or just suppress environmental factors?

A: Have you heard of Milarepa? Have you heard of what his Guru, Marpa, made him do? He had to build, move and tear down stone structures for 12 years! It was pure purification to make his negative karma come out faster and quicker. It was even more effective than prostrations and all those types of practices because he really suffered physically, mentally and emotionally for years. But he took it and look what happened to him! He got enlightened! However, we need to have a Guru of that quality (Marpa) and a disciple of that quality (Milarepa) for that to happen.

For you and me, we can forget it for now. You do not have to build me houses and towers! We use that as an inspiration and example but it does not mean we have to copy it exactly because you and I have to be of that quality. And I am not.

What the Guru can do is set you things to do that you normally would not be able to do. When you do these things you normally cannot do and the motivation is for Dharma, it becomes a purification practice. That is why one of the verses in the *Nine Attitudes* advises us to accept suffering and difficulties and be happy about it. Through that so-called "suffering," we purify so we do not have to experience it later, under an environmental condition that could be harsh.

For example, if we were to have the karma to be very sick and we were near a hospital in our own country with our helpers and friends, we would be able to bear the illness. But if we were to have the same illness in a foreign country that did not have medical facilities and was not clean, wouldn't we be more scared and perhaps suffer more? Wouldn't we rather have our illness manifest here?

Or we might have the karma to have a very nice thick coat and if we wore it in Alaska or Canada, we would be very comfortable. If we ran around Malaysia, at noon with our big coat, it would be pure suffering – the item, the person and the karma can ripen, but the situation, the conditions or environmental factors where the karma ripens can make a very big difference. Therefore, if we do Dharma practice, we are near our teacher and have our Dharma centre and friends around us to help us overcome our problems, we will have the support we need if and when "problems" manifest while we are doing retreats or Dharma work.

The karma has to manifest so it is better that it manifests within an environmental condition where there is a remedy and we will be alright. If we have the latent karma of killing, lying, stealing, cheating or hurting people, the resultant karma could manifest at the time of our death as us taking rebirth as an animal or in a hell realm, where there is no relief at all. If the karma manifests here, it is much easier to deal with and bear because of the environment around us.

Therefore, when the Guru gives us work to overcome our ego, our fears and our karma that creates suffering, we should be happy and accept it. The environmental conditions allow us to suffer it through and to purify it with no negative repercussions.

Q: How do we determine whether something is a manifestation of negative karma or purification?
A: It depends on your attitude, perspective, purpose and goal. Experience of an unpleasant situation and how you take it makes it suffering or purification. If you have been a naughty student and your Guru makes you do prostrations, and you hate every minute of it, that is suffering. If you hate your Guru, the prostrations and those Buddhas that you are prostrating to, then you are suffering and creating even more negative karma from the prostrations.

But if you are doing the prostrations out of your own free will, knowing that you want to purify your negative karma and advance in your spiritual practice, then whatever "suffering" you experience will not make you suffer. You actually become happy and you want more; it does not become suffering anymore. That becomes purification and collection of merit.

There are people who prostrate from their provinces in Tibet all the way to Jowo Rinpoche[34] in Lhasa, thousands of miles away, and it takes them one year to get there. For us, that would be pure suffering. If we did it, it would not be purification! We would be cursing everybody all the way. These people regard it as purification. They cook outside, they collect snow and melt it to make tea. It is cold, freezing, harsh and arid but in spite of this, they prostrate all the way. By the time they get there, their bodies are all cracked, some get snow blindness, some die.

---

34 Jowo Rinpoche is Tibet's most revered Buddha statue, located in Jokhang Temple in Lhasa.

For some people, going to Bodhgaya on pilgrimage is a totally purifying experience. When we went to Bodhgaya a few years ago,[35] it was totally purifying for some who went. They had diarrhoea and headaches all the way, they did not have enough sleep and they were tired, but they were happy and they knew what they were doing. They purified their karma. For people who did not realise what it was about and just went as a tourist, it was pure suffering.

It all depends on our attitude. You may be thinking it is all in the mind. Yes, it is! Whether it is in the mind or not, the mind creates the causes and creates the results.

Q: If I cancel on someone for Dharma, and they get upset with me, do I tell them a white lie? Or let them get upset?
A: Whether you cancel or do not cancel, whether you change something or not for Dharma, it is not Dharma's fault that they get upset. It is the fact that you have cancelled. In this case, if you have cancelled on them for Dharma and they have wrong views about it, there is nothing you can do.

It is not good or bad. That is just the way it is. We cannot make the whole world understand what we are doing.

As for telling white lies, we have to ask ourselves why we are white-lying and to whom. Is it to trick them? Extort things from them? To get something from them? Or to not hurt them while we are on our virtuous journey? If our motivation is to hurt, extort, cheat and lie to them to get something, then it is very negative.

If you were standing in a forest and you see a deer go left, and I am the hunter who comes along and asks you which way it went, what would you tell me? You would tell me it went right, of course! Is that bad karma? No. It would be bad karma if you told me which way the deer went.

Q: Certain elder members of a family may not understand Dharma. How do we help them to not go to the three lower realms?
A: Sometimes we can help them. Sometimes we cannot. Whether they are elderly or not is beside the point. The point is there are some people whose karma and spiritual potential is ripened to receive the Dharma, and some whose karma is not. For example, no matter how nice our

---

35 Rinpoche took a group of students to Bodhgaya, in north India for a pilgrimage in 2004.

pet dog is or how much we teach him the Dharma, he cannot practise. Like the dog that does not have the faculties to understand the Dharma, some people may have the karma not to understand because they may not have the environmental factors – for their mind, their body and their situation – to comprehend the Dharma. Sad to say, there is nothing much we can do for these people at this time.

It would be a different story if they rejected the Dharma outright. If they do not reject the Dharma outright or if they are weak about their rejection, then if we practise, change and transform, there would still be a chance that they would do Dharma if we hung around them often enough. People like that need to see an example; an example will transform their mind. Without an example, it is very, very difficult for them to say that the Buddha is good or this *mantra* is good. They do not have any "proof".

So if we want to bring the people around us into the Dharma, we have to be the courageous one to practise the Dharma by transformation. Then they will think, "Hey, why is it this person was like that before and is now like this? This must be good," and they will become interested. That is the best way.

Q: Can we indirectly help them by making dedications to them?
A: Of course we can. In fact, you can also do it for people who have passed away.

Q: If we do Dharma practice, does it benefit and help our parents, people we live with or people who support us?
A: If a highly evolved being is taking rebirth in a mother's womb and the mother has this highly evolved being in her stomach – for nine months, she feeds the baby, gives it sustenance, keeps it warm, keeps her body healthy for it – does she collect merit?

Q: Yes
A: Is the collection of merit by virtue of the object (the baby), or the person (the mother) and her motivation?

Q: The object.
A: Very good. That is correct. That lady collects merit by virtue of the object. Why is it not because of her motivation?

Q: Because she is not aware that the baby is a highly evolved being.
A: Correct. Therefore, if we do Dharma, and we are living in our parents' house, they feed us, give us our pocket money and take care of us, does it help them indirectly? It definitely does. In fact, if we are living at home and we are doing Dharma practice quietly and skilfully – whether our parents know or not, or like it or not – it definitely benefits them. It benefits them if a highly evolved being is in their stomach. We may not be a highly evolved being but we are trying to become one. Because the motivation is there and we take things from them in a good way, our practice will benefit them.

However, if we are taking things from our parents, we do not have that higher motivation and we break our commitments and vows, it will not help our parents at all.

This is why I always say if we practise Dharma, we can help our parents if we love them enough. If we love all sentient beings, we should practise Dharma. If that is too big for us, we should practise the Dharma because we love our parents. If that is still too big for us because we are too selfish, then we do it because we love ourselves. I give people many levels for them to practise the Dharma because these are all valid reasons to practise.

Q: I've read that some Gurus give initiations as a form of blessing. For example, His Holiness the 14th Dalai Lama gives Kalachakra initiations which some people just regard as a blessing. What makes it an initiation or a blessing?
A: It would be our attitude during initiation. Usually, when we take tantric initiations of any of the lower Tantras (such as Avalokiteshvara, Vajrapani, Green Tara, White Tara, Lama Tsongkhapa, Samantabhadra) we will have to take refuge and *Bodhisattva* vows. We will have a commitment to hold these vows, even if we do not have to recite the deity's *mantra*. Holding the vows is a commitment, but it does not mean that we have to meditate on or do the mantras or any special practices of the deity.

When we take the higher *Maha Annuttaratantra* initiation deities such as Guyasamaja, Yamantaka, Hevajra, Vajrayogini, Chakrasamvara or Kalachakra, we definitely have to take refuge, *Bodhisattva* and tantric vows in that initiation.

But because the Kalachakra initiation has been a very special form of blessing for the public by the current and previous Dalai Lamas, the Dalai Lamas made it an option for the people attending to take it as a blessing or as a commitment. It is not usually like this but His Holiness made an exception.

Therefore, if we go for the initiation and we think, "I'm going for a blessing," it is a blessing, we have zero commitments and we will not take any vows. When His Holiness is reciting the vows, we simply do not repeat after him if we do not want the vows or the initiation.

If we go for the initiation as an empowerment, to enter Kalachakra as our personal deity and practice, then we would go in with that motivation and we would take the vows. Then, when His Holiness is reciting the vows and we wish to have them, we repeat them after him.

People who are not qualified and do not understand what they are doing, do not receive the initiation even when they are sitting in the initiation and reciting the words. It is just a blessing.

Q: What do you think of Gurus who give out initiations as blessings?
A: I cannot criticise or comment. All I can say is I am not for giving initiations to people who are not ready. I did that many years ago. When I first found out I was going to Malaysia to teach, I assumed that because it is Asia and Malaysia, there would be a lot of Buddhists, that people here would know Buddhism and that it would be a part of their culture. I assumed I did not have to teach the preliminaries and could just go into teaching them *Tantra*. When I first came to Malaysia, I went around giving initiations. After the initiations, when I started getting questions from people, I realised I had to go back to the preliminaries.

The reason some Gurus give initiations is because they think most of us are going to go to the three lower realms anyway (this is what Zong Rinpoche said – this is a little frightful, but we should not feel threatened). With or without initiation, we usually engage in a lot of negative actions that will make us take rebirth in the three lower realms. Therefore, it would be better for us to receive a higher-level initiation before we went to the three lower realms, for the seeds to be planted in our mind. We will then have something when we come out of those realms. Some Gurus are of this thought, that it would be better to give the initiation to people although they are not ready. Because I will be here in the long term and I wish to establish a good relationship with my friends and students, I think I can go progressively.

I have also heard some Gurus say that if they give the initiations and plant the seeds of that deity in people's minds, Maitreya Buddha's appearance in the world in future will be an environmental factor for those seeds to open up, for them to receive the Dharma. I do believe this too, I am not against the thought. Even if they have received a Tara initiation, they do not have to wait until Tara appears for the seeds to open – Tara and Maitreya are both Buddhas and anything virtuous will trigger that virtue to open.

I remember that Kyabje Zong Rinpoche gave a lot of initiations when he went to America. To tell you the truth, I only wanted one or two – the ones I received from my first Guru – to repair my vows. I did not want to get any more, but I got it all! When I asked Geshe Tsultim Gyeltsen why he requested so many initiations and why I had to get more, he said it was to plant seeds in my mind. When I think back, I feel so grateful that Geshe-la forced me to go to those initiations because I can now pass it to other people when the time is right. I have no regrets now.

If people do not have to teach or disseminate the Dharma, I would not recommend for them to take a lot of initiations. I recommend taking one initiation and doing that really well. This is why I always tell people in our centre to stick with me and just get one initiation when we are really ready – one *yidam*, one practice, one *sadhana*, one focus, one retreat, and we do that every year. That was the style of Kensur Lobsang Tharchin Rinpoche,[36] my first teacher in New Jersey. He gave only one initiation, and he gave teachings and made people do retreats every year on just one *yidam*.

---

36 Kensur Lobsang Tharchin Rinpoche was the abbot emeritus of Sera Mey Monastery, who migrated to New Jersey in the United States in the 1970s. During his time in America, he also was the abbot of Rashi Gempil Ling Buddhist Temple in Howell, New Jersey, and Tsem Rinpoche's first Guru.

Self

EACH ENLIGHTENED BEING WAS ONCE LIKE YOU AND ME...

– TSEM TULKU RINPOCHE

REFUGE: FREEDOM

> Once you take refuge, you are not entailed to do anything except to be the best person you can be.

THE REFUGE VOWS

The ten refuge vows are to refrain from:

1. Killing
2. Stealing
3. Sexual misconduct
4. Divisive speech
5. Harsh words
6. Idle chatter
7. Lying
8. Envy
9. Hatred and malice
10. Wrong views

There is nothing hard about these vows. Actually, if we are good people, these vows would be effortless, they would not be difficult at all. They are actually quite light. Wait until you see the tantric vows!

If we take refuge and commit to the refuge vows, the benefits are definitely more than if we practised without refuge. When we take a formal vow in front of the Three Jewels – with the Buddha, the Dharma and the *Sangha* – and we say, "From now, I will refrain from these 10 negative actions so I may gain *Bodhicitta* and realisation", then every day we refrain from those actions, all our actions will lead towards *Bodhicitta* and realisation because of that vow and our motivation.

Some of us have fear of taking refuge and taking the vows because we have not seen the value of the Dharma in its full light. Usually, people who are afraid of taking refuge feel that it is a threat to their freedom and they have great fear, so they do not want to be pushed. We have fear of taking refuge vows either because we do not trust the teacher, we do not trust ourselves, or our attachment to money, work, entertainment and fun is very strong and the vows threaten our freedom.

Those of you who think you lose freedom are not in the minority. I promise you: there are many people who feel that when they take vows, they will lose freedom and they are afraid.

It is a wrong concept of freedom. We must ask ourselves why we are free in the first place. And if we took refuge, why would we not be free? If we do not kill, steal or lie, why would we not be free? Why is taking vows that help us and guide us in taking virtuous steps not freedom? If we already do not do those things and we take the vows, our collection of merit from not doing them every day makes us even freer. From not killing, stealing and lying, we obtain beautiful, wonderful results; results that resemble the cause.

Taking vows does not necessarily make someone a Buddhist. If we believe in the Buddha, the Dharma and the *Sangha*, we are a Buddhist and that is fine. Taking the vows is the first step toward liberation. That is why the first, basic set of vows we take – from which the refuge vows are distilled – are called *Pratimoksha* vows. In Sanskrit, *prati* means self and *moksha* means freedom. It literally means freedom! I am not playing with words. The reason we take those vows is to become free. Not taking those vows makes us not free!

If we say vows do not give us freedom, it is like saying we should not have any laws in the land or we should not have any traffic lights. We have freedom because there are red traffic lights and because there are so many rules, regulations, law and jails in our countries. We can walk around and not be robbed every day. We can be sure that if we get robbed, the person will be caught and there will be consequences. Without laws, we do not have freedom, we have chaos.

Taking vows is like a direct counter to prison, just as laws in the land are a direct counter to prison. Laws in the land are a direct sign of freedom. Because we have laws, we have freedom. Because we have traffic red lights, we have freedom. There is a higher chance we will not get run over if we cross the street!

Refuge vows give us full freedom. They help us and bless us to go back to our original self – clarity. By holding the vows every single day, we collect the merit to support our practice, so as time goes on, the vows

> **"Refuge vows give us full freedom. They help us and bless us to go back to our original self – clarity."**

become easier and easier, until it becomes natural for us to hold them; in future lives we will act according to the vows from the moment we are born. Do you think people like the Dalai Lama do not have freedom? I have pure freedom! In fact, I have much more freedom than you.

If we are afraid or think we will not have freedom, we do not have full conviction, we cannot see and do not know the full benefit. Our perception is so limited we cannot even see and perceive what will happen. We are like a frog in a well who thinks that he sees everything. Actually, we are not free at all. Anyway, how many more years will this so-called freedom we think we have last? This is how I think.

When we take refuge vows, it is not a matter of having freedom or not having freedom. It is a matter of achieving freedom and the vows are a method. When we talk about freedom, there are different levels of freedom – small, medium, large. If we want ultimate, large freedom – to go where we want, to do as we like, to have extraordinary powers, to have great compassion, to be loved, to not be controlled by our anger, greed, jealousy, miserliness and fears – we take refuge.

If we are controlled by our money, jealousy, greed, hatred and all these emotions, we do not have freedom. We are actually far from it. Working and slaving for money is not freedom. It is never freedom. As long as we have hatred, jealousy, anger, miserliness and greed – and all of us have some degree of that – we do not have any freedom because those emotions make us engage in actions that create more negative karma and bring negative results.

If we have fear towards refuge – ten tiny little vows, which are natural, ethical vows – then we are not free. If we were so free, what would be the problem? It is because we are not free that we find ourselves caught, we are stuck and scared.

You might say that whether we take the vows or not is a matter of choice. We must realise that having choice is different from having freedom. Yes, it is a matter of choice – we choose to take refuge if we want to get the benefits; if we do not want to receive the benefits, it is up to us. But to say our lives are free in itself is a very different thing.

No one in this room is free. We have no control of our destiny, our death, where we are going to be reborn or even our emotions. We do not have control of our kids or our spouse, we do not have control over our body, our ageing process or our sickness. We have zero control, and the control will get less and less and less.

If we have Dharma friends who are encouraging us to take refuge, we should think of it like this: from the donations we have given to the Dharma centre, the practice and prostrations we have done and our involvement in Dharma, our merit is opening up now for us to take the next step in our spiritual practice.

If we take refuge, nobody benefits, nobody gets anything! We do not have to give money to every person who suggests that we take refuge. If they get nothing back and they are encouraging us towards refuge, we must realise that it is for something positive. We should think of it as the ripening of our good karma, to lead us towards real freedom, a wider freedom.

The refuge commitments

Along with the refuge vows are the 12 refuge commitments, which are very simple:

1. Not to go for refuge to teachers who contradict the Buddha or to *samsaric* gods.

When we take refuge, we have full faith in the Three Jewels that they can and will take us all the way to Enlightenment. Going for refuge with teachers who contradict the Buddha will be contrary to what we learn in Dharma teachings and will therefore, not bring us to Enlightenment; it could even be harmful to us.

Not taking refuge in *samsaric* gods means we should not go for refuge to beings that are unenlightened such as through worldly god practices or spirit practices. We do not need to abandon them because they may have helped us in the past. However, we should understand that these practices only provide temporary help and protection.

We must understand that worldly, *samsaric* gods cannot help us on an ultimate level to leave samsara because they themselves are still within *samsara*. Therefore, we must seek the highest refuge – with a Buddha

– for the most reliable and fullest protection. If we believe that the Three Jewels can bring us to Enlightenment, there is no reason to rely on these other worldly beings.

2. To regard any image of a Buddha as an actual Buddha.

When we see a Buddha statue or Buddha image, we should not think that it is simply an object or a picture. We should think that the Buddha himself is there. It is about showing great respect, reverence and awareness when we around holy beings. It is not that the Buddha needs this from us, but it is for us to develop awareness in the actions of our body, speech and mind.

3. Not to harm others.

This is very simple. I do not think most of us go around harming others, do we? This commitment is about examining all our actions and the motivation behind what we do. We must reflect upon whatever we are doing – even the smallest action – and think about whether it is beneficial to others or if it may harm them.

4. To regard all Dharma scriptures as the actual Dharma Jewel.

This simply means we should respect Dharma books. We should understand that Dharma books contain the instructions to Enlightenment within them. We should therefore have great reverence towards them and treat them with much care and respect. For example, we do not simply throw Dharma books around, leave them on the floor, scribble all over them or allow them to get dirty.

5. Not to allow ourselves to be influenced by people who reject the Buddha's teachings.

This means that we do not allow views of other people to influence us or sway us away from the Dharma if their views contradict those of the Buddha. This does not mean we do not associate with these people anymore. These people may be very close to us but their views or advice may drag us down, encourage us towards negative habits and actions or lead us away from our practice. We do not abandon these people, but we should remain very aware of what they are telling us and stay firm in our practice.

6. To regard anyone who wears the robes of an ordained person as an actual *Sangha* Jewel.

This means that even if an ordained person is poor or young, we should still show them respect and humility. They have taken vows to refrain from negative actions and to live with virtue, and they have dedicated their lives fully to the service of others.

At this time, we may not be able to live as monks and nuns do, fulfil all the work they are doing or hold all the vows they hold. We serve the Sangha, make offerings to them and show them respect because they are doing what we cannot do right now. It creates the causes for us to practise and work in the Dharma like them in the future.

Even if the person in robes is not real (because there are people out there who do, unfortunately, use robes as a guise to get money or other material benefits), it does not matter. The offering and service we make should come from us and our pure motivation. It is for us to develop humility, respect and awareness when we are in the presence of a representation of the Three Jewels.

7. To go for refuge to the Three Jewels again and again, remembering their good qualities and the differences between them.

Going for refuge again and again does not mean we take the ceremony again and again. It means that when we recite the refuge during our prayers and *sadhana* every day, we think about their good qualities.

8. To offer the first portion of whatever we eat and drink to the Three Jewels while remembering their kindness.

Traditionally, when we cook at home, we offer a small portion of our food to the Three Jewels once a day. If we are on the run or when we order something at a restaurant, we can make a food offering with a prayer. We recite the following prayer just before we eat:

OM AH HUM (3x)
GANGCHEN SHINTAI SOL JE TSONGKHAPA
NGOTOP RIGPAI WANGCHUK GYALTSAP JE
DONG NGA TENPAI DAGPO KHEDRUP JE
GYALWA YABSE SUMLA CHOPA BUL

As we make this offering, we think, "I offer what I am about to eat to Lama Tsongkhapa and the two spiritual sons, Gyaltsap Je and Khedrup Je. Whatever I take, may it benefit my body to benefit others. I offer this to you." I am sure we can all do that once a day. We can do that even with a cup of tea.

9. With compassion, always encourage others to go for refuge.

Understanding the benefits of going for refuge, we should encourage others to take refuge also. Dharma is the greatest gift we can give someone because we are offering them the means to gain Enlightenment. Encouraging them towards Dharma practice and refuge is a way for us to offer them this gift.

10. To go for refuge at least three times during the day and three times during the night, remembering the benefits of going for refuge.

If we have refuge, we are always in refuge and we believe in the Buddha, that is enough.

11. To perform every action with complete trust in the Three Jewels.

There is nothing hard about this. We think, "When I drive, I believe in Buddha. When I drink a cup of coffee, I believe in Buddha. When I get dressed, I believe in Buddha."

We must develop that awareness so that when we die, the awareness will be spontaneous. When we think about the Buddha at the time of death, it opens up good conditions for us to take a good rebirth.

If we become used to thinking about the Three Jewels, then when we think about them immediately while we are dying, it becomes an environmental condition for the karma of the prayers, donations and help we have done to open, to push us to take a good rebirth and reincarnation. That is the purpose of holding this commitment now. It is very important. It is not something barbaric.

12. Never to forsake the Three Jewels, even at the cost of our lives, or even as a joke.

Going for refuge provides the foundation of all realisations and attainments. It is the beginning of our journey to Enlightenment. When we forsake or go against the Three Jewels – who we trust to take us all the way to Enlightenment – we are forsaking the highest benefit we can gain in this and all future lives.

If we are able to forsake the Three Jewels – who can lead us out of suffering and give us the ultimate benefit of Enlightenment – it also shows us that we will be able to easily give up everything else in our lives. This will bring us no benefit, either on a worldly level or at the highest level of Dharma.

The benefits of taking refuge:

1. We become a pure Buddhist.

We need to follow true paths that lead to liberation and Enlightenment. Our minds must not be contaminated by worldly concerns and wrong views.

By taking refuge and holding the vows, we are committing to following the pure instructions of the Buddha. This motivation is what makes us become a pure Buddhist.

2. We establish the foundation for taking all other vows.

When we take initiations for higher practices or if we wish to take higher vows – such as the *Bodhisattva* or tantric vows – we are first required to take refuge and hold the refuge vows. Holding the refuge vows prepares us for these higher practices.

3. We purify negative karma that we have accumulated in the past.

We do this much faster than if we do not have the vows.

4. We accumulate daily a vast collection of merit.

We accumulate the merit of not doing certain things because we have taken a vow not to do it. A child does not steal or kill but this does not mean he is collecting merit because he does not know not to do it. If we know the bad effects of those actions, and we then consciously take a vow in front of an enlightened Being, such as a Buddha, not to do those things, it has a lot of effect. Ceremonies reaffirm something inside.

5. We are held back from falling into the three lower realms.

This is on the basis of the 11th commitment – to perform every action with complete trust in the Three Jewels – as explained above.

Also, since taking refuge and holding our refuge vows help us to purify our negative karma, we do not create the causes to be reborn in the lower realms.

6. We are protected from harm inflicted by humans and non-humans.

People who have real refuge cannot be disturbed by any negative forces. Even if we have tremendous karma and are disturbed by negative forces, having refuge makes it very easy to dispel and get rid of them. An analogy of this is like having the backing and protection of a very big minister when someone wants to harm us. We give them a warning that we will call up our minister friend, and he will run.

7. We fulfil all our temporary and ultimate wishes.

When we engage in virtue and virtuous actions, our temporary wishes – such as for basic material comforts and needs – will be fulfilled.

At the same time, our ultimate wish to attain liberation and Enlightenment will also be fulfilled because we enhance and perfect virtuous qualities such as generosity, patience, joyous effort, ethics, meditative concentration and wisdom.

By having faith in the Three Jewels, we will experience both of these benefits.

8. We quickly attain the full Enlightenment of Buddhahood.

When we attain Buddhahood, we attain total and permanent freedom from suffering and harm. This is achieved by totally destroying and removing the three main delusions that afflict us – desire, hatred and ignorance.

Also, when we attain Buddhahood, we attain perfect wisdom and great compassion. From this, we will have the special skills, powers and capacity to help all living beings.

If we establish a strong foundation for our spiritual practice by going for refuge sincerely, holding our vows, removing negative qualities and developing positive qualities, we will easily achieve this goal of Enlightenment.

I do not think that there is anything in here that should make us scared, cause us to worry or make us lose our freedom. I do not think that anything in any of these vows would contradict how we are already living our lives; except that if we take the vows we will have more benefits and the benefits are great. That is something that was taught by the Buddha, so it definitely has benefit.

I took refuge when I was 10 or 11 years old and I have held my vows until now. I never lost any of my freedom. I was jumping around all over Los Angeles in the clubs, as a teenager. I never lost any of my freedom!

You should remember who you are committing to – the Buddha, the Dharma and the *Sangha*. Once you take the vows, you are not entailed to do anything except to be the best person you can be.

QUESTIONS AND ANSWERS

Q: A lot of people take the refuge vows without really understanding them...
A: When people take the vows without understanding, they do not take refuge. Nothing happens. They should take it again. People who take refuge vows without knowing it or without having the right attitude do not take refuge and they do not have any vows. It is just words. If we get the vows from simply sitting in a refuge ceremony without having any understanding of what is happening, that would mean that babies who are there also take the vows. It is not possible.

If we are scared that we will lose our freedom when we take refuge with a Guru, it is not a good refuge. It would be considered that we did not take refuge and we did not surrender. It means we are still holding on and we are still trying to bargain.

Q: Some people have taken the vows without understanding, but later come to understand what it means. Does this still count as having taken refuge?
A: Yes, but we would have broken the vows, since we did not understand them before. If we have broken the vows, we should purify them – this is done by purification methods or by retaking the vows.

Q: People take refuge with a Buddha Shakyamuni statue – what is the difference between that and taking refuge with a Guru?
A: If we do not have any Gurus around who can give us refuge, we can take it with a statue. However, if we could take refuge with a Guru, it would be much better because the Guru would have a lineage and oral transmission to pass on. He can give us teachings and explanations on the value of refuge.

Q: If they take refuge with a Buddha statue even when there are Gurus around, does that still create the merit to receive the vows from a Guru later?
A: If we have taken refuge in front of a Buddha statue because there are no Gurus around – we have no choice and we are dying to hold our vows – then it is permissible. After that, we call ourselves a Buddhist. If there are Gurus and masters around, but we do not see anything that we gain faith or confidence in, it would still be permissible to take refuge with a Buddha statue.

However, this does not necessarily create causes for us to have a teacher in the future. If, after we take refuge, we do not hold our vows, practise, transform ourselves or make fervent prayers to meet a Guru, then we will not. We have to create the cause. By taking refuge and holding our vows, having faith and confidence, and praying to the Buddhas to turn the wheel of Dharma, we will create the causes for ourselves to find a Dharma teacher. For example, in the *Guru Yoga* of Lama Tsongkhapa, we ask him to rain down a vast rain of *shunyata* and great compassion. It is our request to him and to all Gurus to turn the wheel of Dharma on those subjects, so we can study them and gain those attainments.

Q: Sometimes people jump queue and take initiation first before refuge. Is it necessary to take refuge first?
A: No, because in initiations, before taking tantric vows, we have to take the *Bodhisattva* vows. Before taking the *Bodhisattva* vows, we have to take the refuge vows. So refuge is included during an initiation, which means we will have taken it. Since other vows are dependent on the foundation of refuge vows, they are given together as part of tantric initiations.

Q: Is taking refuge in Buddhism similar to being baptised in Christianity?
A: Yes, it is similar to that but even before you take refuge, you can still be a Buddhist.

GLOSSARY

Avalokiteshvara – Buddha of Compassion. Also known as Chenrezig (Tibetan) and Kuan Yin (Chinese).

Bardo – "the state between"; referring to the period between death and rebirth.

Bodhicitta – the determination to attain Enlightenment to liberate all living beings from the painful chains of delusion.

Bodhisattva – an enlightened Being that keeps returning into our world to show us the path to happiness.

Buddha – the awakened one. The term "Buddha" refers to all Beings that have attained full Enlightenment.

Chenrezig - Tibetan name for **Avalokiteshvara**, Buddha of Compassion. (See also **Avalokiteshvara**)

Dakini – literally, this means "sky goers" or "sky walkers" in Tibetan. Dakinis refer to enlightened celestial Beings and highly spiritual women.

Dharma – right conduct: seeing, thinking, feeling, speaking and acting in ways conducive to lasting happiness, as propagated in the teachings of Buddha Shakyamuni.

Dharmakaya – one of the three states of being of the Buddha and is considered to be the state beyond existence and all concepts.

Enlightenment – a state of mind purified of all delusions, with all positive potentials of wisdom, compassion and skilful means fully activated.

Geshe – "professor" of Buddhist philosophy, practice and ritual – a title obtained after many years of ardent monastic study.

Guru – spiritual teacher, mentor and friend. The one who can free our enlightened potential, who can destroy our destructive self-concepts and uncover our naturally clear and compassionate true mode of being.

Heruka – tantric form of Avalokiteshvara.

Kalachakra – tantric deity.

Karma – "action"; the universal law of cause and effect. This suggests that all positive, negative and neutral actions of our body, speech and mind will have a corresponding reaction.

Khata – it is a Tibetan custom to offer a white silk scarf to our Gurus, elders or people we respect, as a symbolic representation of our respect to them. Khatas also symbolise our prayers which we offer to the Gurus or Buddhas.

Kuan Yin – The Chinese form of **Avalokiteshvara**, Buddha of Compassion. (See also **Avalokiteshvara**)

Ladrang – a Guru's household and administrative office. The ladrang forms the headquarters of a Buddhist organisation.

Lama – Tibetan word for spritual teacher. (See also **Guru**)

Lamrim Chenmo – *The Stages of the Path to Enlightenment*, an invaluable practice guide written by Lama Tsongkhapa which outlines the precise steps to Enlightenment.

Lineage – teachings and practices transmitted from teachers to students who, by mastering them, become teachers themselves. In this way, the stream of wisdom and blessing passes unbroken through time, making authentic attainments possible wherever there is a pure bond between Guru and disciple.

Mahasiddha – supremely attained Being. Highly realised practitioners who are known to manifest unconventional means (crazy wisdom) to inspire and awaken others.

Malas – A mala is a string of prayer beads, similar to a rosary. It usually consists of 108 beads, made from various materials and assists in the counting of mantra recitations. (See **Mantras**)

Mandala – a symbolic representation of the universe. To make a mandala offering to the Buddhas is to offer up all that is precious within the universe, and all of one's attachments and aversions, thereby letting go of them. This offering is a very powerful way of accumulating positive imprints.

Manjushri – Buddha of Wisdom.

Mantras – prayers that are the spiritual energy of the Buddhas in the form of sound. Reciting mantras evokes the energy of the Buddhas.

Merit – the result of a positive action done without personal motive. The beneficial energy gained in this way will not be exhausted but propels us further on our spiritual path.

Migtsema – a supreme mantric prayer to Lama Tsongkhapa, invoking the three Bodhisattvas he embodies: Avalokiteshvara (Buddha of Compassion), Manjushri (Buddha of Wisdom) and Vajrapani (Buddha of Spiritual Power). (See also **Lama Tsongkhapa**)

Mudra – hand gestures used in ritual practice, corresponding to the flow of subtle energies activated in spiritual practice.

Oral transmission – permission and empowerment for recitation practice which is passed from Guru to disciple.

Palden Lhamo – female Dharma protector famously associated with Tibet and the Dalai Lamas.

(Six) Paramitas – also known as the Six Perfections. Enlightened qualities that help us to progress in our spiritual practice and eventually attain liberation from suffering: Generosity, Patience, Joyous Effort, Ethics, Meditative Concentration and Wisdom.

Practice – practising the Dharma functions on two levels: 1. The outward practice of making offerings, prayers, prostrations etc. to the Buddhas as a way of connecting to the enlightened mind. 2. The inner practice of transforming negative, harmful qualities (anger, jealousy, greed etc.) into positive, enlightened qualities (patience, kindness, generosity etc.).

Prostrations – a purification practice which can involve half or full prostrations, depending on which Buddhist tradition we follow. Prostrations purify harmful actions of the body and introduce us to the bliss of humility.

Protector (or Dharma Protector) – Beings sworn to protect the Dharma. There are worldly as well as enlightened Dharma Protectors and they usually emanate in wrathful forms that are very helpful in clearing obstacles to our Dharma practice. We are advised to rely on the enlightened Dharma Protectors as they have a pure motivation and greater clairvoyance than the worldly protectors.

Puja – ritual set of prayers and offerings, which clear obstacles and invite blessings.

Rinpoche – meaning "greatly precious one" in Tibetan. Respectful and loving way to address a highly attained spiritual teacher.

Sadhana – a collection of prayers and mantras which are to be recited on a regular, daily basis and which help transform our lives by cutting away negative states of mind and developing enlightened qualities.

Samaya – the sacred bond and commitment to one's spiritual teacher, based on strong faith, devotion and effort.

Samsara – the cycle of existence where sentient beings continue to create their own sufferings and experience it lifetime after lifetime.

Sangha – the community of monks and nuns. On an absolute level, this refers to the field of all enlightened Beings.

Setrap – an enlightened Dharma Protector who is an emanation of Buddha Amitabha. Setrap is the principal protector of Gaden Shartse Monastery.

Shakyamuni – Lord Buddha who, 2,500 years ago, set down the liberating teachings that we continue to follow today.

Shunyata – Sanskrit for "Emptiness", which explains that all phenomena are void of inherent existence as we know it.

Stupa – a representation of the enlightened mind.

Tantra – the practice of taking the result onto the path where we identify with and work directly with the energies of an enlightened Being, instead of our limited concepts of ourselves. Tantra is practised by the most advanced, sincere and committed practitioners.

Tara – a great female Buddha who manifests in 21 forms. She is most commonly known in her Green Tara form, embodying Enlightened Activity, and is extremely swift in coming to our aid and answering our prayers.

Thangkas – traditional Tibetan paintings of deities, to be used for meditation and practice.

Three Jewels – The Buddha, Dharma and Sangha.

Tsa tsas – small portable Buddha statues made from clay.

(Lama/Je) Tsongkhapa – One of Buddhism's most prominent masters from Tibet in the 14th Century, who was especially known for his ardent study, practice and teaching of the Dharma. The founder of the Gelug tradition, Lama Tsongkhapa is said to be the direct incarnations of three great Bodhisattvas – Avalokiteshvara (Buddha of Compassion), Manjushri (Buddha of Wisdom) and Vajrapani (Buddha of Spiritual Power).

Tulku – literally, "Emanation Body" in Tibetan. The title refers to highly attained Beings who have the power to emanate and reincarnate at will, and who have full control of their death and rebirth.

Vajrayogini – embodying the essence of wisdom and compassion, this female Buddha's tantric practice is extremely relevant for our present time since her practice becomes more powerful as our delusions become stronger.

Vajrapani – Buddha of Spiritual Power

Wheel of Dharma (turning the) – teaching the Dharma.

Yamantaka – a wrathful emanation of Manjushri. His practice can cut off the roots of the strongest greed and hatred by destroying the delusion that precedes them.

Yidam – a meditational deity (such as Tara or Manjushri) whom practitioners concentrate their prayers and practice on.

Zen – the top of three parts of cloth which makes up a Tibetan monk's robes.

REFERENCES

Berzin, Alexander. *Relating to a Spiritual Teacher: Building a Healthy Relationship*. New York: Snow Lion Publications, 2000

Nga-la Rig'dzin Dorje. *Dangerous Friend: The Teacher-student relationship in Vajrayana Buddhism*. Boston & London: Shambala Publications, 2001

TRANSLATIONS

Lama Tsongkhapa's Guru Yoga
Translated spontaneously by H.E. Tsem Tulku Rinpoche during the teachings.

Practising Guru Devotion with the Nine Attitudes
Translated by David Molk for Kechara Media & Publications. Previously unpublished.

> "ONCE YOU TAKE REFUGE, YOU ARE NOT ENTAILED TO DO ANYTHING EXCEPT TO BE THE BEST PERSON YOU CAN BE."
>
> – TSEM TULKU RINPOCHE

ACKNOWLEDGEMENTS

With much gratitude from our hearts to our Guru H.E. Tsem Tulku Rinpoche who, to us, is the Buddha, Dharma and Sangha. Without our Guru, we would have never met, much less tasted, the nectar of Enlightened compassion that is the holy Dharma.

Our deepest appreciation to Terence Mahony and Joan Foo Mahony for their very kind sponsorship of this book. Thank you for making these teachings accessible to spiritual seekers all over the world.

Gurus for Hire, Enlightenment for Sale would not have been possible without the contribution and effort of so many, including Thor Kah Hoong, Su Lin Chee, Philip Soyza, Lim Kim Swee, Deborah Pereira and everyone at Kechara. To them, we owe our gratitude.

Finally, we would like to sincerely thank all the special individuals who have taken the time from their busy schedules to read the book in its First Edition and to provide this Revised Edition with their endorsements.

In the actual production of the book itself, both the First Edition and this Revised Edition, we would like to extend our deepest thanks to the following:

Recording and editing of teachings: Loh Seng Piow
Transcription of teachings: Joseph Chan, Jamie Khoo, Susan Lim, Sharon Saw and Shirley Tan
Editor: Jamie Khoo
Compilation and editing: Jamie Khoo, Sharon Saw and Joan Foo Mahony
Cover design: Justin Ripley / 1am Concept
Typesetting and book design: Kelley Cheng & Beverly Chong / The Press Room

KECHARA

Kechara, established in 2000, is a non-profit Tibetan Buddhist organisation under the spiritual guidance of His Eminence Tsem Tulku Rinpoche. It is an affiliate of the illustrious 600-year-old Gaden Shartse Monastery, which is now situated in Mundgod, south India. Gaden Shartse Monastery belongs to the holy Gaden Monastery which now houses more than 3,000 monks and is one of the most elite monastic universities in the world.

The objective of Kechara is to spread the beautiful teachings of Lord Buddha to as many people as possible, in southeast Asia and worldwide. It offers regular teachings by Rinpoche and a range of programmes ranging from introductory classes on Buddhism to regular prayer sessions.

Since its inception, Kechara has grown into several departments:
Kechara Media & Publications – the publishing arm.
Kechara In Motion – a film production house.
Kechara Saraswati Arts – the first Tibetan arts studio in southeast Asia.
Kechara Soup Kitchen – a community action group which distributes food to the homeless and urban poor in the Klang Valley, Malaysia.
Kechara Paradise – four retail outlets in prominent areas of Kuala Lumpur, offering handicrafts and artifacts from the Himalayan region.
Kechara Oasis – a vegetarian restaurant.
Kechara Discovery – a travel consultancy which organises pilgrimages to holy places and sources for statues to complement the selection at the outlets.
Kechara.com – an online e-shop which offers a selection of exquisite items from the outlets, books, DVDs and audio CDs of His Eminence's teachings.

If you would like to know more about Kechara, please contact us through the following avenues:

Kechara
21-23, Jalan PJU 1/3G,
SunwayMas Commercial Centre,
Petaling Jaya 47301
Selangor, Malaysia

Tel: (+603) 7803 3908
E-mail: care@kecharahouse.com
Website: www.kecharahouse.com

INDEX

#123...
1,000 Buddhas – 43, 187, 188

A

abbot(s) – Biography, 63, 124, 126, 131, 165, 179, 197, 198, 218

advertising – 45, 96, 137, 163, 164, 168, 170

alert, alertness – 24, 36, 59, 60, 61, 62, 63, 78, 87, 136, 160, 161, 195

altar(s) – 118, 151, 159

(United States of) America – Biography, Introduction, 25, 36, 107, 128, 145, 175, 198, 206, 210, 218

American – 36, 209

Amitabha – 51, 136, 237

arhatship – 112

arya beings – 177

Ashvaghosha – 40, 60

assistant(s) – 34, 35, 36, 141, 158, 161, 162, 209

Atisha – 92

attainment(s) – 29, 34, 37, 38, 39, 45, 46, 51, 53, 80, 129, 130, 131, 132, 133, 134, 135, 143, 164, 165, 171, 182, 185, 188, 196, 198, 203, 210, 228, 233

Avalokiteshvara – 48, 51, 99, 216, 234, 235, 236, 237

awareness – 26, 37, 40, 62, 66, 77, 156, 161, 226, 227, 228

B

bardo – 205, 206, 234

Berzin, Alexander – 52, References

Bodhgaya – 214

Bodhicitta – 58, 68, 72, 86, 130, 133, 143, 200, 211, 222, 234

Bodhisattva(s) – 43, 86, 122, 130, 133, 134, 141, 155, 178, 195, 203, 216, 229, 233, 234, 236, 238

Bright Hill Temple – 108

Buddha, Lord – 24, 25, 106, 131, 154, 186, 237, 243

Buddha nature – Introduction

Buddhahood – 27, 74, 81, 134, 136, 143, 203, 230

Buddhas – 39, 43, 52, 89, 92, 93, 95, 119, 131, 132, 141, 154, 156, 158, 187, 188, 213, 218, 233, 235, 236

Buddhism – 20, 49, 52, 92, 98, 107, 108, 116, 152, 153, 154, 164, 170, 179, 186, 187, 188, 189, 190, 191, 192, 193, 201, 217, 233, 238, 239, 243

buddy system – 143, 148

Burma – 116, 117

C

Chakrasamvara – 216

centre-bashing – 169-175

chanting – Biography, 25, 33, 75, 145

Cheng Yen, Reverend – 108

Chenrezig – 29, 43, 234

Chogyam Trungpa Rinpoche – 210

committees – Introduction, 130, 131, 132, 140, 143, 149, 159

crazy wisdom – 54-55, 236

D

dakini – 83, 105, 234

Dalai Lama – Biography, 26, 51, 53, 76, 89, 90, 99, 111, 118, 134, 145, 163, 164, 165, 179, 187, 188, 197, 198, 216, 217, 224, 236

dedication(s) – 27, 132, 133, 155, 215

delusion(s) – 43, 63, 64, 65, 91, 92, 93, 112, 230, 234, 238

Dharamsala – 38

Dharma Protector(s) – 39, 59, 89, 131, 236, 237

Dharmakaya – 29, 234

disciple – 17, 34, 49, 52, 56, 58, 60, 63, 71, 99, 100, 108, 187, 210, 212, 235, 236

disrobement – 195-199, 210

divination(s) – 37, 47, 130

Drepung Monastery – 166, 209

E

ego(s) – Introduction, 54, 58, 64, 72, 74, 78, 79, 90, 95, 177, 188, 191, 201, 208, 213

Eight Verses of Thought Transformation – 178

Enlightenment – Introduction, 26, 42, 46, 52, 57, 59, 60, 64, 68, 79, 94, 129, 160, 163, 175, 180, 183, 186, 187, 225, 226, 228, 229, 230, 231, 234, 235

F

faith – 26, 27, 34, 54, 59, 68, 92, 112, 120, 164, 167, 171, 172, 178, 180, 182, 190, 191, 193, 225, 230, 233, 237

fame – 24, 147

fanatical – 60, 61, 62, 64, 81, 99, 163, 170, 171, 178, 186, 190

Fifty Verses on Guru Devotion – 40, 49, 50, 52, 60-65, 66, 80, 156

four completing actions – 187

G

Gaden Shartse Monastery – Dedication, Biography, Introduction, 26, 34, 38, 63, 237, 243

Gaden Tri Rinpoche, H. H. – 122, 170

Gehlek Rinpoche, H. H. – 210

Gelug, Gelugpa – 92, 149, 183, 187, 189, 192, 238

Gen Nyima Rinpoche – 166

Gendun Nyedrak – Biography

Geshe(s) – 61, 66, 165, 176, 179, 234

Geshe Langri Tangpa – 178

Geshe Lharam – Biography, 26

Geshe Tsultim Gyeltsen (Geshe-la) – 25, 34, 61, 180, 198, 209, 218

ghost(s) – 68, 169, 172, 200, 201

gossip – 16, 95, 143

Graded Path – 60, 64

Guru-bashing – 15, 20, 176-181, 183

Guru-desciple relationship – Introduction, Foreword, 49, 52, 53, 58, 67, 69, 75, 80, 81, 94, 96, 99, 100, 205, 210, 239

Guru Yoga – 25-30, 101, 195, 233, Translations

Guyasamaja – 216

Gyaltsap Rinpoche/ Je – 27, 227, 228

Gyuto trantric college – Biography

H

Heruka – 38, 235

Hevajra – 216

Hinayana – 195

I

incarnation(s) – 10, 34, 45, 89, 90, 99, 122, 138, 161, 185, 190, 191, 198, 203, 204, 208, 209, 210, 228, 238

incense – 28, 29, 37, 71

India – Biography, Introduction, 34, 38, 41, 63, 106, 125, 153, 174, 186, 194, 209, 214, 243

Indian – 36, 40, 92, 153, 166, 193

initiation – 40, 53, 83, 96, 100, 118, 131, 163, 211, 216, 217, 218, 233

J

Jangtze Geshe Yeshe – 165

jealousy – 68, 101, 147, 165, 167, 171, 177, 224, 236

Jesus Christ – 43

Jowo Rinpoche – 213

K

Kadam – 92

Kagyu – 183

Kalachakra – 49, 53, 89, 118, 216, 217, 235

Karnataka – 166

Kechara – Biography, Introduction, 66, 111, Translations, Acknowledgements, 243

Kek Lok Si – 108

Kensur Jampa Yeshe Rinpoche – 52

Kensur Lobsang Tharchin Rinpoche – 218

khata(s) – 119, 125, 153, 156, 158, 159, 235

Khedrup Rinpoche/ Je – 27, 227, 228

Khentrul Rinpoche Thubten Lamang– Biography

Kuan Yin – 51, 86, 93, 234, 235

Kyabje Zong Rinpoche, H. H. – Biography, 34-41, 61, 86, 87, 96, 163, 164, 175, 198, 209, 217, 218

L

Ladrang – Introduction, 178, 209, 235

Lama/Je Tsongkhapa – 25, 26, 27, 28, 29, 30, 92, 95, 97, 101, 110, 142, 149, 189, 192, 195, 200, 201, 202, 216, 227, 228, 233, 235, 236, 238, Translations

Lamrim Chenmo – 39, 91, 187, 235

Lhasa – 198, 213

liaisons (changtzo) – 131, 132, 133, 161

living Buddha – 35, 86, 92

Lobsang Drakpa – 29

Los Angeles – 25, 34, 36, 61, 86, 209, 231

M

Maha Annuttaratantra – 216

Mahasiddha(s) – 41, 82, 83, 178, 198, 235

Mahayana – 108, 195, 211

Maitreya – 27, 30, 218

mala(s) – 111, 235

Malaysia – Biography, Introduction, 107, 108, 120, 128, 153, 174, 200, 212, 217, 243

mandala – 26, 29, 125, 184, 185, 236

Manjushri – 43, 93, 108, 161, 201, 202, 235, 236, 238

mantra(s) – 59, 72, 76, 87, 90, 110, 112, 123, 132, 205, 215, 216, 235, 236, 237

mara – 68-69

master(s) – 10, 25, 26, 36, 39, 40, 41, 43, 61, 82, 92, 96, 112, 116, 131, 163, 164, 165, 178, 186, 187, 188, 198, 202, 233, 238

meditation – Introduction, 26, 27, 34, 51, 62, 85, 89, 90, 91, 108, 110, 111, 112, 113, 121, 132, 149, 155, 230, 238

membership – 151, 152, 169, 170, 178

merits – 28, 34, 38, 64, 69, 71, 92, 134

Migtsema – 25, 29, 236

Milarepa – 23, 106, 210, 212

Mohammad – 43

Molk, David – 66, Translations

monastery – Biography, Introduction, 26, 34, 38, 50, 63, 105, 108, 114, 117, 118, 124, 126, 131, 132, 144, 149, 150, 165, 167, 198, 206, 209, 218, 237, 241

Mongolian – Biography

monks – Introduction, 34, 44, 90, 107, 108, 112, 114, 116, 117, 118, 124, 131, 132, 155, 166, 171, 176, 177, 193, 194, 196, 197, 198, 211, 227, 237, 241

mother monastery – 114, 115, 126

Mount Meru – 29

mudra(s) – 25, 236

Mundgod – Biography, 166, 243

N

Namo Sangha Ya – 177

Naropa – 99, 101

Nepal – Biography, Introduction, 174

New York – 36, 52, References

Nine Attitudes (of Practising Guru Devotion), the – 66-79, 80, 212, Translations

nun(s) – Introduction, 90, 108, 117, 118, 180, 185, 193, 194, 196, 197, 198, 227, 237

Nyingma lineage – 192

O

obstacle(s) – 26, 50, 57, 59, 68, 85, 87, 88, 117, 118, 190, 191, 204, 208, 236, 237

Om Mani Peme Hung – 145

oracle(s) – 59, 179

ordination – 116, 117, 176, 193, 195, 211

P

Pabongkha Rinpoche, H. H. – 187

Palden Lhamo – 89, 236

paramitas – 27, 58, 72, 77, 79, 111, 154, 236

Phari – Biography

pilgrimage – 106, 214

politics – Introduction, Foreword, 94, 174, 175, 176, 178, 191

Potala – 89

Pratimoksha – 195, 223

prayers – 25, 26, 27, 70, 108, 109, 110, 111, 119, 122, 132, 133, 145, 155, 172, 177, 203, 205, 227, 228, 233, 235, 236, 237, 238

promoting the Guru – 160-164, 190

prostration(s) – 35, 37, 61, 83, 125, 149, 153, 154, 156, 157, 184, 185, 188, 212, 213, 225, 236

protocol – 60, 62, 66, 153, 158, 159

puja(s) – 59, 82, 98, 117, 121, 125, 129, 136, 165, 208, 237

R

Rashi Gempil Ling Temple – 218

rebirth – 57, 74, 77, 203, 206, 213, 215, 217, 228, 234, 238

recitation(s) – 25, 112, 177, 235, 236

refuge commitments – 100, 225

refuge, taking – Introduction, 52, 60, 100, 101, 125, 145, 223, 225, 229, 230, 232, 233

refuge vows – 89, 176, 195, 210, 222, 223, 224, 225, 229, 230, 232, 233

Reting Rinpoche – 89, 90

retreat(s) – 27, 39, 72, 81, 87, 106, 113, 121, 131, 132, 173, 176, 202, 212, 218

Rig'dzin Dorje – 52, References

ritual(s) – 25, 26, 50, 70, 102, 109, 111, 125, 169, 234, 236, 237

root Guru – 29, 34, 39, 45-46, 96, 99, 100, 101, 203

rumour(s) – 16, 95, 172, 173, 176, 199, 211

S

sadhana – 56, 70, 83, 86, 87, 122, 218, 227, 237

Sakya – 183

Samantabhadra – 216

samaya – Foreword, 41, 69, 71, 80, 81, 83, 90, 123, 126, 182, 183, 185, 189, 203, 204, 205, 210, 237

samsara – 29, 58, 70, 74, 77, 95, 112, 177, 191, 205, 225, 237

Sangha – 110, 112, 114, 116, 117, 118, 139, 144, 151, 170, 171, 176, 177, 194, 196, 197, 199, 222, 223, 227, 231, 237, 238, Acknowledgements

scriptures – 50, 102, 124, 226

sect(s) – 25, 149, 168, 177, 186, 187, 188, 189, 190, 192

sectarianism – Foreword, 174, 186-192

Serkong Dorje Chang – 210

Sera Mey Monastery – 209, 218

Setrap – 237

Shakyamuni – 43, 86, 93, 99, 112, 149, 201, 202, 232, 234, 237

Shunyata – 233, 237

Singapore – Introduction, 107, 108

sponsors – 34, 81, 82, 83, 108, 110, 119, 120, 121, 123, 126, 139, 140, 158, 161, 165, 167, 178, 244, 245

statue(s) – 35, 82, 86, 92, 99, 110, 111, 119, 168, 173, 213, 226, 232, 233, 243

Stupa – 110, 237

submission – Introduction, 56, 58, 75, 157

succession – 203, 204, 207

Sutra – 26, 64

T

Taiwan – Biography, 108, 204

Tantra(s) – Biography, 26, 50, 64, 89, 93, 149, 203, 216, 217, 238

tantric – Biography, 33, 36, 61, 64, 70, 195, 211, 216, 222, 229, 233, 235, 237, 238

Tara – 142, 201, 216, 218, 237

temple(s) – 45, 107, 108, 110, 111, 112, 144, 151, 213, 218

tenshi – 62

tenzin – 62

Tenzin Gyatso – 51

Thailand – 117

Three Jewels – 110, 111, 154, 155, 156, 176, 222, 225, 226, 227, 228, 229, 230, 237

Thubten Dhargye Ling – 25, 34, 36, 86, 209

Tibet – Biography, 34, 41, 89, 117, 119, 125, 153, 161, 164, 166, 176, 186, 194, 197, 198, 209, 210, 213, 236, 238

Tibetan – Biography, Introduction, 25, 26, 35, 61, 82, 110, 116, 118, 119, 125, 126, 153, 159, 166, 170, 183, 191, 198, 234, 235, 237, 238, 243

Tilopa – 99, 101

Tsangyang Gyatso – 198

Tsem Tulku Rinpoche – Biography, 13, Introduction, Foreword, 25, 106, 161, 178, 221, Translations, 241, Acknowledgements, 243

Tulku(s) – 176, 179, 238

Tushita Heaven – 27

Tzu Chi Foundation – 108

U

Umapa – 202

V

vajra(s) – 68, 70

Vajrapani – 216, 238

Vajrayana Buddhism – 52, 236, References

Vajrayogini – 205, 216, 238

Vinaya – 193, 194

visualisation(s) – 26, 86, 92, 111, 123

volunteer(s) – 108, 113, 135, 136, 137, 138, 143, 145, 244

vow – 86, 162, 197, 211, 222, 229

W

West, the – Biography, 90, 169, 204

wheel of Dharma – 43, 233, 238

Y

Yamantaka – 25, 131, 216, 238

yidam(s) – 95, 218, 238

Z

Zen Buddhism – 98

Zhuan Dao, Venerable – 108

www.ingramcontent.com/pod-product-compliance
Lightning Source LLC
LaVergne TN
LVHW041700060526
838201LV00043B/508